MEN ONLY
An Investigation into Men's Organisations

Barbara Rogers is a founder member, and currently Editor, of *Everywoman*, the British current affairs magazine for women. Her first job was in the Foreign and Commonwealth Office in London, her first encounter with a men's club. She has also worked at the United Nations in New York and in the office of Congressman Charles Diggs in Washington. She was a Councillor in the London Borough of Islington, 1982–86, and she has worked for a number of international development agencies and African organisations. She is author of several books, including *52%: Getting Women's Power into Politics* (1983), *The Domestication of Women: Discrimination in Developing Societies* (1980) and, with Zdenek Cervenka, *The Nuclear Axis: Secret Collaboration between West Germany and South Africa* (1978).

MEN ONLY

An Investigation into Men's Organisations

Barbara Rogers

London   Winchester   Sydney   Wellington

First published by Pandora Press, an imprint of the
Trade Division of Unwin Hyman, in 1988.

PANDORA PRESS

Unwin Hyman Limited
15/17 Broadwick Street, London W1V 1FP

Unwin Hyman Inc
8 Winchester Place, Winchester, MA 01890

Allen & Unwin Australia Pty Ltd
P.O. Box 764, 8 Napier Street, North Sydney, NSW 2060

Allen & Unwin NZ Ltd (in association with the Port Nicholson Press)
60 Cambridge Terrace, Wellington, New Zealand

ISBN 0 86358 0831

Set in 10 on 12 point Trump Medieval by Grove Graphics
Printed in Finland by Werner Söderström Oy

Contents

Acknowledgements

A number of researchers gave me invaluable help with this investigation, which I could not have achieved without them. They were: Peter Watson (men's clubs), Bernadette Donaldson (Church of England), Julia Davis (private schools, and statistical research), Bill Blume (Freemasons), James Marsh (pubs and the City), David Smith (armed forces), Linda Vickers (politics), and Stephen Potter (Rotary). I would like to thank also the Equal Rights in Clubs Campaign for Action (ERICCA) and many individuals who set me on the right track.

My thanks to the *New Statesman* for commissioning an investigation of working men's clubs, which became my introduction to this issue. Pandora showed great enthusiasm, and in the end patience: so did my agent Anne McDermid. My colleagues at *Everywoman*, especially Chris and Bernadette, cheered me on. The Press Association library provided a vast array of press cuttings. The Typing Pool co-operative produced a beautiful typescript. And acknowledgements are due, too, to Harleigh and Barry for showing me what football (American or otherwise) was all about.

Introduction

'What you can't see can't hurt you' has always seemed to me a strange principle on which to work for equal opportunities for women. A men-only organisation or club, by definition, is hardly ever even glimpsed by women – yet these are places where deals are done, jobs are offered and important matters of public as well as private interest discussed. It has seemed to me for some time that women, and the cause of equal opportunities generally, need a basic understanding of how these (to us) shadowy networks operate, and how they affect us.

My starting point is not that men should not get together for personal or social ends: on the contrary, men ought to have more male friends, not less. I do not object to a men-only club which is purely social, or even charitable in nature (although I object to any set-up where women are treated as inferiors). The problem, I suggest, lies in the fact that so many men-only organisations provide exclusive access to resources which should be available to all, without distinction or discrimination: community facilities and resources, sports, jobs, business deals, politics, and supposedly 'public' appointments. The question to be asked is: what do the members have that others are excluded from? Does it rightly belong to them, or to all of us?

In a country such as Britain where there is legislation against sex discrimination and unequal pay, and with all the equality provisions of the European Community, it is startling to discover the extent and power of men-only organisations (and those which are mixed but where men are in total control) which render these laws a joke by controlling major information and contact networks far from public scrutiny or accountability. At the moment Britain's Sex

Discrimination Act does not cover any activity which is not in the 'public' or commercial sphere. It simply means that private organisations can discriminate freely in the way they control public life. The connections, I hope, will become clear in the chapters that follow.

It is a daunting task to investigate where no woman is allowed to go: many of these organisations are very poorly documented for such important institutions in our society, and several of them rejected straightforward approaches from me. It therefore became essential to use men as informants and investigators alike, and I am most grateful to my researchers for their sterling work in helping to open up the different worlds of men only to a female scrutiny. Each institution presented a different challenge, and a different strategy had to be developed for getting an insight into each one: each chapter, therefore, is approached in its own way. Having shown the way and charted some of this unknown territory, I hope that others will follow to add more detail where I have already been, and also to investigate for themselves some of the other men-only organisations which I have come across in the course of researching this book, but was unable to include on my own itinerary.

I have aimed to cover the most important men-only organisations, whether because of size or influence or both. I started, in the first section, by looking at the 'informal' male culture and male territory which most of us are aware of — but do not think much about — in pubs, social drinking, and the world of sport. It is important to understand just how well organised they are as men's areas in an ostensibly integrated culture, because they profoundly affect our own relationships with men, as well as our prospects at work. They are the visible end of a largely invisible men-only sub-culture, the informal end of a highly organised set of organisations.

Part Two moves straight into less familiar territory: the mass men's organisations. I look in some detail at the working men's clubs which comprise by far the biggest working-class organisation; the Freemasons, who operate at different class levels but mainly in the middle of the social spectrum; and the Rotary Clubs, which specialise in business contacts. All three are enormously large and powerful as well as operating with varying degrees of secrecy.

Finally, I look at the élite men's networks, organisations and clubs which provide a framework for upper-class men from birth to death. I start (as most of them do) with the private boys' schools and go on to the Very Important Men's clubs, the City of London, and the upper tiers of those linked and also heavily segregated institutions, the Church of England and the armed forces.

This book is written primarily for women. I hope it will serve as a general introduction and outline of the male Establishment and how the big men's organisations work. Most men, I have found, already know at least some of this whether from personal access or from knowing other men who belong. It is important for women to know at least as much as the men do, if we are to work out a strategy for overcoming the discriminatory effects of all this.

Women's organisations – and especially those campaigning for equality – are ironically seen by many people as some kind of aberration, a strange innovation in what we like to think is an integrated society with its roots in the family. If this book manages to tilt our perceptions in that regard it will have achieved much. All the women's organisations taken together are as nothing in resources or influence compared to those of the men, organised as they are around the protection of members' privilege not only within the organisation but in society as a whole. If it is true at the base of society – with pubs, clubs and sports providing the permanent escape route from women, children, and personal involvement with both – it is even more true of what is referred to as the Establishment, which effectively runs the country from largely men-only inner sanctums.

In researching and writing this book I have become aware that I have only touched the surface of this issue. The informal 'buddy' culture in many workplaces, political parties and elsewhere needs much more investigation. So do the organised business, professional and trade organisations, from the dog-breeders' Crufts to the magicians' Magic Circle and beyond, which restrict women's entry to the positions of influence and privileged access. They operate along similar lines to those observed here and require their own investigators. There are, as I found, enough men willing to talk, for whatever reasons, about their club and what it does for them: we only have to find them. We need help from honest men, and there is every indication that it is available to us if we look for it.

PART ONE
Men's Territory

1
PUBS
'Getting away from the wife'

We know about pubs. At least, we know about the ones we've been in. No longer a male domain, pubs have been opened up to women.

Or have they? It is worth stepping back and looking at the pub scene, how it has and hasn't changed since the establishment of 'the pub' as a major social institution in the last century, and the invisible barriers which still persist at different times of day, in different parts of the pub, with different facilities, and between one pub and another. Pubs are very important institutions in Britain, not just as your 'local' where you can relax and be with friends – or go for a drink whenever you feel like spending time doing nothing in particular – but also because they are still very important as meeting places. Political parties, trade union branches and a variety of other meetings take place in the room over the pub, and adjourn downstairs for the gossip.

Last, but by no means least, the pub is important in the context of men-only meeting places because it *is* a public place, however restricted by custom and practice. Observations of how men use pubs can provide us with important clues to the psychology of other men-only gathering places including those which are 'secret', like the masons, or 'élite', like the West End clubs for top men.

Let's start, then, by a little tour of some pubs to refresh our memories of what they are like – including the bits where we are not welcome, and where we also choose not to go. Out of sight: out of mind.

This is an area where the appearance of a woman as observer affects the scene being observed and it seemed best to get a man to survey the scene. So intrepid *Men Only* researcher James Marsh did a pub crawl in one area of London, Whitechapel, chosen after a tour of the East End as fairly typical. It is a mixture of traditional working-class culture with the first signs of 'gentrification' providing a variety of pubs serving the different groups of regulars. The visits were made between 6.30 and 11 p.m. on a Friday night, the time when men traditionally go to the pub for some serious drinking, and women are also more likely to be going out.

The first pub he visited was The Lord Rodney's Head in the Whitechapel Road. From the outside it looked drab and uninviting and it turned out to be a stereotyped working men's pub, austerely furnished (probably last decorated in the 1950s) with few pretensions to comfort and none to style. A few fruit machines were the only diversion from drink that the pub offered. The clientele was *exclusively* male – middle-aged to old men, drinking in small groups or on their own.

He was greeted with a certain amount of suspicion and hostility, both by the proprietor and the customers he approached. They seemed to resent any intrusion on their drinking time and to regard any interest in pubs beyond their function as drinking holes as quite ridiculous. An old Irishman summed up the attitude of the pub: 'I'm here to drink beer. Everything else is fucking nonsense.' This was repeated several times to make sure the point was properly understood.

With persistence though, James managed to get one of the solitary drinkers to talk to him rather grudgingly. He was a married middle-aged man, who worked for the Gas Board and he came to the pub for a few pints after work before going home for his dinner: this was a daily ritual. What he wanted from the pub basically was a place to *drink*, without frills or molestation. He didn't come for conversation, although he found it reassuring that he would see the same familiar faces – men, he assumed, doing exactly what he was doing. He chose this particular pub because it was functional to his drinking needs. Indeed, the pub itself would presumably be attractive only to this sort of (male) customer who demanded a table, a chair, a pint, and nothing else.

When asked whether women ever came into the pub, this man responded: 'One or two of *them* bring their wives sometimes,' implying that this was a sort of exclusive drinking place for men where a few women could count themselves lucky if their husbands chose to 'bring them'.

Did women ever come in without their husbands? 'Not when I'm here . . . maybe later . . . but they wouldn't come *here*, would they?'

Did he ever bring his own wife? 'No . . . she wouldn't like it.'

Did she have his dinner ready for him when he got home? 'Well, yes, usually . . . she knows my habits.'

Pubs like The Rodney's Head are perhaps less numerous than they used to be, but they are there in much larger numbers than we want to notice – small, perhaps a bit scruffy, definitely not welcoming to strangers. Inside they have a strong 'members only' atmosphere. As an outsider, James was made to feel distinctly uncomfortable – and it would be much worse for a woman. This sort of pub appeals to exactly the type of character James found inside, and effectively excludes anyone outside the area, the social class and drinking habits of the regulars.

As a general observation, it is likely that any pub (or social place) which caters largely for the consumption of beer in quantity will be a men's area, since most women would find this very boring as well as feeling very isolated in a pub of this kind even if the men refrained from hostile looks, gestures and comments.

The next pub on the list was The Star and Garter, a pub that used to be very similar in atmosphere and clientele to The Rodney's Head. The landlord here, though, had made a conscious effort to change his customer base. A hand-written notice refuses entry to 'Persons in Industrial Clothing', and the bar itself is done out in kitschy modern style, what you could call 'anti-pub' decor and fittings (fitted green carpets, cafe-style tables, spotlights, and so on). However, there were no women drinking in this pub either. The male customers were younger and in groups, and it had, although with a different generation, a strongly 'masculine' atmosphere, at this prime time – 7.30 or 8 p.m. – on a Friday night. James chatted up one of the regulars, a middle-aged man who ran his own removals business. He was already quite drunk. He claimed that this used to be a 'dosser's' pub but that since the landlord had redecorated he had prevented the 'wrong sort' from coming in and that 'respectable people' now drank here. So it was moving up in social class as well as down in age.

He came to the pub, he explained, because it was a bit 'classy' and he would feel able to bring 'a lady friend' here. Did women come to the pub on their own or in groups without men? 'Sometimes. Not much, really, like a group of birds, but you won't get them in this area. Look around . . . if you're looking for dolly birds, you should go down the road a bit.' He was referring to The London Hospital Tavern, which was in fact on the list.

This man used the pub, apart from a place to drink and be seen, as a sort of recruitment centre. Men seeking casual work often came in and he would give them a couple of days' work, sealing his 'contract' with a round of drinks. Builders and painters he knew also did the same thing in this pub from time to time, handing out odd jobs. This, he thought, was common in this sort of area with high unemployment and the last vestiges of a genuine community.

The Star and Garter was very different, superficially, from the first pub visited – but women were expected to be there only when taken in by an 'accepted' male regular. This was common at weekends, when a fairly even sex ratio was achieved. For most of the week, though, it remained *male* territory despite efforts to 'neutralise' the interior away from the traditional fixtures of the pub.

The only woman in the pub was in fact a young student, working temporarily as a barmaid. She said that the customer mix had changed since the recent refurbishment, and pointed to two other innovations designed to attract what the landlord regarded as 'the right sort'. There was now food at lunchtimes, and wine was available. These particular features appeared to have made the pub more attractive to women – but strictly at lunchtimes only. This is a neutral period in a pub's life, especially if there are offices in the area, when it is not necessarily controlled by its 'regulars' and it can take on a more comfortable atmosphere for women, and the offer of food and perhaps a drink at a reasonable price without pressure to down several pints, in the company of others with similar interests.

James asked the barmaid more specific questions about herself. Did she feel uncomfortable being the only woman in the pub? 'It's kind of funny, I suppose, but you don't notice it really. It's just normal for me.' Did women come to the pub much? 'A lot at lunchtimes, to have lunch usually. I mean, they seem to quite like it here.' And did the male regulars bring their wives or partners? 'No, they're not usually with them, except at the weekend. . . . Some do, quite a lot, then.'

Was the pub hostile to unaccompanied women? 'No, not really. . . . Well now, I suppose it is, because there's none here, is there? It's all men really . . . but it's still quite early.'

Did the men make remarks to her that she could do without? 'It's difficult, really, they do – but then I think it doesn't bother me. I just give it back, but it's OK, it's their problem. I mean, the manager's quite good, I don't have to dress up or wear anything special like some pubs around here – the one across the road, they all wear shorts and low-cut T-shirts. Funnily enough, it's a poser's pub, that one' (The London Hospital Tavern again).

The visit to The Star and Garter brought out an obvious, but still interesting point. Men's drinking and pub-going habits are radically different from women's: the same pub can have a completely different atmosphere at various times of day, and between work-days and weekends, and if a woman came in to a familiar pub at the 'wrong' time she would stick out like a sore thumb (the barmaid is part of the fittings, not an exception as a female visitor would be).

And so to the famous London Hospital Tavern. It turned out to be a fairly ghastly example of the pretentious high-tech, no-character design which the breweries have convinced themselves will appeal to young people. Tropical plants, mirrors everywhere, a plethora of chrome make this kind of pub far removed from any traditional notions of a British pub. Again, the management were doing their best here to exclude a certain *type* of man. Men in 'industrial clothes' would have clashed with the pub's decorative pretensions.

It was now 8.30, but even here the only customers were men: groups of young men, or men who still fancied themselves as young, well dressed and apparently embarking on a night out. Again, there was a strong feeling that this was *male* territory, and that women would be acceptable only on *male* terms. The only women in the pub, in fact, were employees – obviously recruited for youth and attractiveness, and dressed up to emphasise a male-defined 'sexiness'. The manager agreed when James put this to him. 'Yeah, sure, why not? I don't tell the girls what to wear but they know how to fit in. Around here it's important to get it right. A lot of the pubs are really *scummy* . . .' Later on, he claimed, there would be a mixture of men and women but the men always started their drinking earlier.

The London Hospital Tavern is an increasingly common type of pub, especially in the cities. Not *necessarily* a pick-up joint, it's the kind of place where any woman could expect comments and some direct approaches – not the place to get away from it all! James's brief chat with a group of men there revealed that they came because their mates did and because there would be a lot of 'birds' there later on. They were fairly indifferent to the decor but thought it was better than 'sawdust on the floor' and 'lots of drunken old bastards falling about'.

Customers in each of the pubs were scathing about the others in the area, though there was some cross-over between The London Hospital Tavern and The Star and Garter: customers moving on from the latter to enjoy the 'sexy' environment of the former.

James was pointed in the direction of The Grave Maurice as being an 'odd' pub, used by students and nurses, and unusual in the sense that few local residents used it. On entering this pub, there was an immediately obvious difference in atmosphere. It was furnished in a low-key, unobtrusive and comfortably traditional way, the decor not being contrived and pretentious like the two previous pubs. And for the first time there were actually groups of women in the pub and they even seemed to be in a majority, overall. If you go into a pub like this it's easy to forget that it's the exception that proves the rule.

The barmaid, again a student, had some strong views on the problem women face in mixing socially in pubs, both from observation and from direct experience. James asked her about her job and the difficulties of it. Apparently the pub was used a lot by medical students, and although they didn't make the atmosphere hostile to women customers, a minority did seem to regard the bar staff as fair game for sexist remarks. It was not really very different from the kind of leers you'd get in The London Hospital Tavern. 'It just takes a different form that's much more subtle, but it can be very crude as well.'

And it offends you, obviously? 'It offends all women, but most just live with it. I mean, it offends me as a human being because in this particular job men can regard you as just a sexual commodity. You give them their beer but they want you to smile and flirt . . . not all men, and not here so much but it's still irritating. What's funny is that in a lot of pubs round here, and everywhere I suppose, it's somebody's wife doing the serving and they still expect them to behave that way, they don't realise it could be their wives. They don't make the connection.'

And her own experience of pubs, off-duty? 'I don't like them much, they're really boring. It's not much fun watching men drink all those pints and becoming more and more obnoxious. You don't always get obvious harassment but it's always there, you come to expect it. When you see a crowd of men together it's worrying, because they egg each other on, they're like a pack really . . .'

Did she feel that men controlled the atmosphere in pubs to some extent? 'Yes, obvious really, when you think about it, and how you think twice about going in them on your own, even places that you know. When I've done it, even if I'm waiting for friends or whatever, I find myself just making sure I've got a newspaper so that it's like I'm occupied and hidden.'

How much freedom do women have to use pubs? 'Well, you have to choose where you're going very carefully, where you're going to be OK. I don't think women – well, I don't anyway – just go out and drink for the sake of it. It's almost as if they're not *allowed* to.'

What were the alternatives? 'Wine bars are good because there's wine, people don't go there to drink loads of beer. They're private as well. . . . In a pub it's like you're *available*, anyone can just walk up to you. I have been to women-only pubs when it's the right night, though.'

Why was that so different? 'Well, men take that situation for granted, don't they? Drinking together. When women are together like that it does seem perfectly natural: there's no role to play, like trying to be aloof and that sort of thing. You don't feel threatened . . . but they're a defensive thing really, and that's a shame. There's a lot more talking than drinking, and that's a difference.'

None of the women asked said they would feel comfortable going in to *any* pub on their own – a commonplace taken for granted by most men. And there was a lot of stress on this – exceptional – pub being one where women felt at ease. Two women, both secretaries who had travelled some way to meet in this particular pub, said it was the only pub in a wide area that they'd feel comfortable in, just talking. It was also one of the very few pubs they'd 'feel safe' in. One of the women was a Canadian, who pointed out that in Canada it was even worse: bars were intimidating, all-male drinking places, and unaccompanied women would simply never dare go in – even with a newspaper! It was quite rare for Canadian women to go independently to bars even in groups.

This group also drew attention to a particular problem women face when we go out socially in the evenings: that of travelling home late, which to them was a real worry and something that affected the whole business of going out – preventing them from drinking too much and always having to ensure they'd go home in a group.

Pub trends

After this excursion through pub-land, perhaps it is time to assess whether pubs are really, as some claim, becoming more 'family' institutions rather than anti-family, the men's escape holes for getting away from family responsibilities and relationships.

The evidence is mixed. You certainly have the good news: more women in pubs at weekends, more food, sometimes family rooms and garden areas where you can take – shock, horror – children. The aversion to kids, it's easy to conclude, has less to do with publicans' worries about their getting the drinking habit early on than a concern with keeping women back home to look after them while the men are guaranteed a meeting place without responsibilities. There's many a pub still which shows not the slightest interest in catering for children.

Then of course there's the bad news, and the battles still being fought in pubs around the country. Fleet Street's El Vino wine bar, a gossip and contact shop where the drink just helps the wheeling and dealing, fought a protracted legal battle to stop women claiming a legal right to get served at the bar, which is where they were most likely to hear something to their advantage. Having finally lost the case on appeal, El Vino manager Peter Bracken tried (unsuccessfully) to ban the two women who had brought the case. However, he is entitled to ban women who are not wearing skirts – so there is no feeling of being welcomed on your own terms.

El Vino's might be the top end of the trade, but that battle has its parallels in pubs up and down the country where there are sporadic outbursts of fighting over attempts to ban knitting in pubs, stop women breast-feeding in pubs, stop us drinking pints (you're supposed to do it by halves), serving glasses with stems instead of handles, and the rest. We all have our own particular red flag to which we respond with rage: mine was a pub near Holloway Prison where I tried to buy drinks while the publican pretended I wasn't there, and which had a cute little card stuck on the wall: 'We don't serve women, you have to bring your own.' I was getting angrier by the minute and my comments to an embarrassed companion louder and louder. He turned round and served me just in time to stop me throwing the ice-bucket at his fancy mirrors at the back of the bar, in which he'd been keeping a furtive watch on my reactions. The joy of combat . . .

Despite this kind of guerrilla warfare, women versus publicans, there is a general notion that the women are winning and in particular are invading pub territory as increasingly important customers. Take for instance a well-publicised Gallup survey commissioned by Harp lager in 1985, which painted a rosy picture of more women buying more – er, lager actually, more food, bar staff claiming there was less violence (well, they would wouldn't they?). They also, incidentally, found some form of 'entertainment' at 81 per cent of pubs and 94 per cent of clubs: gaming machines (45 per cent), darts (41 per cent), juke boxes (33 per cent), pool tables (32 per cent), dominoes and live entertainment (26 per cent) and cards (22 per cent). The cynical would point out that most of these are used mainly by men, that 'live entertainment' is a euphemism for a stripper and that one of the innovations in some pubs is a GIANT screen to show football matches which is what some of us might have been trying to get away from in the first place . . .

Time to look at some facts and figures. First we need to remember one important reality: women drink much less alcohol, much less frequently, than men. When we do drink, we often have different products from the men. It is the much lower volume that is the most significant factor in women's marginal position in pubs and pub culture (and similarly for other kinds of recreational clubs, as we shall see later). It explains the pub landlords' and breweries' general lack of interest in us and in our interests as customers.

In a recent Government survey on alcoholism comparing a 'high risk' area with a low risk one,[1] the drinking habits of the women – at home or outside – were almost identical in the two areas. This suggests that women's drinking is not subject to the regional and social variation that men's drinking is. In both areas it was found that 45 per cent of women drank less than once a week; only 24 per cent of the men were this abstemious. Of those women who did drink more than once a week, only 20 per cent consumed more than ten units of alcohol a week (equivalent to five pints or ten shorts). Of the men who drank with some frequency (a higher proportion of men in any case) over half drank more than ten units. As with all drinking surveys, this report was obliged throughout to separate male and female data, since they are so different that combining them gives a nonsensical answer. Almost every aspect of social drinking separates women from men in a dramatic, and socially very significant way.

In a market prediction undertaken for the alcoholic drink

trade,[2] it is suggested that the female market for alcoholic drinks (with the possible exception of wine) has now expanded to its natural limit, after increasing during the 1970s. This means that there is no significant profit increase to be extracted from the female market, however much the pubs try to cater for women.

The bulk of the profit to be made in the drinks industry remains − and will remain − selling beer to men. Women overall are *not* a significant part of the beer market, as all the market surveys show. The same report goes in for some interesting speculation about the presence of women in pubs actually *depressing* the profits. The increasing proportion of women in pubs since the 1970s, it suggests, may actually have diminished the consumption of drink among men they were with. More talk, less drinking perhaps.

Brewing Review, the organ of the Brewers' Society − which is the national federation of all the brewers − published in its January 1986 issue some of the results of a MORI survey on attitudes and trends in pubs.[3] These crystallise some of the assumptions which are being formed in the pub trade which underlie their whole attitude to women, and provide other useful information on the changing patterns of pub usage more generally. In 1973, roughly 20 per cent of women polled visited pubs once a week or more: by 1984 it had risen to about 27 per cent, but the figure has fluctuated throughout that period (in 1978 it was 24 per cent, 1981 back down to 18 per cent).

Overall, then, in the last decade, there has been an increase in the frequency and regularity of women's visits to the pub, but not particularly dramatic or even consistent. Men in the same survey show a corresponding pattern of fluctuation (probably accounted for by economic recession, and inflation which hit a peak in 1981), but in 1984 roughly twice as many men (51 per cent) as women were visiting a pub more than once a week (and remember that, once there, they drank a lot more − and men were more likely to be the very frequent attenders so the ratio was a lot more than 2:1).

One interesting finding was that women are now more likely to have a 'local' (52 per cent of women drinkers polled in 1984, 8 per cent up on 1981) which indicates that we are identifying as 'ours' certain pubs where we feel comfortable and 'at home'. This trend, if it continues, would seem to indicate that women are being accepted as regulars in some pubs, although it implies that others will remain firmly fixed in their Women Keep Out ways. You'd be going quite often to the Grave Maurices of the pub world while leaving the Lord Rodneys severely alone. The Stars and Garters would be visited at lunchtime but not in the evening, and the Hospital Taverns would be somewhere to go in a group but definitely not on your own. So in a good three-quarters of all pubs (probably more) men would have free access at all times while women were restricted – even if we were not that conscious of it.

Another point to come out of the survey, which is unsurprisingly given little prominence in *Brewing Review*, is that wine bars are becoming more and more popular (23 per cent of all those polled visited a wine bar in 1984). It is well known, and even the brewers will reluctantly admit it, that the increasing popularity of wine bars has to a large extent been fostered by women as an alternative drinking venue to the pub. The atmosphere and layout of a wine bar, more upwardly mobile in atmosphere than most pubs, is also more comfortable – and a woman is not made to feel so 'available'. As a recent development in drinks outlets, too, it does not have a long tradition of association with men-only drinking. It is another indication of women abandoning the 'integration' of pubs and finding special places to socialise which leave the rest more or less as they were. Interestingly, the statistics for wine bars in this MORI survey is one of the few sets of data that are not broken down by gender. It would just be too glaringly obvious that wine bars can attract women.

Brigid McConville's book *Women Under the Influence*[4] puts a different perspective on MORI survey evidence for women having their own 'local'. It could be, she argues, that 'women's drinking habits are dictated by the men they associate with. A woman will inherit a new "regular" with a new man and when the relationship breaks up she disappears from the scene, losing contact with the whole group.' This certainly looks like part of the explanation – and indicates that for some women even the friendly 'local' is theirs only as long as they are with the man who is the true member of that particular pub family. Without him, she loses that whole social network.

Of course, once in the pub there is pressure to drink alcohol, perhaps more than we really want to in some cases – but as Brigid McConville points out, women are not 'supposed to' be seen drunk in public, although it is fairly acceptable, even sometimes a matter of pride, for men. Women can, of course – and do – get drunk at home on their own.[5] This simply reinforces our isolation and the idea of the 'public house' as men's territory. Public drinking, as Brigid shows, is a part of male culture, and attitudes towards social drinking and drunkenness are shaped by male values. Even the etiquette of social drinking – each man buying his own round in a session lasting a couple of hours or more – tends to exclude women, although in 'our' pubs at least we have managed to modify that and have started to join in by buying the odd round ourselves (as much as we can afford anyway) or buying in smaller groups and even individually.

The brewers' tale

What do the brewers say, faced with evidence that their pubs are, with certain exceptions, pretty much the men's territory they always have been with women allowed in only on the men's terms? We asked two of the major brewers, Watneys and Courage, for their views, with additional comments from the Brewers' Society and finally from that interesting pressure group the Campaign for Real Ale (CAMRA) which has become quite a force for change in pubs. What kind of change, socially speaking? Read on . . .

First Watneys, or Grotneys as their critics have fondly dubbed them: their Public Relations Executive, Debbie Styles, says 'there is no policy' for women as far as her company is concerned. 'We do not have a policy to discriminate against any potential customers, everyone is free to come into a Watneys pub.' Yes, but . . . as she hastened to add, each pub attracts its own regulars who in turn create the atmosphere in that pub (who's welcome, who gets stared at, made comments about, greeted with stony silence or all the other little tricks we all know so well). The implications of Watneys' position are that it sees no point in discouraging the drinking habits of its existing regulars, the basis for its profits, because women just don't have the money or inclination to fill the gap as far as it can see. It is only when a pub is unprofitable or its customers are more trouble than they are worth that the brewery would step in to tart it up in order to attract a different bunch of regulars, perhaps with a new landlord or a couple (playing the old stereotyped Mine Host and Lady at the Bar roles). Debbie offered just one aspect of the brewing trade that the company saw women as having influenced: that of product range, which has diversified considerably over the last decade to accommodate our tastes. And so to Courage and its Public Relations Manager, Stewart Reed. A similar story here, too: he told us the company has never had any specific policy to encourage or cater for its female customers. The changes which have been taking place – and 'the pub trade is constantly evolving' – have had some implications for women but are part of a more general upgrading or uptarting of pubs which only incidentally makes them more pleasant to women. Upward mobility in social class terms looks like a much more powerful motive, in fact. He agreed that the increasing range of drinks, and especially wine, was a specific response to women's tastes (though many middle-class men share them, too). His general conclusion was that the increase of women using the pubs in the 1970s had levelled out and had been pretty static during the 1980s.

Women's support alone, in fact, is not enough to keep a product on tap. Courage had recently launched Miller Lite, a less bulky lager which they believed would be popular with women. Indeed it was, but in marketing terms it is counted as a flop because not enough was being shifted to justify stocking it, and since it is relatively weak and light the men seemed to regard it with contempt as a 'women's drink'. It is now being promoted with a heavy-handed macho image.

This conversation was interesting for the tacit admission that while the breweries were quite happy to sell drink to women when we happen to be there, especially at weekends, it was simply not in their interest to interfere with the prevailing – male – atmosphere where that was firmly established and yielding good profit. Stewart pointed out that from Sunday night to Thursday, the great majority of sales in pubs were to men. 'Women tend to be weekend drinkers. The atmosphere in pubs, in my experience, changes a lot at weekends.'

There is just one aspect of Courage's policy towards pubs which has had a positive benefit for women: an effort over recent years to improve toilet facilities (in the 1981 MORI attitude survey 63 per cent of women polled said this was important to them in pubs, the highest response to any of the questions). But he admitted that in many of Courage's pubs the toilets were still dilapidated, often outside and very primitive.

Asked whether Courage had many women actually managing or running its pubs, Stewart said: 'It's a hard business for women to be in' and added that 'quite honestly, there's only a certain sort of woman who can cope with it.' Offhand, he was aware of 'one pub in London run by two women and there are others', but clearly the brewery believes that running a pub (as distinct from serving in it) is a man's job. Of course, 'the wine bar trade, now there are a lot of women in *that* business', and a great many pubs are actually run jointly by couples.

And so on to the Brewery Society, whose Mr Ripley

repeated the theme: 'We don't feel that significantly more numbers of women are drinking in pubs, certainly not over the last five years, and women who go to pubs don't seem to be drinking significantly more.' What they are much more concerned about is unemployment which is beginning to hit their customer base badly, especially in the areas where it is concentrated. Women, he felt, were certainly not going to replace the men who dropped out because they had lost their jobs.

Apart from anything else, Mr Ripley pointed out, many women just weren't drinking for the sake of the alcoholic effect like many men did. Over a third of the women polled in the Brewery Society's MORI survey had expressed a preference for a soft drink (what a heresy) while over 80 per cent of the men opted for the staple item, beer. The economics of this for the brewers are self-evident. On the other hand, he pointed out, the widespread availability of food in pubs – as well as the wider range of drinks – *was* mainly inspired by women's demands at lunchtime (most of this becomes suddenly unavailable in the evening, incidentally).

So there you have it: the brewers, who after all own and make the major decisions on most pubs, couldn't really care less about their becoming less male-dominated. Put more politely, they have 'no particular policy'. Elements like more food, a wider choice of drink and better toilets and general furnishings have been introduced in some areas (much less in rural areas and the North of England); even these are only done partly for women as such. And on the issue that would make the greatest difference – provision for children – the brewers are not prepared to make any stand (and many 'regulars' are very hostile to the idea). Don't forget, also, that beer advertising (unlike lager and even Guinness, which at one time was trying to reach women) is directed almost entirely at men. The image of the pub in these ads is strictly Men-Only, with the stereotyped barmaid or sexy pick-up there simply as part of the furnishings or amenities for the male customers. In one ad, a girl-friend leaves our hero in disgust; he goes to the pub and she suddenly appears at the door, eyes down, humiliated and desperate to come back. The ad image reflects the reality of a male culture, fantasy and all, at least in the great majority of pubs, of this being male territory – complete with fantasy about women.

There is a big programme, especially in the South of England, of breweries tarting up pubs – gutting their often genuinely old exteriors to install fake-old or glitzy-new yuppie features with lots of brass, chrome and mirrors (for admiring yourself in). These jobs are almost universally condemned but they work, bringing in crowds of screeching trendies (or would-be trendies): money flows freely as the drink, there may be pretentious and pricey food (imitating the wine bars) and the atmosphere is a cross between a very loud party and a pick-up joint. There are women, usually, although definitely a minority: women belong very much in groups here, not on our own. Or you could become a 'bird', as they would put it in The London Hospital Tavern.

This upmarket trend goes together with the increasing emphasis on new, branded drinks, especially lagers with the emphasis on imports. There is also heavy promotion of low-alcohol drinks. The reason is in the profit margins: they are high on branded lagers, higher still on low-alcohol drinks which are not subject to excise duty so the customer pays the same and the pub and brewer pocket the difference. Alternatives are also needed, with higher margins, to compensate for what looks like beer sales drying up – by four million barrels in the last decade, attributed to the decline in the 'sweaty industries' (and mass unemployment in industrial areas: no good being thirsty if you can't afford your pints). So the drive is relentlessly upmarket and towards younger people (at least in terms of the pub image) but it is still aimed at men and masculinity. The fact that men have more money for social drinking, more time to spend in the new trendy pub, and more inclination to drink the night away has not changed, despite all the aspirations to yuppiedom.

Campaign for 'real' pubs

The Campaign for Real Ale (CAMRA) is a pressure group originally set up to persuade brewers and pub landlords to retain and reintroduce traditionally brewed British cask beer. CAMRA's efforts have been quite successful, as most people in the brewing industry will admit. Their role has modified over the years to become, effectively, a general pub-users' pressure group concerned with all aspects of pubs' facilities and management. It is thus the only consumers' organisation which exists for the brewing trade, with a membership of about 20,000.

We spoke to Neil Hanson, CAMRA Executive member and the Editor of *The Good Beer Guide*. He agreed that the average CAMRA member is seen as a 'fat middle-aged beer bore', and that the image of the organisation was largely a masculine one – which was pretty much correct when it started. CAMRA has been going for more than fifteen years now, and its membership has considerably diversified. He is probably not exaggerating much when he says that the organisation is no longer the bourgeois and male-dominated group that it was when it started. Roughly 30 per cent of its members are now women; and on an Executive of twelve there are presently four women. Conversely, of course, that means that over two-thirds of its members are men. Neil Hanson had to agree that, traditionally, women have joined and become involved via male partners and friends, which implies that their entrée into the male world of real-ale drinking is almost all via men. Recently though, he pointed out, women are joining the organisation as 'individuals in their own right' which he claimed reflects the increasing diversity of the organisation's objectives – and women drinking more beer and defending traditional pubs that we know and have 'adopted' as ours too. Much of CAMRA's efforts these days are centred on the breweries' 'obsessive and reckless' refurbishment. There is also the war on chemical additives which is of interest to those who drink real beer.

Neil admits that CAMRA was originally perhaps indifferent to attracting women as members, not as a stated policy but through its core membership who were rather chauvinistic and in favour of the traditional men-only pub atmosphere. Many of them were beer snobs who felt it was only men who had the right and the taste to appreciate proper beer. They were and are very scornful of lager, the 'women's drink'. That element remains in the organisation, although Neil speculates that in numerical terms they may have been outnumbered by women. A large proportion of the female membership comes from the South and East of England though, which indicates that elsewhere CAMRA simply reinforces that anti-women feel to the traditional pub. Because the organisation applies such strong consumer pressure on the brewing trade it could in theory become a way for women to argue for our own needs in pubs, although Neil Hanson admits that this is *not* happening at the moment.

Pub culture

Pubs, and the way people behave in them, for all their importance in social, political and cultural terms, have hardly been touched by academic observers. If you want anthropological studies about male exclusiveness, ritual and how male identity is formed by opposition to the female, then you're looking at extensive works on the cultures of what we now call the Third World. The exotic practices of the British pub (and bars in other western countries) are largely unrecorded and certainly not analysed.

The brave exception, though, proves the rule. There are two important works available as we go to press: Ann Whitehead's twenty-month study of a rural pub in Herefordshire, and its importance in the community as a whole,[6] and Valerie Hey's hard-hitting book *Partriarchy and Pub Culture*, which reviews the historical sources and puts forward some basic theories about how pub culture works – both inside the pub and in the community outside.[7]

An important reason for the lack of studies about men's use of pubs is, of course, the problems that any woman has in quietly observing, or unobtrusively participating in the hardline male pub culture they are trying to study. Ann Whitehead found the The Waggoner's regulars (all of them men) resented any woman's presence, and she was 'allowed' to stay only as an outsider and 'eccentric' under the protection of a friendly man: 'She's like a sister to me.' When women did come in, she witnessed some very threatening incidents of systematic verbal and sexual abuse, and a 'jokey' physical assault in which several men held a woman down and encouraged the abuser, obviously very nasty for the victim. In Valerie Hey's case, she was prompted to study the way men's pub culture worked (as opposed to getting the hell out and finding more 'friendly' places which most of us tend to do) by some bad experiences of her own. In one, she entered a strange pub to meet a male friend who'd forgotten about the arrangement and was then subjected to the experience of being 'stranded like a liberal in the White House. A stranger, unwelcome.' She received unwelcome advances of the exaggeratedly drunken variety. 'Close encounters. I try to keep cool and sophisticated. I fail. Tell him to blankety-blank. The other [male] customers stare at *me*. How dare I spoil the fun! I leave, humiliated and irate.' Ouch . . . don't we all know what that feels like. And it works, practically every time. We don't go back there, which is the whole idea.

Another incident involved two groups of women, obviously well used to giving as good as they get verbally, in different rooms of another pub. One group is bothered by a 'comprehensively drunken' man who pesters them persistently despite warnings: more important, perhaps, is that his companions won't intervene to stop him and accuse the *women* of causing the trouble. In the end the women 'win' by getting rid of the drunk and his mates, but: 'A victory? I am emotionally drained, my "quiet" drink has become a battle of nerves. . . . We feel sickened.' They leave, as does the other group which has had if anything an even worse experience in the darts bar – again from a 'drunk' man supported by his mates.

Valerie also has quite a lot of experience serving in these kinds of pubs which she draws on, together with some Victorian written sources and a Mass Observation study of pubs in Bolton, Lancashire, in 1938–1940 (involving male observers – who completely miss the meanings in terms of male–female antagonism of what they are describing).

Before the nineteenth century in Britain there were taverns, offering food, drink and perhaps a bed for travellers. These all-purpose centres became uneconomic and specialisation occurred: hotels, restaurants, and the pubs. These, as we know them today, are a Victorian creation related especially to the social upheavals and distress of the industrial revolution – as were the gin palaces they were competing with. A retreat from back-breaking labour and appalling housing conditions, sick children, gross overcrowding, noise, arguments, cold and dirt (from which women, though, had no escape), but also a whole social centre and meeting or market-place, the men's club for the new industrial working class. Pubs then sold much stronger brews than any available now. Here was the teeming street life brought indoors into warm, well-lit and comfortable buildings with vendors of food and almost anything coming in, money lenders and plenty of games: betting, cards, dominoes and cock fighting as well as access to newspapers, political meetings, sporting clubs and transport networks based on the pub – not to mention street and community gossip. And, for good measure, there were women available for paid sex in many of the pubs, where some landlords rented rooms for prostitution. They could be brothels as much as drinking places, especially those near army barracks or ports, or where there were large numbers of men who were too poor to set up a family or who were in the 'bachelor trades', forbidden by their employers to marry. Any woman in a pub, then and often now, was assumed to be 'available'.

Even more crucial, perhaps, there was no alternative to the pub as a social and small business centre, apart from its exact opposite: temperance societies and chapel life (largely a women's world). The pub was, as Valerie Hey puts it, 'a masculine republic in every street', a men's playground as well as the hub of the social and public life of the community.

The women were only too aware of this divide. Their hostility to the pub, and the way that men would spend their wages on themselves there at the expense of their families, is well documented (and its formal expression is of course the temperence movement itself). The price paid by many women in their opposition to these male republics, in terms of physical violence and often rape when their husbands *did* come home from the pub, is also a matter of record.

The influence of the pubs on society in general is also very evident. Working-class organisation and the growth of trade unions, closely linked with the public houses, were essentially a male domain as a result. The contrasts in wealth between men and women were greatly increased by the pub habit: it provided what Valerie Hey describes as 'a male right of passage, a right to an exit out of the discomfort. . . . [It] enabled [and enables] men to enjoy better living standards *at the expense of their wives.*' Female and male interests were in head-on collision, very often, as music-hall songs and jokes of the time illustrate all too vividly. It is worth noting, in passing, that in many Third World countries which are going through similar social breakdown in the name of 'development', male drinking habits are seen as the biggest problem by many of the women involved (and they are not short of other problems, needless to say). It is a problem that western male 'experts' have been very slow to perceive since it follows a pattern which they take for granted as a part of their own culture (which lies behind the whole male bias in allocating 'development' benefits in the first place).[8]

Before moving on from the Victorian experience, it is

worth noting an important element in the pub culture of the time which persists very strongly in many working-class institutions and initiations: the idea that to 'prove' his masculinity and therefore membership of the group and access to public life, a man had to drink a lot. The ability to 'drink deeply' was seen as proof of masculinity itself; it was widely and (for the publican) conveniently believed that beer was an essential source of energy both for physical labour and for sex ('puts lead in your pencil' or in the ad-man's version, 'reaches those parts other beers cannot reach'). Complex and secret customs, especially in the skilled crafts, marked what the anthropologists would call the initiation of an apprentice entering the rank of master craftsman, all of it depending on large amounts of drink and drunkenness. These rituals depend on humiliating and sometimes hurting the initiate, then welcoming him into the group – a use of psychological pressure well known to many traditional cultures and to the modern-day cults which are accused of 'brainwashing' their young initiates into total loyalty.

And so to the observations of the late 1930s in Bolton, where many of the early Victorian traditions are clearly in place, although modified to suit the circumstances of several decades later. In some ways the pubs had been drastically changed – much weaker beer, less being drunk in total – but many important elements were the same. Apart from the religious sects, there was 'nowhere else to go' other than the pub. It was still very much a male domain, apart from the barmaid and prostitutes. Wives were 'invited' at weekends into a special room, the lounge, and they could occupy the 'snug', a small private bar which also figures in descriptions of some Victorian pubs. We are told repeatedly in the study that the men came to the pubs to 'get out ow't t'road o' t' wife' and the editor of the Mass Observation study himself concludes that part of the pub's purpose is to be the place where 'men can meet and talk [out] of the way of their womenfolk'.

There were many rooms marked or recognised as for men

only, and sometimes areas within rooms, commonly at the bar and near the fire. The vault, absolutely taboo to women, was where men could do practically whatever they liked. The taproom would be close by, with more of a club atmosphere and offering a variety of games – also out of bounds to women. The force of the custom and practice regulating male and female use of the pubs is evident in the fact that women challenge the system only when they are away from their home pubs. Men are obliged to join in the system whether they like it or not. One man admitted: 'My reason for drinking beer is to appear tough. I heartily detest the stuff but what would my pals say if I refused. They would call me a cissy.'

Valerie Hey sees a tremendous fear from both sexes, but especially the men, about possible 'contamination' by the 'opposite' sex if they do not conform to the group's norm of behaviour. It is men's insecurity about their sexuality, and their dependence for intimacy on the women they feel they need to despise, which is bound up in the deep antagonism they express towards women in general. This is often expressed in terms of contempt for the 'tarts' or 'whores' to be found in the pub itself (their own sexual partners!). Valerie suggests that the relationship (which they initiate) has to be criminalised or made 'taboo' not because it is that different from 'normal' relationships with their wives, but precisely because it is so similar.

The role of the barmaid, 'sexy' or otherwise, is also interesting: Valerie observes that as a very poorly-paid barmaid she was offered a drink by some men (which she took in cash form). The men then assumed that she would listen to their complaints about their wives, and generally offer a sympathetic and non-judgemental ear: 'a perfect construction of male fantasies – maternal *and* sexual, offering a "safe" pseudo-flirtation.'

Finally, Mass Observation found that men 'brought' their wives and sometimes other female relatives to the pub lounge at weekends, and bought them drinks – another common feature of pub culture now. It meant the men could control what women did, where, and how much they could drink (the men often disappeared elsewhere to buy their own drinks). It reinforces the idea that a man is 'free' to spend as much as he likes on himself while his wife has to wait until *he* decides to buy her something: so the imbalance between women's and men's spending power is very much a part of this transaction, and the pub convention that women do not buy their own drinks. The men, incidentally, were effectively required to spend a lot of time (and money) in the pub where the main topic of conversation was about (or more accurately, against) women and women's sexuality, and male control of it. 'Nights out with the boys' or regular stag nights (once a week is still common for many men) were an important part of separating men from the family and ignoring women's demands for joint responsibility. Instead of having to come to terms with a woman on an equal basis, with equal freedom to come and go, the man could be absent whenever demands become hard to deal with, and could be expected to do so regularly regardless of what was happening at home. This may now mean games with the lads, or in 'stag' joints watching a woman strip, seeing porn videos, and generally slagging off women in sexually obscene ways. It matters on an individual, psychological level, but it is also required by the other men in the group: as one man quoted in the Mass Observation study put it, he was in the pub to show he was not 'under the thumb'. 'I'm not like some buggers, henpecked.'

Of course, male 'freedom' is the other side of women's confinement to the home. This can be through the lack of money to go out, or the fact that with him absent she has to be there for the children. It is reinforced by the same abusive pub-based talk about her if she does go out, especially in a fairly small community like the one studied in 1967 by Ann Whitehead in Herefordshire which shows very similar processes, men using the pub for social control of the women, to that observed by Mass Observation in Bolton. In Herefordshire 'going out' was seen as evidence that a woman is a whore, and even women's organisations like the Women's Institute were the target of a constant stream of abuse from the men in the pub.

It's not a pretty story, this pub question, when you look at it in any detail. The kind of study and explanations provided by Ann Whitehead and Valerie Hey are powerful reminders of a side of this society we live in which, for the sake of our self-esteem and peace of mind, we prefer to ignore or avoid. All women, I suggest, are familiar with the feeling of being stranded in a hostile group of men, often with the threat of whatever abuse or violence they may want to use if they don't like you being there or what you are doing, even though it may be what they take for granted for themselves. Participating in a conversation, picking up useful bits of information or perhaps jobs, relaxing with friends or a quiet drink on your own . . . forget it! If they treat you like a whore, that after all is what pub culture is all about.

Does it matter? What do the mainstream pubs offer, after all, apart from having to drink a lot, being with some perhaps very boring companions who can't talk about themselves with any degree of honesty, and often not very comfortable or pleasant surroundings which may be dominated by the blast of loud music or the squawks of the computer games machine?

It does matter. Public houses are often, still, the only available public meeting places: trade union branches and local political party meetings are still held in the upper room of a pub more often than not. Many women, especially if they have never been before, find the idea of going into a strange pub and finding the room very off-putting – enough to keep many away. And many meetings held elsewhere, once they are formally ended, 'adjourn' to a pub where those in the know (and who don't have to relieve babysitters or aren't too worried about the cost of a few drinks) get down to the real business of who's going to be proposed for what position, and what strategy can be adopted for pushing a particular point of view.

Pubs matter because they are, in many areas, still a very important source of hot tips – not just on which horse will be first past the post but on what jobs are going. As illustrated by the customer in The Star and Garter, a pub is often the place where casual jobs are to be found on a fairly regular basis. Certain pubs are also a source of information on where to find scarce housing for rent in the area – and some are well known to those who participate in such things as the place where the keys to Council flats are handed over in return for cash. To say this is not to condone the practice, but to remind ourselves of the adaptability and usefulness of pubs in allowing 'unofficial' and often illegal transactions which, needless to say, are handled mainly by men.

Pubs matter too in terms of more regular kinds of activity: office gossip, what promotions are going, buying a useful colleague or boss a drink, deciding what we all think about so-and-so, or finding out useful bits of information about the job when it's very competitive and there is no formal training. Remember El Vino's and the tremendous fight by the management to keep women away from the bar? Well, the pubs of Fleet Street are of crucial importance in this kind of manoeuvring, and explaining to young trainee journalists the tricks of the trade – and its unwritten rules – as a study of the profession by Roger Smith has underlined.[9]

As women in a man's world, we can't decide to move the kinds of transactions that take place in pubs to those few where we feel at ease (the Grave Maurices – and that unpublike name surely gives the game away). We have to enter the less congenial pubs, using the security of being with a group wherever possible. We have to have the kind of time available, especially after work or after meetings, that the men have (meaning: no responsibility for children or other family members). We have to be able to afford to buy our round, or accept favours when men buy us drinks which just reminds everybody of our different 'dependent' status. These and other subtleties, which many men are hardly even aware of, mean that some of the women have to drop out of the work/social scene. Those who are left are isolated in a sea of men, unless they work in the few predominantly female jobs. And so we battle on.

Let me reiterate that of course not all pubs are the same. There are pubs we can even call our own local (though that is often conditional). But apart from the importance of pubs in many aspects of our lives, we should be aware of how the 'pub culture' of the male drinking operates – since this is also the basis for the many other male clubs and institutions to be surveyed in this book. Many of them are closed to women by far more rigid rules and formulas than even the worst of the pubs, often with an added barrier of secrecy designed to make us unaware that they even exist.

There is quite a lot of overlap between pub culture with its group of 'regulars' and unwritten rules on one hand, and working men's clubs, Rotary and the élite men's clubs of London's West End on the other. In the pubs, one man or even a small group will often take it on himself to harass women who are intruding (or men who do not conform, come to that). In the working men's clubs, as we shall see later, the same kind of thing happens: a self-appointed group of male custodians write and rewrite the men-only rules to exclude women, more or less off the top of their heads – and are allowed to do so by the other men, who are passive on the subject but will very rarely try to stop what is part of 'being a man', and to their advantage as well (in the short run, anyway). In Rotary or the Freemasons, the rules are more fixed and there is a hard core of men – in Rotary and the Church of England – who will threaten to break up the organisation rather than have women in it. In the West End clubs, the members don't even have to bother: it's the club servants who enforce the rules on the rare occasions where these are challenged.

2
THIS
SPORTING LIFE

Sport is big business, founded on the impulse for sociability, feeling part of a team, using one's physical skills and enjoying one's leisure time. But it also divides people over their use of leisure: partly this is a division along class lines (rugby v. soccer, golf and cricket v. snooker). Most importantly, though, it divides men from women.

It is very doubtful whether women have the kind of undiluted leisure-time that men do, which is available for sport. Sport, that is, in the public arena: not just as participation in physical recreation, although this is obviously very important for some women as well as many men, but as a spectacle put on for their entertainment: showing top professionals playing games which they have themselves been taught. Spectator sport enjoys prime-time TV and radio, pages of coverage in newspapers, and of course a whole conversational language which is used mainly by men, talking to other men. It is a mass-marketed, commercial phenomenon, as well as a personal and social one. Company sponsorship is worth £150–£200 million a year. British TV stations alone spend at least £40 million a year – and for the BBC that's a quarter of total production – on sports coverage, mainly soccer, cricket, rugby and snooker.

Most sport takes place mainly in a male environment. This is self-evident in the games like snooker and darts which take place mainly in pubs, and in the predominantly male parts of pubs at that – or in the working men's clubs which we shall be reviewing next as we move more towards the overtly men-only organisations. It is apparent in the fact that the main spectator sports in Britain, soccer and cricket (and rugby in some areas), are taught almost exclusively to boys. Girls' team games, like netball or rounders, are a joke commercially and with rare exceptions are not spectator sports in the same sense. As well as learning how to play the games themselves, and what the rules are, the boys are being prepared for a lifetime of interest as spectators. Women are not necessarily excluded from this spectator interest in men's sports – there are some very keen football and cricket followers, and of course players, among women – but we remain a very small proportion of sports fans. Many women are fairly uninterested in these games, and some positively hostile. 'I'm quite happy for him to go but I don't really enjoy motor racing,' said one woman. 'It's just that it's the only outing he's interested in.' 'I quite enjoyed the football matches once or twice for the novelty, but it's not a sport I've played and I certainly didn't feel part of it all,' said another. 'I could feel all the agony and ecstasy in the crowd about their team but I hated the sexual insults and I felt very exposed among all those men, not one of them at all.'

The male nature of sport – and especially of competitive team sports – is evident in the fact that men get almost all the TV air-time, most of the financial support, facilities and sponsorship (with the exception of tennis at Wimbledon once a year). Having tried to raise questions in a local authority about the allocation of public open space to football pitches and 'kick-about areas' in a supposedly equal-opportunity London Council, and having asked for simple monitoring of the use of sports centre facilities by women and men, I have seen at first hand the intense resistance by men officers and councillors alike to any questioning or exposure that challenges 'their' regular access to facilities that they themselves use, dedicated largely to their own sporting interests, and their unwillingness to consider women's claims on the space or budget available. 'Women can play cricket if they really want to' or 'we've already got a netball pitch in this borough' are about the limit of their understanding. Enough courts for a tournament, changing rooms, perhaps facilities for spectators, refreshments, even a bar are way beyond their ken if women's sports are on the agenda – while all these are provided without question for the men's. They fail also to take into account the discrimination against girls, which means that those who *would* like to play soccer or cricket are barred, especially if they are any good – which has happened repeatedly with Football Association bans on outstanding girls playing in mixed soccer teams.

One of the features of men's organisations, and the way they interact, is continuity of interests and social life from childhood to old age: from public school to Oxbridge to a good job via a club to public life, for instance, all done through the same or similar group of other men. This is rare in women's lives. The constant transitions that women experience between full-time, part-time and unpaid work, or in different social circles depending on their job, where they live, whether they have children or sudden switches to activities favoured by a man they are associated with, is reflected in the fragmented experience of sport and leisure. There is an almost complete loss of sport when girls leave school: the team sports they have learned there are not taken seriously elsewhere, or supported by local government facilities or programmes; there is very little media coverage of good teams or players to keep alive an interest in netball, hockey or lacrosse (let alone rounders). Precisely the opposite is true for men's sports: what is learned at school is available through work-related or other sports clubs afterwards, and the same sports are shown on the television and take up pages of the newspaper. Competitive sport at amateur level is important as a place for men to meet, playing in an all-male team with universal rules that all the men understand, followed by a booze-up afterwards with a verbal replay of the game. Women – as spectators – are perfectly acceptable, but it is a cold and disheartening role standing on the sidelines and cheering on your team: how many men, I wonder, have ever done it for women's teams? Most women, I have noticed, vote with their feet – in the opposite direction.

Like pub culture, sport is sacred to the idea that a man has no home responsibilities: everything away from the job is his 'leisure' time. Think for a moment, for example, of the different experiences of a weekend for many couples: for women it is housework, cooking, for many also taking care of the kids (taking the boys perhaps to the sports centre . . .) and cleaning up after everybody (including hubby or partner). For many men it's watching a game, at the ground or on TV, and perhaps Sunday morning playing it, usually in a men-only and strictly no-children atmosphere. Sons may be brought in to give them the general idea of how a man spends 'his' weekend ducking out of the housework. (When did you last see a woman 'gone fishing'?)

As a result of the amount of time and undivided attention that many men spend on sport there is a whole language of familiarity with the latest scores, the star players, who deserves to be promoted or demoted, how the man's own team is doing: a never-ending stream of comment and prediction that makes up a male language from which most women, since they are not giving this amount of time and loving attention to it all, are simply excluded. 'What's the latest score?' 'What d'you think of them dropping Smith?' 'Are Grimsby Town going to be relegated?' 'Did you see that try . . . ?' And since all this takes many men away from home, family and especially kids, it is as if many couples were living in different worlds. No wonder that, as Ann Whitehead remarks about the couples she studied in Herefordshire, this absence of shared leisure interests is a huge barrier between women and men, while it is the main channel of communication (on a fairly superficial level, at least) between men. She observes: 'There is not much to talk about and for what there is, husbands and wives do not always share the same language.'[1]

The predominance of sport and sporting events in our society is extraordinary, a vast topic of conversation between men as well as a huge business and media phenomenon. It feeds the male culture of heroes, villains, team spirit, winners and losers, rankings and 'scorers'; it also derives from that scene. Just as the decision-makers in local government cannot or will not see sport other than in terms of their own sporting interests, so do the decision-makers at national or even international level. It is extraordinary, for example, that while the audience figures (minus almost all the women) put sport well out of the top categories, it is given a priority out of all proportion to its real popularity. This is particularly true of cricket, which can take up hours of television time for a very small male audience. Jonathan Martin, head of sports and events at the BBC, commented recently that he did not approach coverage in the normal business terms: 'If we did, I would put a red pencil through quite a lot of output,' especially the Saturday afternoon sports programme, golf and cricket.

It is interesting that as soccer and cricket become overexposed and boring to all but the most fanatical, diversification takes place not with women's sports but men's snooker and even (men's) American football where all the rules have to be carefully explained – if one men's sport palls, try another. . . (Sports have different meanings, incidentally, in different cultures. Soccer is a mass men's game in Britain but an 'alternative' sport to macho American football in the US – played often in informal mixed teams.)

In Britain there have always been different sports for different social classes. Among the upper classes the language is quite literally sprinkled with terms from cricket, shooting, golf and yachting (and probably other sports of which I, as a complete outsider, do not understand the references) while in a more working-class group of men it might be boxing or wrestling as well as soccer. (Women may play or watch sports, but it is not a part of everyday language for us.) At all class levels, if you don't know the language or simply don't know what they are talking about you are established as an outsider: a term that, in sport, means an almost certain loser. You're not 'keeping a straight bat' and someone is likely to 'bowl you a googly'.

Kathryn Stechert, in a book on men's business culture, *The Credibility Gap*, points out that sport does not have to be a big part of a man's life to be used commonly as an opening gambit in making contact with other men. She quotes one man: 'Sports is a safe topic of common interest. It's just natural; everyone's interested in sports.' What he meant was every man: many women simply would not understand 'going to the mat on this one', 'You're going to have to make some hard calls' or 'This is the Dave Kingman board'.[2]

Michael Korda, in his book *Male Chauvinism! How it Works*, is another writer who has looked at the role of sport as part of a separate – men's – language and culture. He is describing the American scene, with particular reference to business, but his book has much wider application. Sport, he suggests, symbolises the values of strength and courage which men want to see themselves as having:

Here, at any rate, was an activity in which men could effectively reassert their membership in the male group, and from which women were as a rule generally excluded. It is hardly surprising that sport should have taken on, in Western society, such an importance that its rules, its language, its legends, have passed into the male consciousness. . . . Men talked of sports, thereby excluding women from their conversation, they admired sportsmen, and identified with them, which women were in no position to do, they used the terminology of sports, as many older businessmen still do. As a general rule, when an executive speaks of 'our team', he is unlikely to be including the women in the organization in his thoughts.

In reality, he reminds us, many men do not participate in sports – or they play games like tennis or golf where there are some women around (who may well be better than they are). So it's not actually being active that's the key, it's 'nostalgia for the locker room and the trials of physical strength that the major team sports vicariously provide, the old romanticism of muscle and physical daring . . .' We are talking here about fantasy, all the more powerful for being a shared fantasy with other men. Although some men do it, the *real* point of sport for men in groups is watching it and talking about it. As Korda observes, very much to the point,

Most men are more concerned with knowing and reading about sport than doing it, and it is a woman's ignorance of sport that attracts their ridicule, rather than her inability to play. The male identification with sport has its effects in the *confining* of women, their sense of being limited.[3]

If you have ever found yourself regularly sharing the same space as a man who watches football (I thought the American variety was staggeringly boring until I met Match of the Day) with a total, rapt concentration that excludes you totally, then you will know what this confinement is all about. Your presence is forgotten. He'll be discussing it all later with men friends who saw the same game. And having a real live relationship in which the woman is not supposed to be on the sidelines . . . It can be a great shock to discover that 'the game' comes first, last and always, and you have to fill in the gaps regardless of your own interests and preferences about time and place.

But let's go back for a moment to the whole question of leisure. Sport shows how much leisure-time people have, and also how much money to spend on themselves. Having your own time and your own money is an important element in the segregation of women and men in our society, and in the formation of men's clubs of all kinds. Both 'free' time and 'free' money have a great deal to do with whether or not you take responsibility for your children, and also for your older or disabled relatives or friends. If you 'spend' your time and 'spend' most of the money you have on work – paid or otherwise – keeping your home nice and looking after other people, you are likely to have precious little left

for yourself alone. It is perhaps *the* difference, in this supposedly 'sharing' society, between women and men.

Sport is not a free commodity in our society. Possibly the
nearest you could get to that would be the old-fashioned
idea of rambling in the countryside (when you could get to
it) with no special equipment. These days, you'd look a bit
strange doing that without the flashy boots, rucksack and
all-weather gear (not cheap) that you're supposed to do it in,
and getting there could cost a fair amount and be quite a has-
sle if you haven't got your own car. It is even more so for
anything that's more obviously a 'sport'. It's big business:
sports-related consumer expenditure in Britain runs at over
£3 billion a year – that's for equipment, clothes and court
fees. You also, in most places, are not supposed to bring
children – unless, that is, *they* are playing and *you* are
transporting or minding them. So sport is accessible only
with quite a lot of money to spend on yourself, as well as
functioning as a playground for those with lots of 'free'
time. A bit like a pub, really: very much a men's area. Only
you have to work up a sweat before you start drinking.

The problems that so many women have in getting any
leisure worth the name, let alone getting access to sport to
fill that time, have been surprisingly little documented.
There has been much comment, of course, about the growth
of 'leisure' for 'modern man'. It is based very much on the
pattern of men's jobs, not women's all too common double-
shift of job and home.

A study of the community-based 'Action Sport' programme for the British Sports Council states the problem of
women's lack of leisure and opportunities for recreation
(particularly sport) in simple terms. Most women have
much less 'free' time than men, particularly where there are
any family responsibilities. It may come in 'scattered and
unpredictable amounts' unlikely to fit in with the hours at
which organised recreation is available. Money, like time,
'belongs to the family rather than to the individual woman:
money for becoming a member of a sports centre, is a real
and abiding barrier.' Just as important, 'women are likely,

through formal education and social expectations, to be less well trained than men in many of the skills that make leisure pursuits accessible and enjoyable.' There is a massive female drop-out from sport at the school-leaving stage, then when a woman has her first baby, and when she retires from her job. There can be considerable harassment from male users and attendants at sports centres, sometimes a lack of private changing facilities for women, and the risk of travelling alone, especially after dark, probably on public transport. It *is* possible to get women involved and enthusiastic, the report stresses – but this means drastic changes in the timing of sessions, training of staff and provision of women-only sessions which, like the Action Sports venture itself, is expensive – and not integrated into present sport and recreation provision.[4]

It might not be overstating the case to see it as a matter of women's sport belonging to a different culture from men's sport, an alien invasion of a man's world that often cannot last except as special projects or perhaps as 'keep fit', on the margins of sports centres and public provision generally.

Rosemary Deem, in her book *All Work and No Play*, stresses the close relationship between men's 'free' time and women's 'unfree' time. 'The sporting activities of many men depend on the services provided by women – from cooking Sunday lunch so that a morning male football match is able to go ahead unfettered by domestic responsibilities, to washing sports kit and giving verbal and emotional encouragement to sportsmen. Women, she observes, also tend to get worn out by childcare and the double shift on the job and at home, and do not have the energy for anything except 'positive' leisure. A lack of self-confidence is also an impoortant deterrent, together with the character of sport itself. 'Women's lack of interest in sport is as much due to the stranglehold which men have over sport (its image, its management and participation) as to poor facilities.'[5]

This is not to say of course that no women are involved in sport at all. Many are, though less than 5 per cent of us have sport as part of our weekly routine. But the pattern of sporting activity, where it exists, is very different from men's, with team games in particular very much in the minority for women. Certain kinds of sport which are done informally, on your own or with one or two others – jogging, cycling, swimming and hiking – are prominent for women. It may not be a coincidence that these are seen as 'non-threatening' to the sporting establishment, with its base in the specialised sports pitches and leisure centres. The General Household Survey for 1983 shows that the most popular sports among women are walking, swimming, keep fit and darts. For men they are walking, snooker, swimming, darts, football, golf and squash, a list of which includes several sports that take place mainly in an all-male club atmosphere.

There *are* women who are working hard to push back the frontiers of 'male' sports. Women are starting to play football, for instance. There is a move in some areas for educational authorities to teach 'male' sports to the girls as well. There are 'open house' days at sports centres for women to come and try new sports and equipment. In almost all sports the women are battling for more facilities, more of the money and recognition, and more media coverage and sponsorship. They have a very long way to go.

Sports clubs

Anyone involved in 'male' sports is all too aware of men organising to keep women out, and in some cases to push back gains that women have made. The main area where this takes place is in clubs, formal or informal, perhaps best defined not merely as areas where women never go but also as meeting places that men control. Men may proclaim them as men's places only when women start to encroach, possibly quite 'innocently' – not recognising that place or territory as one that men want to keep for men only.

Sports clubs and venues are all too often in this category. Women involved in the sport, whether as participants, spectators, or really just accompanying a man who is the *real* fan, are often excluded from certain areas which become formally or otherwise 'men only'. There are men-only parts of football and cricket stands, often in the best position to watch the game, and with better facilities; their main purpose, though, seems to be as an 'élite' or 'set apart' place for men to go and feel important. In case this seems a bit of a joke, and often it looks that way, it should be remembered that this is also the VIP area where important (male) guests are entertained.

There are men-only parts of the stands at football grounds, and of course the men-only bars and viewing rooms at Lords and many county cricket grounds. A private box at Lords is an excellent place also to entertain male contacts: a particular speciality is companies wanting favours from Government, who invite senior civil servants and possibly ministers to their box for a day's cricket, booze and men-only food. One woman visiting a cricket club with her husband came face to face with a not untypical sign: 'No women or dogs beyond this point.' She also remembers a joint invitation to a North of England football club: 'We were about to be shown into a beautiful oak-panelled lounge when the chairman asked if I would like to go to the ladies' room. Thinking a quick trip to the loo was in order, I agreed. I was then pushed into a room full of women. Instead of the plush lounge there were folding chairs and paper napkins.' The way back to the men's lounge was then blocked by officials.[6]

The more upwardly mobile sports are also very important for men's informal contact, drinking together, the usual sporting and sometimes sexual conversation (about women, that is, not themselves): in short, for sounding out useful-looking 'contacts' for personal use and mutual advantage. Many a business deal is developed at the squash court or the golf course (bank managers for instance may 'have' to belong).

Perhaps the most systematic study of discrimination against women in sporting clubs at the time of writing is the Report of the Australian State of Victoria's Equal Opportunity Board, *Discrimination in Sporting Clubs.*[7] The Board considered submissions from the clubs and from their members, and paid particular attention to benefits which discriminatory clubs derived from public facilities and subsidies, derived from both women and men.

Many golf clubs, for instance, were leasing public land and getting rate concessions. Yet they would allow women to join only as second-class members (at a lower fee, but there was no option of paying the full fee). They were excluded from the courses at times when the men were most interested in playing, excluded from some facilities – anything from the bar to the car park – and not allowed to join the committee that made up these and other rules. The situation was so polarised in some clubs that female members 'were afraid to even discuss the questionnaire with the club committee for fear of damaging relations with the male members'. So women who were bank managers, for instance, would be in the position of not having access to the most valuable potential clients at the times they were using the club, and if they did manage to find a way to use the club effectively in the same way as their male counterparts the rules could be changed to block that particular route, without their having any say. Of the 200 clubs that responded to the survey, 198 had some form of discrimination and only two offered equal rights to women and men. Interestingly but not surprisingly, 'discriminatory practices are found to be worst in the large metropolitan clubs which are the oldest and most sought after'. Many of these clubs were started by men, for men only, and women had been allowed in as 'associate' members only 'as a way of getting extra revenue'. Virtually all the club managements were very reluctant to give equality and 80 per cent of the most discriminatory ones had no plans for any changes at all.

A test case against a British golf club taken up by the Equal Opportunities Commission in March 1986 challenges the very similar practices in Britain. The EOC is backing a male member against the club at Pruhoe, Northumberland, over the prohibition on men taking reduced-rate and second-class membership – the *only* one open to women, as is the practice in the golf clubs up and down the country. Restrictions on the women include men-only rules in bars, snooker rooms and dining rooms, restrictions on where they can walk and sit, and other detailed and humiliating reminders of their separate and inferior position in the club. Again, we find the most 'prestigious' being the worst. The Royal and Ancient at St Andrews, the golfing Mecca, has a complete men-only rule for the whole place except in very exceptional circumstances. Needless to say, this also undermines women who are serious about playing the game itself, including those playing at a high professional standard: the big money and the TV coverage are for the men's game only. Needless to say, this is the experience of the top women in every team sport, and many individual sports. Less money, less facilities, less coverage and less sponsorship.

Rather similar to the golf clubs in snob and business value are yacht clubs, which are also examined in the Australian report. The 'Commodore' of one key club is quoted as saying that women's compulsory 'associate' membership means merely that 'they can't vote on important matters which don't really affect them'. Many clubs had 'family' membership which includes one first-class, one second-class and junior membership. Guess which is which. Again, the most discriminatory were some of the oldest and most prestigious: just the place to buy a drink for the boss, or pick up key business or future employment contacts. The Royal Yacht Club of Victoria, with its superb facilities and even more superb clientele, excludes women even as associate members. Women are allowed as guests only, and banned from the members' bar. They argued they were 'not the worst'.

The theme of discriminatory sporting clubs and organisations, from rugby to cricket and from bowls to snooker leagues, repeats itself drearily and endlessly – not to mention the way that restrictions on women in pubs disadvantage women in the pub sports of snooker, darts and . . .

would you believe, skittles? (A women's skittles team was banned from a pub in Bristol in 1986, the excuse being that they weren't drinking enough.) The women's darts champion, who married the men's champion, gave up the game recently with: 'Darts is a pub game. Pubs are male territory.' We return to snooker – which as a pub and clubs game *and* now Big Money and Fame, is a very important case study in its own right – in the context of the working men's clubs.

For now, let us just glance at two interesting aspects of the sporting club scene: the use of 'macho' sports to sell tobacco by association with masculinity; and the use of sporting symbols and clothing to promote recognition and communication, as well as status marking, among men.

First, the tobacco sponsorship. It is no secret that tobacco and cigarettes are advertised by associating them with sport (sponsored by tobacco companies) and by getting the name of the brand on to television as well as radio and print by enforcing the use of the name in the sponsored event and by putting the brand name in a position which shows up well to the TV cameras. What many of us have not registered is that tobacco sponsorship of sport is highly targeted. It involves only 8 per cent of all sports sponsorship, and 15 per cent of all the sport on television. The sports are picked with care and the events themselves then heavily promoted: the image is 'men's' sports, including motor-racing (the Marlboro logo on a phallic-symbol racing car), snooker, football and cricket. Prohibited officially from advertising smoking as a 'manly' activity, the tobacco companies have carefully identified certain sports, and high-profile men-only contests in particular, as being clearly identified in men's minds with masculinity itself. Smoking itself, the message is, proves you to be 'manly'.

And speaking of identification, there is the whole fascinating area of how sporting colours act as symbols for men: at the mass level this would be football team scarves and at the élite level dress codes – using ties in particular – which those 'in the know' will recognise. Tim Heald in his book *Networks* identifies the striped tie, which is well known to identify 'old boys' of private schools and Oxbridge, as being often the mark of belonging to a sporting fraternity.[8] Originating in the different colours used by the rival teams in formalised sports (rowing, cricket, rugby and soccer) as they emerged in a private-school boys' culture in the nineteenth century, the ties were a life-long symbol both of which group you belong to, and also of what your status is or was within it. The obvious example is the different stripes of blue used to show former members of Oxford and Cambridge sports teams. A particularly prestigious and common tie is the 'rhubarb and custard' yellow and red tie of the Marylebone Cricket Club (MCC) – which you join on connections and money without even having to play the game itself. Tim Heald notes that 'most such ties, because of their sporting origins, tend to be vivid' but it is interesting that the MCC has produced a more discreet 'crested' tie which is very popular because it goes well with the sober atmosphere of the City boardroom or office.

Any men suspected of buying and wearing one of these ties by mistake, or claiming the status when they are not entitled to it, will be challenged on the issue by an irate member of 'the club'. A lot of Americans who just thought the colours looked nice tend to get challenged if they encroach on territory where it is recognised as a powerful tribal mark. Why all the fuss? Heald describes it in terms of a language:

To an outsider the striped tie is a totally alien tongue and may mean absolutely nothing. If, however, he or she has a smattering of the language, the wearing of the tie – whatever the stripes – suggests that the wearer is a person of substance and sociability . . . for the wearer, the tie confers the sort of self-confidence born of belonging to an organisation or sharing an experience from which others are excluded . . . Among those who understand the language, communication is at its most sophisticated. At its simplest the information is straightforward. Wearing the MCC tie tells anyone who has reached the equivalent of an 'O' level in sartorial linguistics that the person wearing it is interested in cricket.

Nevertheless its wearing establishes some sort of rapport not only with fellow MCC members but also with those others – and there are still some – who follow the game.

Since he is very much the sort of man who *does* wear his MCC tie, he has found it a useful ice-breaker at drinks parties, good for introducing himself in the officers' mess at the prestigious Chelsea barracks, and 'it has led to some entertaining conversations with strangers on trains . . . and who knows what benefits may flow from the first response?'

Very useful. Identifying fellow-members of your club, having a 'safe' conversation, perhaps picking up tips or contacts in the course of an engrossing conversation about men's play. Of course, some women could talk about cricket (or football, or whatever) on this kind of level, and certainly a number of women participate in the sport, in women's teams – but it is very much an open question whether we can get any of the social, non-sporting benefits from our knowledge of the sport. An equal conversation about sport between a woman and a man who meet casually, and who see this as something that may lead to 'who knows what benefits' (of the non-sexual variety) is almost inconceivable. Women just can't wear the club tie.

Sport and the power of exclusion

Sport is very largely for men, particularly in team games. Does it matter? Should we care? Why would women want to play rugby anyway? (Some do, and theirs is a rough game even by the men's standards.)

The answer is simply one of discrimination. Sports taught to girls in school are not provided for in later life, unlike the situation for boys. Facilities, sponsorship, media coverage are all lacking. Where women play the same sports as men they again encounter discrimination, harassment and inferior facilities as well as less money. In leisure centres, supposedly for everybody, we find a pattern of provision designed with men in mind. The whole concept of sport and recreation is geared to amounts of 'leisure' as well as money which are almost entirely the province of men. Personal relationships between women and men are sacrificed to men's sporting interests. Men talk sports, results and personalities not only as a form of social interaction but on the job as well − a subtle but effective way of excluding women, most of whom do not follow it all and cannot participate. Worst of all, there is outright discrimination and segregation practised in many supposedly 'public' sporting facilities as well as private sporting clubs, many of them the key to important work-related contacts.

It is outrageous that women are treated in this way − loss of sport means loss of fitness and health, as well as fun. Perhaps worst of all is the continuing bias of the media, especially the television companies, towards men's sports to an irrational degree which far outstrips its real popularity among the population as a whole. Sport, something we all take for granted, turns out to be a vehicle for a separate men's culture, and also the context for some highly discriminatory clubs. Which brings us to our next section, on the world of the mass-membership men's organisations.

PART TWO
Mass-membership Organisations

3
CLUB HIJACK
Working Men Only

My grandparents spent every evening in the club for years: their whole life was the club. When my grandfather died, the club sent a wreath to the funeral and had a two-minute silence for him.

My grandmother went on going just the same, and she died two years later. There was no wreath, no letter, nothing to show that they even recognised that she had died. I was pretty upset about it and I went to ask why they'd not done the same for her as they had for him. They said it was the policy, they always did it like that.

This woman's story, about one of the thousands of working men's clubs in Britain, is echoed by hundreds of letters to the Equal Rights in Clubs Campaign for Action (ERICCA). Both women and men have written about their shock and distress caused by the pettiness of clubs originally set up for the whole community, which are now controlled nationally by a clique of men determined to keep women out of decision-making and full participation in club facilities.

Women who had attended regularly with their husbands have found themselves barred from the club, where only men could 'officially' be members, following their husband's death − when they most need the companionship and support offered by the club and the women as well as men within it. They become virtually non-persons − in their home town. Other women on their own find that there is no way for them to join the club at all, and many single mothers who badly need a social centre where they can take their children are kept out.

'The rules' are invoked constantly by club committees to exclude members of their community whose face does not fit. People can be excluded without any reason being given. Rules can also be used to keep in line those men who are (privately) very critical of the clubs' policies towards women. If they lose their club membership they also forfeit the card issued by the Club and Institute Union (CIU) which gives them access to clubs and their activities on a regional or even national scale.

With an atmosphere of intimidation in some of the worst clubs, there is also a streak of petty vindictiveness (not unlike the golf club syndrome). A dog is given the CIU card which no woman is allowed to have. Games facilities are open to children but not to women. A club's AGM is called off when a woman arrives. White lines are painted on the floor which women are told not to cross. There are many other nasty power plays which would seem merely childish if they were not so far-reaching in their effects.[1] They are a constant reminder to women that in the club, the social centre of their own community, they do not 'belong'. It is not *your* club: keep out, you're only a woman.

A big business

Working men's clubs are a very British institution, and they operate on a huge scale which many British people are unaware of, through the Working Men's Club and Institute Union. They provide the community and social centre in many villages, towns and cities. Their stronghold is the older industrial and mining areas but there are community centres all over the UK, in many areas where you would not expect to find such a working-class institution, which if you look closely are labelled 'affiliated to the WMCIU'. And that means discrimination against women, since it is a condition of affiliation.

For a community-based organisation, the network of working men's clubs are very inward-looking. All my attempts to get hold of their basic literature (officially available to anyone who asks) was met with a blank refusal from headquarters until the man in charge agreed it (he never did). I got the same response to my requests for an interview. For much of my inside information I am indebted to members of ERICCA. I also obtained some very interesting information from the files of the Registrar of Friendly Societies (once I stopped looking for the CIU, which they now call themselves), and discovered them under their real name the WMCIU. These files show that the Registrar is failing to enforce the law which was written to cover the activities of working men's clubs, a law which could be used to stop the discrimination against women in the club world and, therefore, for many people, the whole community. Women are blocked by the WMCIU's Rule 12(e). This reads 'Associate and Pass Cards may not be issued to lady members'. It is these cards that open up all clubs and their facilities to male members of the organisation.

The WMCIU rules the network of working men's clubs with a rod of iron. There are overwhelming pressures on clubs to affiliate in order to get the franchise 'how to' formula, discounted beer and advice where necessary. One member explained:

'It's like having a Little Chef restaurant. Everything is thought out for you: you get cheaper beer than a purely private club, and you can book entertainers on the club circuit. You also have a structure and network to refer to if there are any problems, and more income from the bar since you can let in anybody who has a CIU card. The inter-club competitions are all organised through the CIU, and they bring in a lot of people and therefore income.'

Individuals can also be attracted to join a club with CIU affiliation because it is like a certificate or status symbol:

you know what to expect, and it gives you access to clubs with, ironically, a 'family' atmosphere. Because WMCIU affiliation is in practice essential to operate a viable club, with very few exceptions, clubs are very nervous of being disaffiliated and are far more careful not to offend their own Big Brother than the Government's Registrar of Friendly Societies to whom they are officially and legally accountable.

The WMCIU club network is big business, with its four thousand or so clubs, four million men affiliated to the CIU individually, and an estimated two to three million women belonging to the clubs but denied CIU cards. Combined turnover runs into tens of millions a year, and in many areas the clubs have crowded out the pubs in the search for business. The WMCIU's own headquarters income is over £2 million a year, with over 100 staff and assets of about £3 million – over and above the combined assets of the clubs themselves, which must be enormous.

These men are no amateurs. Club Union House, the head-quarters office at Highbury Corner, North London, has all the trappings of a successful company with its soft carpets and indirect lighting, hardly consistent with the traditional image of the working-class community centre for mining and industrial areas where the clubs have their roots. It has more than a touch of the secretive about it: when I visited the supposedly open-access District Surveyor's office which occupies the top floor I was challenged by the WMCIU receptionist, instructed firmly to take the lift up, and watched with great suspicion as I re-emerged later via the staircase.

All my attempts to get an interview, comment or even the most basic information out of the WMCIU, extending over several weeks with innumerable phone calls, met with determined resistance. Despite the organisation Rule 21 that the annual accounts should be 'supplied gratuitously on demand to every member or person interested in the funds of the Union' and the Registry's model rule that all rules be supplied to 'every person on demand' for not more than 10p, I was informed that *no* information, accounts or rules were available, despite repeated requests. Questions, requests for interviews and even attempts to contact the Secretary, Mr Johnson, or *his* secretary were met with a blank wall. 'We'll ring you back,' became the standard response. I'm still waiting. The same phenomenon of extreme secretiveness has also been encountered by many women who are 'lady members' of their local club, when they try to get copies of the club's rules or accounts. All of this is in flagrant breach of the Government's regulations as well as the clubs' own rule-books.

The WMCIU and its network of clubs throughout Britain is unique: there is no comparable organisation anywhere else in the world. Its influence goes far beyond the clubs themselves: this is a nation-wide recreation, sporting, and educational business. In education, the clubs predated local authority schools as a source of basic literacy for the crowds of people moving from the countryside into nineteenth-century towns and cities, swept along by the industrial revolution. The clubs also provided a very popular library service when there was no other source of books. Scholarships have been provided on a large scale – the key to social advancement – and the programme continues today with popular Summer and Spring Schools and dayschools for thousands of people every year on a wide variety of topics. There is a six-month correspondence course in club law, administration and accountancy which leads to the Club Management Diploma, held by some 12,000 men. Health and social security provision has also been a vitally important benefit to members, with the clubs raising funds for those injured or bereaved in mining or industrial disasters as well as maintaining permanent, men-only convalescent homes – vitally important before the NHS was introduced. All these benefits are mainly or exclusively for men.

The WMCIU promotes more sporting contests than any other organisation in Britain, dominating competitive sports such as snooker and darts – both of these now a route to fame and fortune, where women would be competing equally with men if given equal access to practice facilities and matches.

Many new 'rules' invented by club committees have been aimed at the women who win snooker matches against the men, and who have suddenly found themselves excluded from practising the game or playing in the club leagues. Bans on women playing snooker and darts are being directed particularly against those women who already play in leagues and can beat many of the club men. The trigger for Sheila Capstick's formation of ERICCA (for 'a woman's right to cues') was her sudden exclusion from the snooker room of her club in 1978 which came when she was just getting good at the sport. The committee invented a rule to bar women from playing snooker, claiming that it had always existed but been forgotten. Her comments: unprintable. The same happened to Ruth Nunn, a retired hospital worker who had twice beaten sixteen men to reach the final in a knockout snooker competition; she suddenly found herself banned from playing in her own club in 1982.[2] 'Pathetic' was her reaction.

Even some 'independent' sporting bodies participate in the clubs' discriminatory policies. The Newcastle and Gateshead Snooker League, which involves fifty-six clubs of which nineteen have 'men-only' games rooms, used to allow teams including women to arrange their matches in their own clubs or a neutral club, whenever they were drawn against teams with men-only facilities. In 1981 the League announced that the men could now 'win' the game if they were based in an exclusive club and were due to play against mixed teams. The pattern is not invariable, though: in the Exeter area, for instance, no club is allowed to participate in the snooker league if it refuses to allow women to play.[3]

There is no reason why one of the women now coming into the game could not become a future professional champion, given equal practice and competition facilities. Top snooker coach and referee Brian Halter, who has coached many girls as well as boys, thinks women are potentially just as good, if not better. He argues: 'The day will come when both the youth champion and the professional champion is a woman.'[4] The Chair of the Billiards and Snooker Control Council, Sam Brooke, has also called for fairer treatment of women who play snooker – in increasing numbers since many become interested by watching the men play on TV.[5]

The issue of competitive sports, especially snooker, is a crucial one for the clubs. Not only are club competitions, leagues and trophies organised by the WMCIU, which make this a key attraction for many of the men joining clubs – the promise of a chance at the big time or at least a bit of status on the regional circuit – but the snooker table is also a star attraction in the daily life of the club itself. No expense or care is spared in maintaining the level of the table, cleaning and ironing the cloth and checking the cushions for their spring. It is the inner sanctum, the heart of the club: only the privileged are admitted to this prized facility. And when they feel like it, the men put women firmly in their (subordinate) place by inventing new rules and restrictions to keep women out – especially if they look like competing and winning on equal terms.

'Above and beyond the law'

The whole issue of club rules is a murky one indeed. For despite their name, working men's clubs are *not* in fact men-only. Only one club in the whole country, the Wallsend Social Club, actually excludes women from membership. The rest are clubs run by and for the whole community, but controlled by the men on many individual club committees, and at national level through the WMCIU and its men-only Affiliation Card. Even if a club is commit-ted to equality – and some are, with women on the club committee and given equal membership rights – it cannot issue an Affiliation Card to the women which will be recognised by the WMCIU or any of its member-clubs. Indeed, to do so would be to court expulsion from the

Union and the threat of the club's collapse through loss of the various facilities it provides.

The national Union, like other 'private' organisations, is exempt from Britain's Sex Discrimination Act, as a 'private' club or organisation, an exemption which does not apply to racial discrimination. The WMCIU's Rule 8 also states that a club 'may be suspended from all or some of the privileges of membership or expelled . . . for refusing admission to an Associate of the Union on grounds of colour, race, nationality or ethnic or national origins'. It is ironic that refusing admission to women, on the other hand, is a requirement of membership: a club risks suspension or exclusion for *not* discriminating.

It must be added, though, that racial discrimination is in practice still very common in the clubs, since they can exclude people from membership without giving any reason. In some clubs only one member's objection is enough to keep someone out, which means open season for discrimination of all kinds.

'The rules' of all these clubs are often very elusive and secretive. In theory, the reverse *should* be true: under the legislation club rules should be strictly regulated and open to inspection. Since this is possibly the largest single organisation in Britain, there is special provision for working men's clubs in the Friendly Societies Act 1974, and all individual clubs as well as the WMCIU itself are required to register with the Registry of Friendly Societies (in London for England and Wales, and in Edinburgh for Scotland). Annual accounts as well as current rules have to be formally registered, and the rules are invalid until this is done.

The Registry has itself issued model rules in the form of 'Rules for a Registered Working Man's Club'. But there is in practice little attempt to regulate the activities of the clubs or even their rules, when these are inconsistent with the model rules or applied in a way which appears to contravene both the letter and spirit of the law. Complaints about clubs' use or abuse of 'rules' to exclude women arbitrarily from facilities are in fact the most frequent communications received by the Equal Opportunities Commission, but at the time of writing these have not been taken up with the Registrar of Friendly Societies.

I picked out for examination three Yorkshire clubs which are known to have discriminated against women, citing 'the rules': Highfield House Social Club in South Elmshall, the Wakefield City Working Men's Club, and the Elmete Social Club near Leeds. All three had identical 'rules' relating to women – as members and visitors. This 'rule' had clearly been circulated by WMCIU, since the three clubs were all using its standard printed rule book, with minor amendments, and had all pasted in a pre-printed addition to the book as follows:

Lady members shall not be entitled to attend general meetings, or vote at elections, and shall not be eligible to hold office or propose or second candidates for office or introduce visitors. *They shall be subject to such special regulations as the committee may from time to time make regarding lady members.* The number of persons admitted to membership under this rule shall not result in them being significant in proportion to the total membership. (Emphasis added)

This, on the face of it, is in violation of the legal requirement that club rules can only be amended by a general meeting of the club after due notice is given, and are invalid until they have been submitted to the Registry of Friendly Societies and accepted by it for registration. I asked a Registry representative about this discrepancy. He expressed surprise at my discovery of a 'grey area' in their own records which had 'never before been raised'. He strongly denied any suggestion that a club committee could do whatever it liked to women members, and added that if a club was using a rule to change the rules outside the normal procedures it would be 'going outside the law'. Since that time, however, the Registrar has taken no action and the clubs continue to break the law with impunity.

The Registry *can* get heavy when it wants to, as when it moved in on irregularities at the New Cross Building Society, forcing it to close down. But it seems very reluctant to challenge the working men's clubs. A representative of the EOC told me that it, too, would certainly want to get involved if the clubs were doing anything discriminatory 'above and beyond the law', although it had not itself considered the rules of registry for the clubs as a discrimination issue. It is perhaps a question of bureaucratic non-communication, coupled with a fear on both sides of tackling the politically powerful WMCIU. A representative of the Registry wrote to me, with classic double-negative ambiguity: 'I would suggest as a general proposition that it would not seem inappropriate for such regulations to be made as will ensure the comfort and well-being of both sexes.' This is simply not good enough.

One of my legal informants, however, pointed out that although a 'men-only' club is legal, and exempt from the Sex Discrimination Act 1975, any club which admits women as full members and then makes them second-class members either by the rules or by administrative action (by withdrawing certain facilities, for instance – or painting lines on the floor and forbidding women to cross them) may well be in breach of the Act. It may in any case, he advised, be unlawful under the Act to exclude women from competing in snooker competitions.[6]

A history of conflict

The question of whether the club committees' and the WMCIU's rule-making is legal or not is the latest twist in the club movement's conflict-ridden history. Groups of men have worked to take over a movement started, and kept going, largely by women.

The clubs were originally founded over a century ago by women and men in the working-class and trade union movements, and those in the temperance movement (which was largely female in both membership and leadership). They were 'distressed at the way wives and children of working men were being degraded'. The concept of the clubs as educational and recreational centres in opposition to the pubs, with alcohol banned, did not last long since it could not work financially. But the idea that working-class people needed their own social centres away from the pubs *did* work as long as beer was available – albeit in a 'family' atmosphere which was far better from women's point of view than the pubs which, as we have seen, were virtually men-only, with prostitution often thrown in.

The founders wanted women to participate fully in the educational and library services, as teachers as well as students. The founders acknowledged 'the very valuable influence of educated women' in their projects. It was one of the men involved, Rev. W. T. Marriott, who called for the clubs to be exclusively male, the equivalent of the upper-class London men's clubs such as White's and the Carlton. The conflicting ideals of full participation by the whole community, and the élitist notion of men-only clubs, were present in the movement from the beginning.

It was the élitist faction which gained control as the clubs became more like pubs, and educational activities declined. There were moves by the many clubs to expel women, or exclude them from full membership. The Council of the Working Men's Club and Institute Union was moving backwards from its initial balance of eight women to fourteen men in the 1860s to an all-male body by the turn of the century. Two of the early Secretaries had been women; it is now inconceivable for women to hold any office because of the 'men-only' rule on Associate status.

The battle has raged constantly since then. It was an incident in a Manchester workers' club in 1903 that sparked the militant suffrage movement. It arose out of the takeover for a men's club of the Pankhurst Memorial Hall, built by the Independent Labour Party (ILP) in tribute to the late Dr Richard Pankhurst – a supporter of women's emancipation as well as a strong socialist. His daughter Sylvia, then 21, was commissioned to decorate the interior and did so with great commitment to the symbolism popular at the time: a peacock's feather for beauty, the lily for purity and the rose for love. The Pankhurst family then heard that the building was to be made a social club for men only. In great anger, Mrs Pankhurst told her women friends: 'We must have an independent women's movement. Come to my house and we will arrange it!'[7] It is sad that while the women's suffrage movement sparked off by this calculated insult won the vote for women, eighty years later the clubs themselves still remain under men-only control with women having no vote in their own clubs.

The well-documented history of women's full participation is often denied by many club men. In 1980, for example, the Secretary of the Wakefield City WMC claimed that it was the men who had built the clubs in the first place and were wholly responsible for their success: 'Why should the men let the women take over . . . let them do these [club activities] in clubs they have helped to build and not in the clubs which men have worked hard for and built up . . .'[8] The WMCIU's General Secretary, Mr Johnson, wrote to the *New Statesman* in response to my report on the clubs: 'It is necessary to establish, as the title suggests, that the Working Men's Club and Institute Union Ltd. was originally a men's organisation in which men's clubs were predominate [sic]'.

The men's power-base in the clubs now is not the membership as a whole (who have *never* been consulted about discriminatory rules) but the thirty-one-man WMCIU Executive, allied with the club committees, most of them all-male, to bypass the annual delegate conference which is in theory the policy-making body, and where women demand equal rights. There was an interesting example of this tactic immediately after the Second World War, mentioned by the WMCIU's historian George Tremlett. Faced with rising demands from the membership, and a 1946 conference decision, to set up a convalescent home for women similar to the four already provided for men, the Executive found every excuse for refusing to implement the decision. This included the pretext that there was so much need for a women's home that just one would not be enough to meet the demand, so it should not be built. After an unexpected ballot of the club committees to back up the Executive's refusal to implement the policy decision, a fifth and very expensive home was opened for men only – only to close down shortly afterwards for lack of demand.[9]

Exactly the same tactic was used in the WMCIU's ballot of club committees in December 1983 which resulted in 'overwhelming defeat' of the proposal to give women equal rights. This took place in the face of mounting concern about the lack of debate on the issue among delegates to the annual conference, who had been consistently denied the opportunity to debate the topic, and survey evidence that most men now wanted equality. The Executive was claiming to support abolition of the men-only rule, although at the 1982 conference Derek Dormer, the President, had called the equal rights movement 'the enemy' and claimed that the campaign to admit women to CIU affiliation was 'a failure'. 'But we are not sitting back on our laurels and saying we have beaten back the enemy. We will continue to watch the situation.'[10] The ballot was much criticised for being organised with no notice or prior debate, following a 'special conference' in October. ERICCA members felt strongly that there had not been proper consultation and that a secret ballot of the whole membership would have produced a decision in favour of equal rights. Support had been growing, they reported, over the last few years with many of the men starting to change their minds on the issue – but prevented from raising it at the annual conference, the official policy-making body. 'We've had letters from lots of men – some of them anonymous – about the vicious things that have been said to their wives,' one activist told me. But such is the threat of expulsion that they do not dare to complain.

There are plenty of indications that the men who control the club movement are feeling very threatened by the principle of equality. At the 1981 national conference there was an ostentatious padlock on the women's toilets; when seventy women entered the gallery a man grabbed the microphone to warn the other men, and the meeting was suspended while the women were kicked out. Pickets outside were met with abuse: 'Start your own clubs', 'Women aren't allowed in – it's the law', 'There are only two places for women: one's in bed and the other's in the kitchen', and a variety of obscene references to women's bodies.[11] 'But if they were on their own they'd creep in without saying anything!' the picketers laughed.

Petty vindictiveness and spite, and the feeling of a personal privilege under threat, seem to lie behind the constant rule changes to remind women of 'their place'. They give a special kick to the parish-pump tyrants who can exercise a bit of power in this way. The women involved see much of this as very childish and not worth bothering with, but they also observe that the men who go on to the club committees – for which there is little competition – tend to be those with unrewarding jobs, or none, who use the club as their personal outlet for bossing other people around.

A dead end?

What the committee men cannot control is the logic of the clubs' faltering finances. Clubs have been closing all over the country, with a number of the very big ones going down as the boom days of cheap beer and clubs' popularity as entertainment centres in the 1960s turn to hard times. Men are less and less interested, it would seem, in coming to the club every evening and weekend to 'get away from the wife' – and they now have many other ways of doing this if they want to, anyway. Married couples go out together, whether to the club or not, or they stay at home and watch much better snooker and darts on TV than they could ever see at the men-only matches in the club.

The pubs, too, have been recovering ground lost to the clubs by selling real ale, something the clubs have not managed to organise. The price differential on their beer supplies, previously the clubs' secret weapon, is now almost negligible. Meanwhile the cost of almost everything, including 'turns' to attract the members in for an entertainment evening, has rocketed for the clubs. Former stars of the club circuit have turned to television, and the cost of getting big-name entertainers like Shirley Bassey or Matt Munro has become astronomical.

One very objectionable phenomenon, the introduction of strip-shows in some of the clubs, is seen by others as a measure of the desperation felt in those faltering clubs which are clinging to the anti-women principle. It is common, it seems, for (all-male) club committee meetings to be held on Sunday mornings and for the strip-show to be put on immediately afterwards. However, it further undermines the prized 'family' image of those clubs as well as alienating women; many of the traditionalists, men as well as women, oppose the strip-shows bitterly.[12] They exploit the unemployment and poverty of local women, many of them recruited through Job Centres in the North East of England. 'I was terrified the first time I stripped before an audience,' one of them told a visitor. 'It took a month to get over my fear of taking my clothes off. I couldn't stop my legs shaking. Even now I wonder, "What's going to happen tonight?" ' Audiences of men only are getting harder all the time, it is reported: 'Now that they've seen it all before, they want the girls to go further each time,' observed the stripper organiser. It is the exact opposite of the clubs' basic function as a social centre for all the family, and a place for women in particular to feel safe.

What is perhaps the most important factor for the clubs, which makes this trend unlikely to succeed in the end, is the important role that women have always had in keeping the clubs alive and well. Clubs literally cannot survive without women members: their subscriptions, their purchase of drinks at the bar (usually drinks with a higher profit margin than the men's beer), their bingo and use of the gaming machines, their loyalty, their very successful ladies' nights, their family outings, events for the elderly, fund-raising, and the organisation of 'ladies' committees' which are reliably reported to be far more business-like and well supported than the male equivalents which theoretically run the clubs. 'The men are afraid we'll take over,' suggested one of the women.

Not only would most of the clubs have to close if the women left, but they are being made increasingly conscious of this dependence. The awareness may be unwilling, as in the case of the Park Social Club in Scunthorpe, which found that it was losing business to neighbouring clubs because of a ban on women using the club in the afternoons. It granted a four-day 'amnesty' over Christmas and New Year 1981–2 which was very popular with the men as well as the women, and went on to lift the ban altogether and grant women full membership rights. In many areas, the former men-only rule in the bar is now being dropped – also largely for financial reasons.

The trend to abandon the barriers against women is accelerating as financial pressures increase, and also when members leave. Some of them walked out in protest at what they saw as the WMCIU's 'rigged' national ballot on the exclusion of women, others moved to more open clubs because of their own club's 'petty apartheid' discrimination. Meanwhile *new* clubs are starting up, which from the beginning are based on the principle of equality. They avoid the term 'working men's club' like the plague, despite being affiliated to the WMCIU; they actively recruit women into full membership; and they have women as well as men on their committees. A new club in Coventry made ERICCA's Sheila Capstick a life member. One thing they are prevented from offering on an equal basis, though, is the WMCIU Affiliation and Pass Card, the guarantee of access to other clubs.

This is a situation where private clubs wish to give equal treatment, but are prevented by an outside body which is to all intents and purposes a commercial organisation. The Sex Discrimination Act exempts private clubs – but what if a private club wishes to observe the law and is prevented from doing so by another organisation? It would be interesting to consider whether a club could go to court, perhaps with EOC backing, to claim the right to give equal opportunities if it so wished.

Unlike the men-only brigade perhaps, those campaigning for equal rights in the clubs are strongly committed to keeping the movement going in spite of all the problems – the reason why they have not gone for outright war with the men. They argue that the clubs provide a crucially important social and sporting facility for the whole community, a meeting-place for different generations, and a tradition of working-class organisation which women in particular want to build on – in strong contrast to the élitist tradition that the WMCIU now represents. 'Pubs are not the answer for women,' one activist told me.

'It is much easier for women to use the club than go into a pub on your own. There is much less chance of harassment since everyone is known and there is much less anti-social behaviour. Clubs are, or could be, the best place for women to meet and get organised, whether on their own or with men.'

With equal rights, they could be the centre of a lively and well-organised community, caring for *all* its members.

Political discrimination

Equal rights in clubs are also related to equal rights in the political process: they have crucially important links with all the major political parties in Britain.

Probably the most important area of influence for the WMCIU clubs is in Labour politics, especially of the organised, more right-wing variety. Most Labour Party members know how much wheeling and dealing is done over a pint, especially when it comes to selecting candidates. In many Labour strongholds those pints are drunk in clubs which exclude or restrict women. Many of the Labour MPs from safe seats in Wales, Scotland, the Midlands and North of England are members of their local working men's clubs, and probably have a stake in promoting club objectives. Male Labour MPs declaring their club membership in *Who's Who* include Dennis Canavan (Selkirk West), Don Dixon (Jarrow), Roy Hughes (Newport East), Austin Mitchell (Great Grimsby), Stan Orme (Salford East), Barry Sheerman (Huddersfield), Dennis Skinner (Bolsover), Harold Walker (Doncaster Central) and Michael Welsh (Doncaster North). (Many more, incidentally, than these declare membership of the real élite clubs of London's West End, which look better on a *Who's Who* entry.)

The WMCIU has never been shy about cashing in its political assets with the Labour Party when it has been in government. It has played the key role in campaigns to keep down the tax on beer 'for the working man' through thick and thin, while showing no comparable concern about the price of food and other basic necessities of life for the *whole* of the working-class family. It has worked to preserve the privileges of its affiliated clubs in a variety of ways, in the face of any local as well as national Government attempts at regulation which it does not favour. No problem, then, to make sure that the Labour Government which put through the 1975 Sex Discrimination Act worded it along the lines of the Race Relations Act (which has since changed) to apply only to 'the public' – and so allow clubs and the WMCIU to discriminate as much as they liked with regard to their own 'private' membership. The Minister responsible, Merlyn Rees, was representing Leeds South in the heart of club territory (although he admits in *Who's Who* only to belonging to that most expensive of the London clubs, the Reform).

The decision to introduce what was called the 'working men's club exemption' into the Sex Discrimination Act made a mockery of the principle of sex equality for the millions of members of the club network. It has had particular impact on working-class communities who were left very much the poor relations where equality issues were concerned. Whether it was intended or not, the clause ensured that those clubs that *wanted* to treat all members equally, but were dependent on their WMCIU affiliation, are being *forced* by the national body to discriminate. The importance of this in the communities concerned is underlined by George Tremlett (who later became a prominent Tory politician in the Greater London Council), author of the WMCIU's official history, *The First Century*, published in 1961. He had no doubt, he wrote, that the clubs were and are a major organisational force in all areas of working-class life: 'The organisation that gave the working man somewhere to meet his fellows, somewhere to look to his future, and somewhere to decide his destiny.'[13] When I tracked him down at London's County Hall over two decades later, Tremlett reaffirmed his view that the clubs were of vital importance to the Labour movement as well as to community life. (Labour clubs, incidentally, are quite different, much fewer and poorer, and seem to be strongholds of equality in the club world.)

Although the WMCIU clubs are closely associated with the Labour Party, the political influence of the non-CIU clubs goes even further than this. There are a number of Liberal clubs, several of them also affiliated to the WMCIU, which are very similar to the rest both in activities, atmosphere and the degree of their discrimination against women. Several of them do so of their own volition, as well as in the matter of issuing WMCIU cards to men only as required by the organisation; some, though, are among the more . . . well, Liberal of the clubs.

Even more important is the vast network of Conservative Clubs, which have their own Association of Conservative Clubs (ACC). These clubs operate in the areas where the WMCIU is strong, along very similar lines, but also carry the principle of discriminating against women in clubs across the length and breadth of the country, including the rural and suburban areas where WMCIU clubs are few. They go much further in their discrimination, too, since several Conservative clubs will not admit women at all. The Conservative Party has always been heavily reliant on social organisation, through their clubs as well as other activities, to keep the party's membership base intact in the absence of the kind of *political* involvement that underlies membership of the Labour and Alliance Parties. The clubs are therefore very important to the Conservatives – as well as notoriously anti-women.

Some of the worst discrimination cases which have led to ERICCA pickets have involved Conservative clubs, often regarding exclusion from the snooker room. George Tremlett cheerfully admitted to me that they are just as bad as the WMCIU clubs. 'There is something very backward about men in clubs,' he told me. Margaret Thatcher (an 'associate member' of several Conservative clubs) has herself let it be known, via a letter to a Hampshire club, that she is unhappy abut the discrimination – although powerless to do anything about it. Conservative politicians, if they are women, can be excluded from certain activities or rooms in Conservative clubs in their own constituency. Jean Brinton, a Conservative county councillor, was not allowed to join the Medway Conservative Club in Rochester in 1981, the President claiming that 'the women at the club do take a keen interest in things, but I'm sure they are happier with the men actually making decisions'. Party Vice-Chairman Emma Nicholson, responsible for the Conservative women's organisation and parliamentary candidate for West Devon, was barred from the Conservative club in Tavistock, which excludes women altogether, in 1986. She gate-crashed anyway, but was careful not to use the men-only toilets.[14]

The ACC claims to be encouraging its member-clubs to treat women equally, but the results are distinctly unimpressive – in contrast to the prompt action that has followed publicised incidents of exclusion on racial grounds, when enormous pressure is brought to bear to overturn racist decisions.[15] Mrs Thatcher's Conservative Government decided in 1981 not to support a Private Members' Bill introduced by Labour MP Andrew Bennett, on behalf of the campaign for equality in clubs and with backing from the EOC, to amend the Sex Discrimination Act on this point along the lines of the relevant section of the Race Relation Act.

If you wonder why women are finding it such hard going in politics, then, the clubs and their discriminatory practices provide an important part of the answer. This alone – quite apart from the hurt and bitterness which the actions of petty club dictators cause to many people, especially women, who need the clubs and their companionship – makes the club movement, and the WMCIU in particular, a high priority for action if the clubs are to be saved as a viable resource for working-class and genuine political organisation across the country, and across the whole political spectrum.

What is to be done?

The hijack of a major working-class community facility by a relatively small number of men-only men, and the same phenomenon in politically important Conservative and Liberal clubs, is incompatible with equal opportunities in our society and full participation by women in politics and the community.

It is long past time that men who participate in clubs which exclude women from some or all of their facilities be called to account: particularly delicate, perhaps, is the position of MPs of all parties who belong to a club like this. What, in particular, have the left-wing Labour MPs to say in their defence when they would like to be seen as defenders of equal opportunities? They could learn from fellow MP Roland Boyes who admitted: 'I've spent a lot of time in workmen's clubs and I'm very proud of them, but women do needle me on the equality aspect' – and he had decided to campaign for equality.[16]

More far-reaching than this is the importance of putting pressure on the Registrar of Friendly Societies[17] to take much more seriously its responsibilities for regulating the working men's clubs and their rules – especially in the case of the many clubs' rule that they can change the rules outside the legal requirements. Many of the club members are unaware of the Registrar's responsibility in this regard, which is perhaps why so many have been complaining – fruitlessly – to the EOC. Every time a club committee changes the rules without going through the proper procedures, or refuses to provide basic information on request, there should be a complaint to the Registrar. His rules for the settlement of disputes in clubs, incidentally – which provide for genuinely independent arbitrators – are incompatible with those of the WMCIU – which makes club committees both judge and jury.

The scale of the clubs' abuses is such that the Registrar should set up a full inquiry into the workings of the clubs and invite all members with complaints to appear or give written evidence: this could very usefully include representation from the EOC.

The EOC's own proposals of March 1988 for changes in the sex discrimination legislation would – if and when a Government decides to back them and provide the necessary legislative time – have a major impact on the working men's clubs, although less so on men-only Conservative clubs. The proposals include bringing into the scope of anti-discrimination law all private members' clubs which, on or after 1 January 1988, have had people of both sexes in membership. The time-clause is deliberately included because of the strong possibility that women could be excluded altogether, as an answer to demands for equal treatment. The EOC, clearly, understands the clubman's mentality.

4
FREEMASONS AND BROTHERS

Freemasons belong to the most secretive of the men-only organisations, which operates in Britain and many other western countries very much like the British secret services: on the basis of 'deniability' for all their activities, regardless of the truth of the matter, and a denial also – in the face of all the evidence – that they even exist, in many cases. None of the Freemasons is supposed to reveal the existence of the organisation, their membership of it or any details of the activities. They meet in closed Lodge meetings complete with rather creepy rituals, and can also recognise each other by a variety of codes or 'secret signs', of which the most commonly known is the 'funny handshake' as non-members (who encounter it often in some areas of work and business) describe it.

The problem for outsiders, especially women, is to find a way of understanding Freemasonry which avoids the extremes of paranoia about masonic plots round every corner, on the one hand, or the opposite extreme of dismissing any allegations of masonic activity, on the other, as somebody else's paranoia. Many of us already know, in fact, something about these men and their existence is hardly in dispute: for details of how they in fact operate we owe a great debt to intrepid investigator Stephen Knight, who in his book *The Brotherhood* obtained unprecedented co-operation from otherwise loyal members of the organisations who, dismayed at the abuse of the connections made possible by masonic activity and the potential for cover-up contained within its secrecy rules, revealed an enormous amount to the author about just what *was* going on. Knight was leaning over backwards to be charitable about the masons, especially at the beginning of his investigation: some of his discoveries, however, are damning indeed. The publication of his book brought masons out of the closet to some extent, with public statements from United Grand Lodge in London's Long Acre denying some of his charges. It would appear, as Knight suggested, that leading masons are themselves worried about the abuses which are occurring within the organisation and feel that a little more openness might help them deal with it. However, so far the occasional open statement (claiming for instance that Freemasonry is nothing but a charitable organisation) has been on a token level, with a full open-door policy awaiting what would amount to a revolution among the masons. And the vested interests of many members in the present murky situation are just too great for this to be at all a likely prospect.

For now, then, any discussion of Freemasonry relies very heavily on findings of Stephen Knight since he is the one and only person to date who has undertaken the exhaustive research which is necessary for an informed judgement on the masons. Some of his findings are controversial, to say the least, and his theory about masonry being the perfect vehicle for Soviet KGB agents to infiltrate British Intelligence, while plausible seems to come straight from the Peter Wright *Spycatcher* school of reds-under-the-beds.

I shall concentrate here on those which are corroborated by our own informants, and other sources where they are available.

Masons old and new

The Freemasons of today love to claim an unbroken and mystical secret tradition which extends over not just centuries but millennia. But, as we see with a number of men-only organisations claiming tradition as their own, the masons of today are more like beneficiaries of a hijack, in the much more recent past, of someone *else*'s tradition. The organisation and practices of the skilled medieval stonemasons who designed and built the great Gothic cathedrals of Europe are the pretext for modern 'masonry', not a genuine forerunner.

All too little is in fact known about the original, medieval masons – builders in stone. Few records were kept, instructions were mainly verbal, skills were passed from one to the other. Perhaps the most painstaking reconstruction of their traditions and ways of working is that of John James, who examined the great cathedral at Chartres over many years and slowly pieced together how it had been built, and then went on to compare the construction of similar cathedrals and churches. He found, among other things, that successive building teams first bent the axis of the nave at Chartres and then straightened it – a major variation which is also found in the smaller churches, some of them with bent axes and others with straight ones.

'This suggests some fascinating possibilities about the masters' traditions,' he concludes. 'They must have flowed through the ages independently of their patrons, and have evolved as concepts and theories within a culture of their own ...' The traditions continued up to the end of the sixteenth century, when professional architects started to take over design down to the smallest detail and the builders became mere technicians.

If the masters evolved, and passed on exclusively among themselves, a tradition for expressing sacred ideas in stone, we would have to accept the presence of a parallel culture within a medieval society, running alongside but seldom mixing with the Establishment of clergy and nobility.

In particular, the stonemasons had the knowledge of gematria, a system of translating letters into numbers – an ancient idea probably invented in the sixth century BC in the Euphrates region and developed as a Christian symbolic system by philosophers in Europe and used also by musicians and poets.[1] If it was a separate culture with its own form of science and construction methods, this *may* seem at first glance to have a parallel with modern masons. But medieval and modern are quite different traditions. The medieval masons were below, and separate from, the formal hierarchy of Church and State: a form of trade union. Freemasonry as it operates today is closely allied with that same Establishment, in its modern form.

It would be very rash, incidentally, to assume that the real masons were men-only like their modern imitators. At Chartres, for instance, there is a record indicating that when the first permanent controller of works, Simon Dragon, died in the thirteenth century, his daughter applied for the job on the grounds that it was her traditional hereditary right. The Chapter had to have a special investigation into the matter to determine whether the appointment should be hereditary; there is no mention of her involvement as a woman being particularly remarkable or posing any problems.[2]

So what happened? The leading investigator of the modern British Freemasons, Stephen Knight, has reviewed conflicting claims against the available evidence and concluded that it all started with a simple takeover as a fashionable piece of exotica by the gentry in seventeenth-century England and Scotland of what had by then become a moribund organisation here and elsewhere in Europe. The British variant, with many embellishments and the invention of 'authentic' ancient traditions, was then exported around Europe and eventually, through empire-building, practically the whole world – with particular strength in the United States, where many of the Founding Fathers were masons, as were several presidents (Washington, both Roosevelts, Truman, Johnson and Ford – according to Tim Heald).[3] Hence the masonic symbol of the eye and pyramid on US dollar bills.

In parts of Europe it became a vehicle for anti-government plotting, and played a particularly important role in the unification of Italy. In Britain, and many other countries, it is almost literally a pillar of the Establishment, complete with royal patronage. Freemasonry, it seems, is what the members make of it. It can be different in different places, and practically all things to all men: either extremely moral or extremely immoral, a social centre, charity, or source of personal privilege and corruption. Almost the only constant feature of latter-day Freemasonry has been the rigid exclusion of women from what is in all senses a brotherhood of men, a place where women do not participate and are not taken into account.

Freemasonry as we know it (or don't, officially, know it) was created in Scotland and then in England on the basis of what seems to amount to a fraud, although very few details are available on it. Stephen Knight demolishes the claim made in the modern initiation ceremony to the First Degree that men today are joining 'a just, perfect, and regular Lodge of Ancient Freemasons', a movement 'founded on the purest principles of piety and virtue'. The official masonic calendar dates back four thousand years to when the movement is supposed to have begun.

The original masonic lodges, which were medieval in origin, were first joined by a few gentry some 300-odd years ago, mainly from 'curiosity, antiquarian interest, and a kind of fashionable search for an unconventional, exclusive social milieu – rather like a jet-set fad for frequenting working men's pubs'. The whole thing then became fashionable as well as useful, as 'accepted' members started to outnumber the now dwindling number of 'operative' masons while the entryists soon became tired of associating with artisans and formed their own gentlemen's lodges which went off in a completely different direction to those they were claiming as providing their ancient pedigree. Rituals and convenient myths were taken over or written from scratch. The spirit and much of the letter of the 'Old Charges', histories of the origins of the genuine craft of masonry and lists of rules for the guilds, were unceremoniously dumped. A rule of secrecy about the Lodge and the whole movement was brought in, with suitable blood-curdling oaths attached, which were very much at odds with the simple Christian promise to obey the guild rules 'so help you God'. It was a process of gentrification and mystification of an old structure which had already outlived its purpose: 'a peasant's cottage ripe for development as a luxury weekend home for the well-to-do' is Stephen Knight's description of it.[4]

Fashions change, and Freemasonry went through a period of decline in Britain about which Horace Walpole, a mason himself, wrote in 1743: 'The Freemasons are in . . . low repute now in England. . . I believe nothing but a persecution could bring them into vogue again.'[5] They became a target for derision and mockery, but with the Industrial Revolution the brotherhood came back as a convenient organisation for the serious (male) social climber, who was able to exploit connections running all the way up to the royal family, and the enormous circle of instant 'brothers', in the great struggle to make money and get a step ahead. The explosion of membership in the nineteenth century was mainly from the middle and professional classes, supplementing what had been largely a gentry-based organisation. The First World War further boosted recruitment, as did the Second.

There are now 600,000 men in Freemasonry in England and Wales, a further 100,000 in Scotland, and between 50,000 and 70,000 in Ireland. The number of Lodges in which they meet is around 8,000 in England and Wales, 1,200 in Scotland, and 750 in Ireland. The movement is astonishingly concentrated in certain professions and in particular areas: in London alone there are 1,677 Lodges, hundreds of them in the financial centre of the City where they are virtually all organised around financial institutions, clubs and workplaces.

Freemasonry is overwhelmingly concentrated in areas where there is strong competition for the available jobs, promotions or contracts. It is a system based on a form of nepotism, where instead of your liberal brother or other relative being given the advantage, it is the 'brother' in the sense of organised brotherhood: you scratch my back, I'll scratch yours.

One area where it can be observed in flagrant operation is in business, and particularly in sales. As one man (not a mason) told me, 'You get these funny handshakes all the time, practically every rep who comes in the door. I just think it's a joke and I do it back to them. They seem to expect me to buy whatever they're pushing, just for that.' A joke, yes – although all those sales men would not be giving the masonic handshake to other men if it wasn't working for them – at least some of the time. A sales rep is always looking for some edge on competitors in order to reach sales targets: if brotherhood will do it, it's worth trying that on too. It's a bit less of a joke, though, when you realise that women trying to sell in that market are going to be losing out. A man can use the signs, if he knows them, whether or not he is a mason; a woman can't, because we are automatically excluded. It's a powerful symbolic system of advantage which goes on under our noses but is almost never obvious unless you're really looking out for it.

A lot of back-scratching among small business and sales men also goes on in the Lodges, following the regular and supposedly secret ritual. As one lapsed mason told Tim Heald, the whole thing has been full of 'local grocers and undertakers dressing up and addressing each other by grand titles'.[6] One of Knight's informants particularly referred to local GPs, estate agents, 'tradesmen' and so on benefiting from preferential dealing within the Lodge, especially in small or medium-sized towns rather than big cities. Other categories which he found to be particularly involved were bank managers and clerks, and self-employed men who rely on 'contacts' for their work: accountants, architects, builders, restaurant-owners, taxi firm proprietors, insurance agents, travel agents, and shopkeepers of all kinds – not to mention of course those sales reps, whether locally based or working round the country. Many men told Knight that they had joined mainly to get an edge in business or job interviews.[7] It can also be very handy for street-market traders, who can organise all kinds of deals among themselves via Freemasonry, to the disadvantage of non-members. It is very often business associates who invite men into the organisation.

There's not really much mystery about the masonic equivalent of the nod and the wink: using masonic code-words, arranging the feet with toes pointed outwards in a square, or the famous handshake with thumb pressing on or between the other man's knuckles (depending on which 'degree' you claim). Among the explanations given to Knight by those involved were:

'Membership of Freemasonry is used considerably in the field of industry and commerce – because of the sign one can give which is unnoticeable by anyone else. You can make it known to the other person that you are what they call on the square, and if the other person is on the square he will recognize the sign, and that can influence either you being able to make a sale or, if you are applying for a job, it can make the difference between whether you get the job or not.'

'I have got business from two people as a result of being a Mason. . . . Once it was actually in Lodge after dinner. I was sitting next to a man and he said, "Well, what's your business?" and . . . did some business. But after I came out of Freemasonary he didn't want to know. I had another case where I didn't really intend to convey that I was a Mason in any way but I obviously did so quite inadvertently because it was the natural way for me to shake hands. And as a result of that I got that particular client, but it faded when I resigned.'

'Looking back, although I didn't think anything about it at the time, I suppose it was wrong. But quite a few times I know I got contracts because I gave a masonic grip. . . . You'll find that nine out of ten architects are Masons – and there is no getting away from it, I would put in a tender and when I did so, I'd shake the architect by the hand. "Oh," he'd say, "you're a Mason. The contract is yours."[8]

It is not just individuals or small businesses which are involved in the preference system, however: Knight mentions the phenomenon of large 'masonic' firms, and the outrageous but very well informed Russell Russell, writing in *The Tatler*, tells us that the masonic network is used to promote otherwise unqualified men with little initiative or flexibility on to the boards of large companies.

Extremely senior Freemasons are a doddle to spot. On any board of directors the dullest and most humourless, most pompous and pernickety, will be the Freemasons. If they're all masons, he'll be the most senior.

In any British company, the tedious I Speak Your Rulebook apparatchiks are the masons. In some companies, of course, this means nearly everyone in senior positions is a mason; it's probably what's wrong with British senior management and the real reason why there's only one woman on the board or no woman on the board.

Men, even if they are not masons, can be – and often are – approached to join the brotherhood *after* they have achieved an important promotion or a seat on the board, provided they have not criticised the brothers openly. Women, by definition, cannot: our presence in any numbers would dilute the power of the organisation which is in any case fairly contemptuous of women.

Russell points particularly at the Automobile Association and British Airways as examples of how the system works. The AA, he points out, is 'very light on senior women, very heavy on tedious old duffers, very keen on I Speak Your Rulebook' – and it has two masonic Lodges related to it. He explains this partly, as in the similar case of British Airways, by the armed forces background and culture of the organisations, the forces having their own very strong masonic links.[9]

Public sector, private deals

In the public sector, concern and investigation has focused so far on three related areas: the legal system, the police, and local authorities. The Masonic Year Book (an open-sounding publication which is not in fact published outside the movement and has been withheld even from the British Library) shows considerable numbers of our judges to be senior members of the Freemasons.[10] They include Lord Templeman, one of the Law Lords; John Latey, the most senior High Court judge; and John Arnold, who hit the headlines with some extremely reactionary views and inaccurate claims when giving a lecture which he thought would not be reported.[11]

One masonic judge of very long standing told Knight that over 50 per cent of his colleagues in the High Court, Court of Appeal and Law Lords were masons, with the proportion even higher when he had first joined – and that the reduction was 'not necessarily good'. There is considerable controversy over the extent to which masonic judges favour the many defendants, barristers and others who signal their membership of the brotherhood in the course of a trial. Knight cites a number of cases where this favouritism seems to be the only explanation for otherwise bizarre judgements.[12] Sally Hughes of the Legal Action Group feels that non-masons, and especially women seeking divorces from men who are in the brotherhood, are uneasy and apprehensive about losing out if the case is tried by a masonic judge. 'Even if freemasonry in fact has no influence, citizens should be given no grounds for suspecting partiality in judges,' she told one reporter.[13] A farcical situation arose in 1986 which demonstrated that masons generally expect masonic judges to be biased: in a row which became public over the proposed sale of the Royal Masonic Hospital. When the masonic protesters were seeking a judge to hear their application for an injunction, and one judge's name was mentioned, he was quickly turned down by both sides because he was a mason and so likely to be partial. The rebels were searching for a non-mason to hear their case.[14]

One of Knight's 'moles', a senior police officer and a Freemason, told him that the 'unseen intimacy' between police and judges was 'most damaging to society and to Masonry'. He particularly pointed to the 'overwhelming majority' of magistrates being masons, the regular masonic appeals to them by masonic police officers, and the unwarranted advantage that they gained by it. 'It's just that I can't see that this famous impartiality of judges can exist under these circumstances.'[15]

It would seem in fact that many of these men reached a position where they could judge others via the same masonic system. Knight argues that the second-rate or frankly mediocre barristers are the ones who are desperate to become judges by a certain age; the brilliant ones, with a few exceptions, can do much better by remaining QCs and earning vastly greater sums in their specialised areas. The means by which the second-rate barristers get their promotion as judges is simply to join what they euphemistically refer to as the 'Bar Golfing Society' – an interesting euphemism for masonic lodges attached to the Inns of Court. 'Initiation unlocks a door and allows them admission to the right place where they can be seen by the right people,' comments Knight. And, of course: no women. One Freemason, employed at a senior level in the Lord Chancellor's Department, claimed to Knight that 'Freemasons make the best judges', and described with approval the system of

getting on intimate terms with scores of influential judges, big names many of them, and with large number of my colleagues in the Lord Chancellor's Department. And this is right and correct, a right and proper method for men of integrity to come to the Bench.[16]

And women of integrity, by this reasoning, should be kept out. The comment was from an allegedly impartial and unbiased public servant.

Solicitors, incidentally, are not left out of the deal. They seem to have an even heavier involvement in masonry than the barristers — with whom they of course deal via the brotherhood system, in an almost tailor-made channel for getting round the rule that barristers should not openly tout for business but wait to be discovered, as many of those outside the system, especially women and ethnic minority barristers, are forced to do often for years on end. Once in the closed meetings of the brothers, it is a problem that is easily resolved since no one will report your touting.

Solicitors, especially outside London where legal work can be hard to get, join the brothers for their own interests too. Knight reports interviewing 'countless' solicitors who used the organisation to get on close terms with the business men in their area, and to gain personal contact with police, magistrates, their clerks, and any local or visiting judges. One, who objected strongly on grounds of ethics and his Christian convictions, joined reluctantly only after failing to get business — and under pressure from his colleagues in the firm who promised that it would bring him clients. 'I was initiated and within days clients began to contact me out of the blue. Within a few weeks I had more than I could cope with.' He was very troubled by the system, though, and he left. 'Most of my clients melted away as fast as they had appeared. They were all Masons.' And in case of trouble with the public watchdog of solicitors' behaviour and ethics, the Law Society (which also decides who gets legal aid, for instance to sue a negligent solicitor), the brotherhood offers yet another protection. 'The Law Society is one of the most masonic institutions in the world,' announces Knight categorically, and he discusses several cases of miscarriage of justice to illustrate the point.[17]

If the law is heavily influenced by the brotherhood system, the same is at least equally true of the police. It is this connection which has tended to dominate the news items about Freemasonry since the publication of Stephen Knight's book, and there has been particular emphasis on the Manchester force, including the suspension of John Stalker while trying to complete his investigations into the RUC's 'shoot to kill' policy in Northern Ireland, and subsequent departure from the police altogether; and the difficulties experienced by Chief Inspector Brian Woollard. Woollard was a police officer in North London who was removed from the CID after reporting the discovery of illegal masonic influences at work in a local government fraud investigation in the London Borough of Hackney.

Russell sums up the problem which Woollard's case raises:

The rights and wrongs of the case hardly matter now. What should matter is the difficulty Woollard had in having his own treatment – and the case itself – inquired into by parties unconnected with Freemasonry. His immediate superiors were masons; there were masons handling the case at the DPP; the then commissioner Sir David McNee was a mason, so was the Home Secretary, Lord Whitelaw, to whom he appealed. His own union, the Police Federation, had several masons in positions of influence. He could not be sure that lawyers he might approach would not be masons, nor the MPs.

One doesn't have to be a conspiracy theorist to find such a state of affairs unhealthy and against natural justice. Again, it doesn't matter whether all these people would conspire against him through loyalty to the Craft. It simply matters that he should have the right to an inquiry that is patently free of the influences of which he is complaining.[18]

Stephen Knight makes the important point that it is not just the reality of nepotism within the brotherhood that counts, it is also the firm belief among large numbers of policemen that by joining they can get promotions or favours, they will fail to take proper action against 'brothers' who break the law, and themselves evade disciplinary action if they break the law or police regulations. Knight cites many examples of apparent favouritism, and concern among non-masons and masons with integrity at the sapping of morale and discipline within the ranks, as well as instances of widespread police corruption which has been linked to masonic networks. One former police officer who was prepared to be named, Det. Supt David Thomas of Monmouthshire CID, wrote to Knight:

During my 32 years' police service I saw a great deal of this secret society in action, not only in my own force but also in the many others I visited as honorary secretary of the detective conferences of No. 8 Police District, which comprises the whole of Wales, Monmouthshire and Herefordshire. Sometimes my visits took me to other areas, but wherever I went the story was the same. 'Are you on the Square?' or 'Are you on the Level?' are all naive enquiries as to whether or not one is a Mason.

Thomas suggested that it was not the number of officers involved that was striking, but the fact that they were so senior: '. . . that small percentage forms an important and all-powerful group, the majority of whom are senior officers of the rank of Inspector, or above. Their influence is incalculable.'[19] The pattern varies from one force to another, and in the more heavily masonic ones the proportion of masons, even in the junior ranks, is very high.[20]

We are all affected by rising levels of crime and the erosion of police discipline and effectiveness (as measured by the clear-up rate of recorded crime). Women in particular are affected by the levels of violent crime, including sexual assault and rape, and have for a long time been very reluctant to go to the police given the very male nature of the force, itself perhaps related to masonic ideas and influence. Public pressure has resulted, in some areas, in improved procedures for dealing with victims of rape and sexual assault, although many policemen's attitudes are still uncomfortably close to those of the assailants: she asked for it, she's lying about the assault, she enjoyed it really . . . Although no study has been attempted of the effect of joining the brotherhood on individual men's attitudes to women, there is some evidence that it can be extremely damaging, especially where police attitudes are concerned. One woman who married a man she had known all her life, who joined the Metropolitan Police and rose to a senior level, found that he started battering her and their children and taking an extremely nasty attitude to rape victims. She blamed the Freemasons as well as the macho police culture to which the organisation contributes:

After he joined the Masons he just stopped discussing *anything* with me and started all this 'women should be pregnant and in the kitchen' stuff. I was horrified to find that after a few years within the Force, being promoted and becoming a Mason, he regarded all women – including myself – as second-class citizens.

After her separation from him she found that other women she met who had been married to masonic police officers had had very similar experiences.[21]

It should be noted, incidentally, that a Metropolitan Police guidance note was issued in 1984 on the issue: 'The discerning officer will probably consider it wise to forego the prospect of pleasure and social advantage in Freemasonry so as to enjoy the unreserved regard of all those around him.' The guidelines express concern over the 'exclusivity' of the brotherhood system and the 'mystery' surrounding membership. However, no disciplinary procedures were established to penalise a man jeopardising his chances of 'unreserved regard' and it is uncertain whether the guidelines have had any real effect. The *Observer* newspaper produced secret masonic documents to show that shortly afterwards a new masonic lodge was formed by 'Brethren, all of whom had served as Police Officers in ''C'' or St. James's District of the Metropolitan Police'. (One subsequently became a civil servant at the highly masonic Ministry of Defence, the other became a private investigator.) The 'Manor of St James's Lodge' was so named because, the documents record, 'The term Manor was the colloquial expression used by the police officers when referring to their own district or place of duty.'[22]

If police Lodges are organised around specific 'manors' in what seems to be an organised move to control their operations, this is even more true of local authority networks of the brotherhood. Lodges situated in or near the Town Hall or County Hall provide contact points for men who are not supposed to be in close contact with each other on a social or professional basis: officers with councillors, and outside contractors or other interested parties with either or both. Strict impartiality is the basis of the National Code of Local Government Conduct, especially when deciding on contracts, planning applications or licence applications which are of direct financial benefit to the recipients. Another important principle is declaration of an interest, and withdrawal from the meeting for that item, by councillors who have a personal financial or other interest in the application – for instance, if they belong to an organisation which is seeking planning permission, or are closely related to the applicant. The brotherhood allows these rules to be completely disregarded: rarely if ever has a councillor (or officer) declared an interest because of his brotherhood with an applicant or contractor, although it exists in innumerable cases.

Stephen Knight, who documents a number of instances – including those which involved large-scale corruption, such as the 'Poulson affair' in the North East, as well as much smaller-scale connections – suggest that 'the vast majority of councillors and officials join these [local government] Lodges . . . because they believe it increases their influence over local affairs'. He points out that they undermine the principles of democracy and public accountability, as well as the legal obligations of councillors and officers alike. This is not incidental to the business of the local government Lodge: that is its purpose.

It is also intended to by-pass the supposedly objective procedures for appointments and promotions within local government. In one typical instance I encountered, in Islington, a local government officer in the computer section would arrive for work on a certain day in the month wearing his best dark suit and patent leather shoes and leave at 3.30 in the afternoon for his Lodge meeting, where many others including Chief Officers would also appear (in work time, incidentally). He was not considered very good at the job but clearly expected swift promotion: when it did not happen he disappeared to a different local authority which was presumably better organised for the brothers' benefit. The Lodge meetings took place semi-openly yet attempts to get officers to declare their membership, amid concern about possible abuses, were getting nowhere.

Clearly, there are some authorities which are highly organised by the brothers while others are relatively free of influence. One senior source in local government told me that the Freemasons have a particularly tight hold on the City Council in Leeds, where both officers and councillors arc members and favours are freely exchanged which disregard the party lines which supposedly determine how policy is formulated. Another Council with heavy masonic influence, this source added, is Southwark, where the housing maintenance department showed such irregularities involving stolen goods and links with local criminals that the police were called in with a view to prosecution. There was ample evidence. But one police officer insisted, I was told, that the Council officers had to give some kind of sign: 'Isn't there anything you'd like to tell me on this matter?' Prosecution was eventually vetoed by the Department of Public Prosecutions.

The fact that masonry is secret, known to be working against equal opportunities, and under great pressure in some authorities can have a bizarre effect. A senior officer of great integrity, whom I knew to be a mason but of the honest kind who would never do favours on that basis, was pursuing an inquiry I had been pressing for into allegations of improper behaviour involving Council officers. He met with one of those who had been making complaints, who also happened to be a mason: the complainant told me he'd automatically given him 'the handshake' which was returned. But because of the tensions surrounding the brotherhood in that particular authority the officer completely rejected his fellow-mason's evidence and sent him away with a flea in his ear, so to speak. That, in my view, was as bad an effect of the brotherhood system as the – much more common – favouritism it usually invokes. The inquiry got nowhere. The guilty men carried on as before, threatening the livelihood of those (including several women) who had complained. Until Freemasonry comes out of its closet, and can show that members are not showing favouritism to each other, the cause of honesty and integrity in local government is battling against the odds from all sides.

Attempts are being made, of course, to open up the local government Lodges to public scrutiny. It is not simply membership of the brotherhood that is in question, it is the deliberate construction of an organised group of men with a common, undeclared interest, attached to a particular public authority. The fact that it meets very often on Council premises and in working hours is very much under challenge, together with the fact that the brothers do not declare their membership alongside their other interests which are supposed to be on the record. Manchester City Council decided in 1986 to ban masonic meetings in the Town Hall, and announced a register in which all officers and members of the Council were to disclose membership of any organisation, including and especially secret ones.[23] Other, mainly Labour-controlled, Councils have announced similar action – although there is strong doubt as to whether officers will be prepared to make such a disclosure, preferring perhaps to retreat behind the wall of secrecy and ambiguity about who is, and who can be *proved* to be, one of the brothers. In a weighty report to the London Borough of Hackney by Andrew Arden on alleged corruption, malpractice and the involvement of Freemasonry, he repeatedly emphasises the climate of distrust and suspicion – which might or might not be justified – arising from any suggestion of meetings by interested parties behind closed doors. With local government under attack from national Government, he points out, it is essential to tackle 'the concern that comes with the concept of "public accountability", with which *any* additional loyalty *may* conflict'.[24]

At the other end of the scale, there is concern among

British Labour Party members of the European Parliament about a masonic Lodge set up by EEC officials and MPs. Their notion was rejected by the Political Affairs Committee without a debate, despite the charge by Terry Pitt that 'the interlocking of senior members of the parliament and the administration is classic freemasonry'.[25]

Or, as a restaurant owner in Grimsby told Stephen Knight, you join the masons to make sure of the favour you need (in his case regular renewals of his drinks licence):

We help each other. Why not? It's what it's all about innit? I mean, you come to me, you scratch my back and I'll scratch yours. I'd be a bloody masochist if I didn't take advantages like everyone else, wouldn't I? We're all human.

Except that, by his reckoning, men of integrity (masons or otherwise) who refuse to use the system are not human. Neither are the women who also need a licence or whatever else it may be which should be allocated on the merits of the case, and in the public interest rather than the private ones of the brothers.

This use of a private network to influence a public authority is perhaps the most striking aspect of Freemasonry. Russell and Knight both point to public authorities and nationalised industries as prime targets. Both mention National Health Service hospitals, the Central Electricity Generating Board and the Post Office in particular, and Knight's more detailed list includes British Steel, the Coal Board, British Rail, regional electricity boards, the Atomic Energy Authority, London Transport, the ambulance and fire services and the prison service, as well as the Bank of England and major institutions of the City of London.[26] In the health sector, Knight reports that a masonic trust fund has channelled £600,000 to the Royal College of Physicians and the Royal College of Surgeons, while the masonic system influences the promotion of its members to senior jobs controlled by those organisations. Knight quotes the ex-masonic Lord Porritt of St Mary's

Paddington (named by Russell as highly masonic) as admitting 'It would be hard to deny that some people have been helped.'[27] As with the police, it appears that the widespread belief in masonic influence among junior male doctors in important teaching hospitals, where the jobs which lead to senior hospital jobs are subject to intense competition, leads many to feel that they have to join the hospital Lodge if they are to stay in the race and find the best way of currying favour with the all-powerful consultants. It is not just a matter of promotion, one man told me: if you fail to get the next vital link in your career you could be out of hospital medicine altogether. One (male) applicant for a consultant's post at the London told me:

> I've been doing that job on a temporary basis and was more or less promised it, and I *know* I didn't get it because I've been so outspoken about how corrupt I think the masons are. The really frustrating thing is that I don't even know for sure who is and who isn't.

This describes very well the problem that women encounter when they become aware of masonic organising which deprives them of jobs or other opportunities: it can't be challenged without making matters worse, and there is the uncertainty about just who is involved. It can feel like a taboo subject which *nobody* wants to discuss.

For men in this position, there is a degree of choice: to speak out, or keep quiet. For women, there is no choice on offer. Women are also at risk if they offend one or more of their male colleagues who are in a Lodge. The well-publicised, organised attack on the position of Wendy Savage at the London Hospital has been linked with the masonic network in and around that hospital.[28] Wendy Savage's case also involves the élite clubs of London's West End, and is examined in Chapter 7.

Stephen Knight became very interested in the brothers' organisation around national Government and the civil service, and cites the celebrated vote by Transport House

Lodge in 1935 to make Clement Attlee leader of the Labour Party. Unfortunately Knight died while in the middle of researches into Civil Service links, and while he does mention the Ministry of Defence and appointments to Permanent Secretary positions as particularly influenced by masonry, his statement in *The Brotherhood* that 'this area of masonic influence warrants a book in itself'[29] is left as a tantalising suggestion that this most important of national institutions is at least as heavily influenced by the brotherhood system as the others.

Good, bad and indifferent

Freemasonry is a hugely varied organisation, very much a matter of what the members make of it – from the very good to the very bad. Stephen Knight, seen by the masons' hierarchy as 'the enemy', is anxious to point out the benefits that many men get from it in terms of social contact, especially if they are lonely or depressed. He mentions one such case, where a man had lost his wife and sunk into depression and hopelessness. A few years later, having joined the masons on someone's introduction, he was 'a completely changed man'.[30] It could have been anything: friends, voluntary work, evening classes could have had this effect. But in his case and others, it just happened to be Freemasonry. I have also known senior male officials in local government who were known to be masons but, I am convinced, did it for purely social reasons: they were men of great integrity in their public service but they desperately needed friendship.

Freemasonry offers regular meetings with elaborate ceremonies, a solid and reliable routine. Archdeacon Hoyle, an Anglican and keen mason, has claimed that 'men in particular have a psychological need to be involved in ceremonial acts'.[31] There is also the ready-made circle of other men operating a mutually supportive network as strong as traditional neighbourliness, and as close as a warm extended family, when the men may well lack either or both as well as having less than ideal relationships with those supposedly closest to them, especially their wives and children. One member told Knight that masonry appealed especially to more isolated men who do not take part in local affairs, belong to clubs, or do any voluntary work.

For them Freemasonry is an avenue through which they walk to the path of helping . . . of unselfish deeds – that means charity, that means helping, that means lending the car to somebody, taking them into hospital, or . . . helping, it might be with money, it might be with a job . . .

A member of the City of London Corporation, Frederick Clearey, insisted that the Lodge he belonged to, his old school's, 'engenders a very fine spirit, cementing members of the Lodge with the school. . . . In my experience it has generated an enormous amount of friendship, goodwill and charity, which is what Freemasonry is about.'[32]

It must be added, though, that the much-touted masonic 'charity' is not primarily for society as a whole. It is an insurance policy as much as a charity, being for the benefit of the brotherhood itself, or for its individual members and their immediate families: the Royal Masonic Institution for Boys, the same for Girls, the Royal Masonic Benevolent Institution, the Royal Masonic Hospital and the Masonic Foundation for the Aged and the Sick. Knight tells us that in 1980 £932,000 was given to charities by United Grand Lodge (and individual Lodges gave their own direct contributions). Over two-thirds of that was for masonic institutions.[33]

Another perspective on Freemasonry is to view it as a perhaps snobbish but basically harmless vehicle for social climbing. Russell suggests that in Freemasonry 'bores and name-droppers thrive';[34] rituals, fancy dress, pompous titles and a secret language gave the illusion of importance. Then there's the heady (to some) notion of being a 'royal' organisation which is indicated by the title of the masonic institutions but also by the membership of real live royals – although, to their bitter disappointment, Prince Philip is nominal and refuses to attend, while Charles won't have anything to do with it. Still, the Queen is 'Grand Patroness' although as a woman she wouldn't be admitted as an ordinary member, and there is the Duke of Kent as the nominal Grand Master: a figurehead only, not the real leader (but that's royalty for you). British royalty has patronised masonry since 1874, when the Prince of Wales became nominal Grand Master, and Knight suggests that this is why masons have felt safe in not taking a blind bit of notice of all the legislation dating from 1797 concerning secret societies and illegal oaths. Royal involvement, Knight concludes, ensured – then and now – 'the impression of total reputability'.[35]

It's not all sweetness and light and play-acting, though. One of the most fascinating discoveries that Stephen Knight made was that there is an ultra-secret group of masons who are horrified at the abuses being made of the system by, at best, irresponsible careerists and, at worst, by outright criminals. The problem is that the system is wide open to abuse, as Russell points out: 'Freemasonry has ample potential for mischief. It can, by virtue of its obsessive secrecy, be a vehicle for conspiracy, for corruption, for personal gain, for victimisation. Such things are virtually impossible to prove.'[36] The whole network operates on a cell system: a member knows only who belongs to his own Lodge (although he can identify individuals by means of the secret signs). It is entirely conceivable then that one Lodge could be all brotherly goodwill and charity, and the next full of criminals operating the system (and the police and law officers in the Lodge) to their own advantage. Many 'social' members can quite innocently protest that masonry does no harm to anyone, while the evidence is that this is very far from the truth, with the Lodges organised around particular work places, and those used by criminals, the nub of the problem.

The innumerable cases of abuse described by Stephen

Knight would seem to suggest that the standards of the brotherhood generally, although not of course all its members or Lodges, are deteriorating fast. A typical comment from one of the concerned 'honest' masons, a Detective Sergeant in the City of London police, was:

'I've seen Masonry used for rotten things in the force in recent years. I'd never have believed it was possible if I hadn't seen it and heard it myself. What sickens me is the filthy distortion of the principles of Freemasonry. It's not meant to be for this, it's really not. But Masons are being promoted over the heads of non-Masons left, right and centre. . . . It's forbidden to talk about politics, religion or business in the Temple, but these yobbos – they shouldn't be in the police, let alone the Craft – they're using the secrecy to get into corners and decide who's next for promotion and who they can place where to their own advantage.'

Much of it, he added, was about protecting their own backs if they broke regulations, but there was also 'actual criminal stuff' which included failure to press charges against criminals 'as a result of little conferences at Lodge meetings'.[37]

A broader perspective on abuses across the board was given to Knight by a 'very senior' civil servant who was part of the organised group trying to halt abuses of this kind, in the face of outright refusal by Grand Lodge to acknowledge the problem or do anything about it.

Standards have been falling for 20 or 30 years. It is too easy to enter the Craft, so many men of dubious morals have joined. The secrecy and power attract such people, and when they come the decent leave. The numbers of people who would never have been considered for membership in the fifties are getting larger all the time. If only five per cent of Freemasons use – *abuse* – the Craft for selfish or corrupt ends it means there are 25,000 of them. The figure is much closer to twelve or thirteen per cent now.[38]

That adds up to over 60,000 men using the system for their own personal advantage, above and beyond the 'normal' help that members of the brotherhood would be expected to give each other.

It can get extremely vicious: not just police corruption and bent judgements to permit and encourage crime (a recent case involved police, judges and Jockey Club members in a betting swindle known as the Flockton Grey),[39] but the hounding of individuals, often to suicide or personal ruin. As explained by the senior civil servant, the brotherhood system could easily be used by individual members or organised groups to collect supposedly confidential information about the target. It uses a procedure set up to make discreet inquiries with a view to *helping* members in difficulties – as well as exploiting contracts with men willing to do favours with no questions asked because that was their own reason for joining, and they could expect to get one back. The individual concerned can then be blackmailed, harassed or have evidence of serious crime planted by masonic police; deliberately embroiled in a hopeless legal case by a masonic solicitor; refused credit by being placed on a list of bad debtors, have their mortgage foreclosed, or their telephones cut off; or be harassed by local government employees on some pretext – quite apart from action at work like blocking promotions or firing the person. With this kind of extreme discrimination, any complaint would be seen as far-fetched: 'You can get no help because your story sounds so paranoid that you are thought a crank, one of those nuts who think the whole world is a conspiracy against *them*.'[40]

This also describes quite neatly the problem for women in identifying and then confronting the difficulties with getting a job, a promotion, a contract, a sale or whatever it is in the face of an organised and often quite ruthless brotherhood. Women are all too readily identified as 'paranoid' if we complain about any form of discrimination. How much more so if we complain about an organisation like Freemasonry. 'You can get no help because your story sounds so paranoid. . . .' As Russell puts it: 'People who feel, wrongly or rightly, that they have been victims of a masonic conspiracy – it may be failure to gain promotion at work, or a licensing application before magistrates, or a council contract – can never find the proof, have no redress.'[41] Except that, of course, unlike the many individuals who become the unfortunate victims of the brotherhood system, women as a group *can* help and support each other in finding out what we can about how it works, and who is doing what in a particular situation, once enough of us understand the problem.

Oddfellows and sodfellows

It is indeed a strange business, Freemasonry. But at the same time it is closely linked with the other men-only organisations mentioned in this book – and many more for which there is no space. Similar men-only secret societies include the Knights Templar, the Order of St John of Jerusalem (whose charitable project is the St John Ambulance), the Rosicrucians, the Catholic Knights of St Columbanus (which has played an important role in organising the Labour Party for right-wing ideas and individuals), the Oddfellows, the Order of Eri, and many others. All of these are probably open to exploitation by the unscrupulous in the same way as masonry: for instance, the Manor of St James's Lodge, mentioned earlier, was officially recorded by the Freemasons as having been 'sponsored, appropriately, by Prior Walter Lodge No. 8687, a Lodge comprised of members of the Order of St John, which has a close affinity with the police service.'[42] And the Knights of Malta, nominally based in Rome (banned in Britain for some time and re-established here in the eighteenth century through the 'Order of St John') sparked off a farcical series of imitators recently based on its recognition in international law as the only 'sovereign entity' without any territory but with embassies in some forty countries. They have been described by an irreverent observer in Rome as 'a corporation with no known consolidated balance sheet' but thought to be richer today than in the fourteenth century when they 'owned' France and practised piracy and slaving. They are now 'another élitist club with funny admission rules' and a form of flamboyant drag 'so outlandish that any infidel adversary would topple off his horse or his turret in a fit of terminal laughter'.[43]

A variety of imitators of the Knights of Malta have set themselves up to issue and sell diplomatic passports, possibly to organised crime for arms and drug-smuggling; one, claiming to be the 'Sovereign Order of the Coptic Catholic Knights of Malta', even conned the Seychelles into giving its recognition for an 'embassy', a cover for South African operations, which was far bigger and grander than the British Embassy. Jonathan Goldberg, counsel for one of the men involved, told the jury at his Old Bailey trial for fraud that the whole thing had exploited the absurd snobbery of the British. 'People with false titles and fake passports were given VIP status and able to run up enormous bills at the Ritz, where you or I would be thrown out for not wearing a tie.'[44]

Perhaps it would be uncharitable to suggest that the charge of exploiting our snobbery is just as true of the genuine Orders as it is of the racketeers. What, for instance, are we to make of the media's obsession with titles side by side with a growing disregard for accuracy on anything else? Much more serious, however, are similarities between these secret organisations generally and the Orange Order in Belfast, the vehicle for anti-Catholic discrimination and Unionist terrorism against Catholics in Northern Ireland. Paul Keel reports in *The Guardian* that the Order has 80,000 brethren, who are organised in lodges 'on the model of mainland masonic lodges'.[45] There is nothing new in secret, men-only organisations being a vehicle for discrimination and terrorism, as the activities of the Broederbond in South Africa and the Ku Klux Klan in the southern United States illustrate only too vividly.

On a more prosaic level are the similarities and connections of British Freemasonry with all the other men's

organisations here. There are many men who will deny that
Freemasonry is anything special, or even set apart from the
world of men's organisations. Faced with pressure for Nor-
wich City Council officers to declare whether they were
masons, the Norfolk provincial Grand Master, Colonel
Dicker, declared the policy 'ridiculous' on the basis that
masons were no different from Rotarians or Lions.[46] Knight
tells us that on a local level there is much 'cross-
fertilization' between Masonry and the Round Table, Rotary
Clubs and Chambers of Commerce. 'Most of the male
members of these organisations – and Chambers of Commerce at least contain an increasing number of women –
are Freemasons as well.'[47] There are Lodges linked directly
to private schools (some to Old Boys' Lodges, in fact) as well
as professional organisations, City Livery companies and
other men's organisations.

One police complainant about the Freemasons' tendency
to expect favours from fellow members who are police officers has pointed out that the same is true of Rotarians,
Lions and Round Tablers. Another police man saw no problem with this in terms of his decisions about promotion
which judged membership of any of these as adding points
in a man's favour:

I've got to make a judgement on your characters, and I've got to
take a gamble. . . . And the more I know about you that causes me
to be in sympathy to your cause – the school, the rugby club, the
golf club, Freemasonry or whatever it may be, the more I will be
inclined to take a chance. . . .

A barrister ranked Freemasonry with any other kind of club,
'and I wouldn't put Freemasonry much higher than a dining-
club incidentally', as a place to 'meet people'.[48]

And women? Well, there is the annual Ladies' Night when
wives and daughters have to doll themselves up in expensive long dresses and the works: none of your trousers or independent opinions wanted there. There is also a small,
unauthorised women's version of Freemasonry with, at

most, a few hundred members who cannot begin to compete with the hundreds of thousands of men or with the splendour of their connections, Queen and all. It is easy after all to copy the ritual (or most of it – perhaps not the baring one breast and rolling up a trouser leg to prove you're not a woman) or to make up your own version of the men's mumbo-jumbo. No doubt the mainly business women who belong do derive some benefit from knowing each other in such intimate circumstances, but it certainly isn't the real thing – a nationwide network which reached into practically every aspect of business and public life.

Perhaps equally important, if not more so, is many women's recognition of how important Freemasonry is – to their husbands and sons, and therefore to them. There is a perhaps common instance I have heard about where a single mother was struggling to bring up her son in the 1940s and 1950s, and got him apprenticed to a jeweller: at the same time she moved heaven and earth to get him the right introduction to the Freemasons, who would guarantee him a living in the trade, and scraped together the cash necessary for him to join. It paid off as intended: the brothers have kept him in (very lucrative) work ever since. Enough to employ a young woman, a brilliant goldsmith and jeweller – who will never belong – to do much of the work for him.

Women needed to clean up?

The Freemasons and other secretive organisations based on mutual help among the 'brothers' have to be taken very seriously as organisations working against women, and against equal rights in general – however farcical they appear when you catch a glimpse of them in their closet. It is high time all those men 'came out' and announced themselves as members of their secret lodges and groups. It is long past time that public authorities, from local Councils to central Government, conducted a clean-up campaign to require employees to disclose membership of *any* organisation, and to make it a condition of employment that employees should not participate in any undisclosed organisation, particularly one where they are together with work colleagues and business contacts behind closed doors – and doing some *very* strange things to each other.

Until we get the men out into the open we cannot possibly claim to have an open, accountable and democratic society, nor can we claim a public service sector free of corruption. The single most useful step, perhaps, would be the formation of special police units which can be guaranteed mason-free (women only? – the female 'masons' are minute, and a bit of a joke). We would also need a special unit of the Department of Public Prosecutions along the same lines. We need more women taking charge of this and other issues of public concern, if anything worth while is to be done: effective action would, in turn, remove the invisible barriers which so many women have encountered, often without realising what was going on, in their efforts to achieve positions of responsibility.

5
WHEELING AND DEALING
Rotary Clubs

Rotary Clubs: do they or don't they (promote each other's businesses)?

> Let ev'ry good knight raise his helmet and glove!
> To carry our message of service and love . . .
> The grooming of man is a duty we claim,
> Let's carry on business with fame to our name.
> The man with a smile is the fellow we need,
> Who loses himself in the shaming of greed.
>
> Vive le Rotary!
>
> *Songs for the Rotary Club*

It is easy – perhaps too easy – to make fun of the Rotarians, this conservative band of ageing men who meet weekly in clubs all over the US, Britain and many other countries for lunch, a speaker, and to let their hair down a bit, if they have any, among their own kind. The bank manager sits next to the grocer who throws things at the undertaker, and they all say silly things, throw bread rolls at each other and sing songs like the one above. George Bernard Shaw was once asked to address a Dublin meeting on 'Where is Rotary Going?' Declining, he answered that the only place it was going was 'to lunch'.

But Rotary *is* important (so are the similar Lions Clubs and Kiwanis). Rotary is an organisation of business *men* which rigidly excludes women, and the original principle of promoting each other's businesses through cultivating personal contact is still very much the basis of it. There is, besides, another reason for taking Rotary seriously; their promotion of what can only be described as a cult of maleness, a cult of Man, which is very evident in Rotary publications. The organisation's own descriptions of itself are fascinating and unintentionally very revealing – especially on the twists and turns of 'business advantage' as the main motive, the crusading zeal behind an ill-defined 'ethics' – and above all the importance, to them, of being male. British Rotary were happy to open up their files to a sympathetic (male) researcher.

'Boy in Man'

Particularly in the 1920s and 1930s, Rotarians also had an almost reverent attitude to maleness as seen in 'the Boy'. The Rotary historian, David Shelley Nicholl, emphasises very strongly the 'Boy in Man' idea which was, and remains, the universal lodestone of Rotary's appeal, legitimising for grown men the renewal of the 'gang'. The benefits of the gang to a boy, which included 'pals' of his own age and kind and loyalty to a gang's standards and ideals, are 'essential elements supplied by membership in Rotary' and 'an essential part of man's urge to join Rotary', although as he admits, 'it is an instinct all too easily perverted to causes of conquest and tyranny, as Nazi Germany was all too soon to show'. Rotary coexisted happily with Hitler's Third Reich in pre-war and wartime Germany.

The cult of the Boy beneath this ultra-respectable front is

a means of returning to the world of risks, of personal relationships and of personal choices which being a respectable business man had sealed off. As they grow older, Nicholl explains, men 'erect a wall of innocence – of non-seeing – around our lives to sustain us against cruelty, disappointment and decision. . . .' Boys 'accept consequences for their actions.' So do girls, of course, 'but the years give them no refuge. Women are far less innocent than men; life gives them far more of the consequences.' But it is not to women that men turn to break out of their lonely and loveless cocoons and reach true humanity, but boys. 'To recapture the careless bravery of boyhood is thus a universal longing to which men of success of every race and creed and political belief are happy to admit. . . .'[1]

Unsurprising, then, that Rotary should back work with and for boys, providing a big element in discriminatory provision for children and young people that favours boys over girls – not just in recreation but in skills that will be useful in the future world of employment. The message is that boys deserve, and get, better than girls. The Rotarians backed the Boy Scout movement from the very beginning, but not the Girl Scouts or Guides. With financial help and the individual participation of many Rotary members, scouting for boys was spread rapidly around the English-speaking world. Writing in the April 1919 issues of *The Rotarian*, George Wyckoff of the Boy Scout executive in Indiana claimed: 'Truly the Boy Scout is a Rotarian, as the Rotarian is a real Scout.' To drive his theme home, he wrote: 'When God made the first man, he made the world significant, but when he made the first boy, he made it interesting.' A poem in the same issue went even further:

> O, but I like you,
> You sun-tanned boys,
> You brown-clad boys of mine.

In case of doubt, it was made clear that this meant white boys. In the 1920s the Rotary Club of Selma, Alabama, entertained 120 farm boys to their lunch every week, 'all white boys in the county' being eligible.[2] Racism remains a problem, incidentally: in 1982 a court order was required to force the 350-member Rotary Club of Birmingham, Alabama, to remove the limitation on membership to 'any white male person of good moral character'.[3]

Meanwhile, women remain very much on the outside of the Rotary world. We are hardly mentioned in their publications at all, except for the lawsuits in the US. The value assigned to women seems to be that of the founder, Paul Harris, who claimed of his wife that he didn't know her true worth until he married her and by then it was too late. There is more than a hint that in fact he, too, preferred boys.[4]

Founded in 1905 by four business men in Chicago, Rotary International now has one million members world-wide, participating in what it defines as 'a world-fellowship of business and professional men united in the ideal of service'. In Britain and Ireland there are over 1,200 clubs with about 55,200 members, organised as Rotary International in Great Britain and Ireland (RIBI). Predominantly centred in North America and Western Europe, with a strong presence in Asia, Rotary invites into membership only those who 'are in a position to influence the conduct of their own particular businesses and their vocations as a whole'.[5]

However, not all business men can take advantage of Rotary membership: their presence has to be in the interests of existing members. They cannot apply, but have to be nominated by existing members and are rigorously vetted (without their knowing) before being elected. Membership is also restricted by the system of 'single classification' by which only a single representative of a trade or profession can be admitted to any local club – so no member is associating with his competitors, but only complementary businesses.

Who, why, how

Inside 'the club', it is still a cosy Rotary world. On 17 February 1986, in France, Jean Paul Morval became the millionth member of Rotary International. A chief engineer of Unimetal, a French steel manufacturing firm, 'Rotarian' Morval is fairly typical of the type of man being recruited.

He was joining a movement with members in over 160 countries and geographic regions, with a young wing of 210,000 (including, ironically, young women) organised through Interact and Rotaract. While women are excluded from membership of Rotary International, wives (known as Rotary Anns by English-speaking member husbands) also meet in 'Inner Wheel' groups and are expected to attend a number of Rotary socials with their husbands.

The twenty-five regional magazines and the monthly journal of the whole movement, *The Rotarian*, help to bring a surprisingly high degree of homogeneity to this international organisation. Rotarians are proud of the fact that they can walk into any Rotary Club meeting in the world and feel 'at home'.

In order to gain admittance to his local club in Thionville, Jean Paul would have had to have gone through a procedure which would be familiar to most Rotarians. Firstly, he would have to comply with the Constitution of RI, of which Article IV, Section 3 states in part that:

A Rotary Club shall be composed of men with qualifications hereinafter provided and no Club shall be qualified for membership in Rotary International unless the qualifications of its active members are as follows:

They are adult male persons of good character and good business or professional reputation, and
(1) engaged as proprietor, partner, corporate officer, or manager of any worthy and recognised business or profession;

or

(2) holding an important position in an executive capacity with discretionary authority in any worthy and recognised business or profession;

or

(3) acting as the local agent or branch representative of any worthy or recognised business or profession having charge of such agency or branch in an executive capacity.[6]

Jean Paul should have been unware that his name was being put forward for Rotary by his friend Jean Bertrand, a past-president of the Thionville Club. Bertrand first had to submit a suggestion slip to the secretary of the Club, who would then pass it on to the 'classification committee'. This assesses whether admitting the proposed man would conform to the principle of having a single representative of each type of trade and profession. This condition of membership, although somewhat relaxed in recent years, has been a consistent feature of the organisation since its foundation.

It is for this reason that the Rotarians insist on secrecy in the initial stages of recruitment – not only, as they thoughtfully point out, to prevent prospective members being 'wounded' by rejection, but perhaps more from their own very lively fear of legal action being taken by those who are turned down. There was evidently a dearth of chief engineers in the metal trade in the Thionville Club since M. Morval made it to the next stage: the Information Committee.

He would have been given a briefing on what was expected from him. He would have to meet weekly for a meal, almost certainly lunch; the minimum attendance is 60 per cent of all functions. Considerable efforts would be made to make him feel at home: the Rotary Information Service sets out 'integration' procedures which include introducing the new member to other Rotarians 'at every opportunity', sitting with him at different places to prevent cliques forming, asking him to talk about his business at an early opportunity, and publicising his 'life story' in the Club bulletin.

Jean Paul would have been informed, too, that the Rotary ideal is that of 'Service above Self' and assured that this meant personal activity in one of the four branches of Rotary service (club, 'vocational', community or international) rather than financial contributions to charity.[7]

Election takes place with all club members participating, two 'black balls' being sufficient to rule out membership. But Jean Paul would also have been told of the pitiless attitude of the Rotarians to failure in business. If he was to go bankrupt or his firm should liquidate, his 'classification', and thereby his membership, would be terminated.

This rather ruthless policy of confining membership strictly to men in executive positions who can help each other's businesses has been subject to a great deal of criticism. The Rotarians are holding out against any fundamental change to the 'single classification' principle on the grounds of not 'embarrassing' members. They claim:

> For ordinary social reasons a Club must be composed of men who can mix together without financial embarrassment. Further it is assumed that Rotarians, as men with executive responsibility, are in a position to influence the conduct of their own particular businesses and of their vocation as a whole. The idea of a Rotary organisation for employees has been suggested, and it may be that steps will one day be taken to encourage its establishment.[8]

While the same guide goes on to state that leading representatives of trade unions are eligible for membership, this defence of the 'single classification' system sits rather uneasily with the assertion that the system of membership is merely to make sure that each club has a 'genuine cross section of local business and professional community.'[9]

'The right to develop business deals'

There was no such reticence about seeking personal advantage among the founding fathers of the Rotarians. The first Rotary Club was formed in 1905 by Paul Harris, a lawyer. The initial grouping of four members had been brought together in a conspiratorial campaign to establish . . . the first men's public toilet in Chicago! Their name derived from their habit of meeting near each other's offices by turn in pursuit of this ambition, and the broader one of making friends and business allies in the violence and corruption that was Chicago at the turn of the century.

By its second gathering, the Club had defined two of the cardinal principles; that members should represent different and non-competitive firms, and each should either own such firms or enjoy high executive authority. Each new member would give a talk on 'My Job' which would outline his interests and ways of operating.

David Nicholl in his history of Rotary International, *The Golden Wheel*, states unequivocally: '. . . the right to develop business deals within the Club . . . was at this time the principal purpose of the Rotary Club's existence, apart from forming friendships – and those friendships were related to deals.'[10] Not only were such transactions made, but a detailed ledger of transactions between members was carefully kept to make sure each member *was* giving business to the others. This record was kept secret, however, for fear of retaliation from outraged competitors.

The membership of the Chicago club was confined originally to the middle professions, with men predominantly in their 30s who were just getting established. The occupations of its founding members – lawyer, coal merchant, mining engineer and tailor – were typical of those who were to follow in its early years. But the establishment of a brother club in San Francisco saw a marked shift towards big business, with the very first meeting being addressed by a steel magnate and the Vice President of the California Gas and Electric Company. It is this element that dominates national and international Rotary today, although at local level members obviously include small business men as well as, more recently, local employees of the multinationals.

Business methods, too, were more thrusting in the San Francisco club. It started the practice of 'boosting': members would continually praise their own and each other's products and services in the meetings, touting for reciprocal business – and usually getting it. (This profitable ritual, it was suggested, was the real reason for calling the organisation 'Rotary'. It gave a new slant on the idea of 'wheeling and dealing'.)[11] There were also 'boost weeks', including one when all the Rotarians' wives were urged to besiege city stores demanding a cosmetic called Skin Jelly, thus 'boosting' sales astronomically. Any employee of the club was paid for 'business getting'. Inter-member deals were not only reported but actively negotiated during the lunches, and merchandise was displayed on the table between the knives and forks.

It was a winning formula, the original 'How to make friends and influence people'. New clubs were being set up everywhere in the US, with the advice of Paul Harris to his organisers being direct and to the point: 'You will find that one of the readiest avenues to the heart of prospective members will be the business advantage route.'[12] The first National Convention of Rotary Clubs adopted as its fifth and final objective (since dropped): 'To advance the business interests of the individual members of the affiliating clubs.'

The practice of 'boosting' became so notorious that Sinclair Lewis based his 1922 novel *Babbitt* on the typical middle-class businessmen of Rotary, renamed the 'Booster Club' (one of the names actually proposed for the original Rotary) in fictional Zenith City, in the American Mid-West.

At each place was the Boosters' Club booklet, listing the members. Though the object of the club was good fellowship, yet they never lost sight of the importance of doing a little more business. After each name was the member's occupation. There were scores of advertisements in the booklet, and on one page the admonition: 'There's no rule that you have to trade with your fellow Boosters, but get wise, boy – what's the use of letting all this money get outside of our happy fambly?'

According to Sinclair Lewis, men like his hero, a Mid-Western estate agent called George F. Babbitt, belonged to everything in sight:

the Rotarians, the Kiwanis, or the Boosters; to the Oddfellows, Moose, Masons, Red Men, Woodmen, Owls, Eagles, Maccabees, Knights of Pythias, Knights of Columbus, and other secret orders characterised by a high degree of heartiness, sound morals, and reverence for the Constitution. . . . [The motiviation was] firstly because 'it was the thing to do', secondly 'it was good for business, since lodge-brothers frequently became customers', thirdly, it enabled ordinary American men to assume 'such unctuous honorifics as High Worthy Recording Scribe and Grand Hoogow', and fourthly, it meant that the 'hen-pecked' American male had a legitimate excuse for being away from home whenever there were meetings or other business to attend to.

It was a fancy excuse, though Sinclair Lewis does not list this as a factor, to get out of household chores and looking after kids. He does however make fun of the pretence that high-flown 'ethics' were the object of the exercise: 'a thing called Ethics, whose nature was confusing but if you had it you were a High Class Realtor [estate agent] and if you hadn't you were a shyster, a piker, and a fly-by-night.'

It wasn't only in the brash new towns of America that 'boosting' was the main diet of Rotary Clubs. In Britain and Ireland the same history records that business advantage predominated in rules and procedure. 'Far from being coy about this or feeling any need to be, Belfast members were required at each meeting to announce what business they had given, or received from fellow members. . . .'[13] And in Brighton, members could be expelled for not putting business their colleagues' way.

However, crude and open 'boosting' was already declining in the *public* utterances of the Rotary movement. As early as 1911, the Second National Convention of Rotary Clubs was claiming that 'no obligation, actual or implied, to influence business exists in Rotary'. The change had come with success. The business benefits of Rotary membership were now widely known and needed no advertising to recruit members: the problem was now to keep them out. Not only that, but retaliatory action was now being taken against overtly 'booster' clubs such as San Francisco by disgruntled non-member firms.

By the foundation of Rotary International in 1922, all mention of business advantage had disappeared from its official aims and objectives. The emphasis was now very much on 'service' – although this is so vaguely defined in Rotary that it really will not do as an explanation of its activities. Representatives insist that Rotary is *not* a charitable or fund-raising organisation, although there are obviously elements of both in the activities of many members and clubs. But they insist that, unlike the Lions or Kiwanis, Rotary members are *involved* in community activities and do not simply write cheques to maintain their charitable credentials. Certainly there are favourite Rotary causes, including a polio vaccination programme in many countries, Christmas carols (mechanised, these days) to raise money for local charities all across the country, sponsorship of youth activites and exchanges, and so on. But this is more a legitimation of the business interest base than a replacement of it: a joint activity to promote friendship and co-operation, worth while in itself certainly but not the reason for the organisation's existence. If you hear Christmas carols at full blast in the shopping centre, that's Rotary for you; a routine form of charity based on privileged access and a standard formula, rather than an innovative, thoughtful and empathetic one.

Rotary comes from a culture and ideology where no contradiction is seen between business interest and the highest religious and moral ethics. Indeed, they are one and the same in the view of those business executives who favour the high moral tone which, as an additional benefit, reinforces their position of élite within their own community.

The cause of Rotary ethics in the cause of business was spread with an evangelistic fervour in the early days. Consider for instance this hymn to Rotary's conquests by William Stead, one of the founders and popularisers of the organisation:

The United States of America has capitulated to the demands of Rotary. Not content with this, the cause is urged ever onward. The

Dominion of Canada and the British Isles give way to the crusader's demands. Paris is ours and today the slogan is 'on to Berlin, Vienna, then to the Antipodes'. . . . The ambitions of our conquest know no limitations save the limitations of the civilized world. Unlike the conquest of the Napoleonic forces, our conquest is, and will continue to be, in the interests of men and the principles which make for the practical idealization of trade.[14]

This was written shortly before publication of a runaway inter-war best seller, Bruce Barton's *The Man Nobody Knows*, which swept the business community in North America and Britain with its portrayal of Jesus Christ as 'the founder of modern business' and 'the great advertiser' whose first priority must always be 'my Father's business'. The Gospels were seen as carrying the essential lessons of good sales methods (even interpreting 'Let there be light' as a prophecy of electric light – or neon advertising signs?) It is very much a Dale Carnegie philosophy: win friends and influence people by being a nice guy, which will also conveniently mean you can sell practically anything to anybody. If you pray hard enough, God will make sure you win in the great business competition known as life.

It was a time of great upheaval, of fierce and often bloody conflicts between big business and its employees. How could the Vanderbilts, the Rockefellers and the Fords – or even the smaller fry working on the British scene – claim a high moral tone while hiring thugs to beat up or even murder trade union leaders and attack crowds which included women and children, for demanding better wages and conditions? The argument that business interest was sacred was a large part of the answer (so too, of course, were the charitable foundations set up with part of the multi-billion dollar proceeds). It is a convenient association of self-interest and community interest which remains very vigorous, and is at the heart of 'service' business organisations such as Rotary today – although of course the extremes of conflict in which the individuals are involved are much less evident now. And no Rotarian would admit to any conflict or interest being involved in his membership of a charitable organisation which also protects his personal interests to the detriment of others'.

Whether this convenient ethic produces the true 'fellowship' that Rotarians seek is something only individual members can answer. For perhaps the strongest presentation of the other side, we have G. K. Chesterton's assault on Rotary:

It is a form of comradeship that is gross, common, vainglorious, blatant, sentimental and, in a word, caddish. . . . There is something vulgar about such companionship. It lacks spiritual dignity. . . . Why is there this debasement of human friendship? Without the admiration of something better than ourselves or each other, we become a mutual admiration society and a very paltry collection of snobs.[15]

'Forbidden to use the privileges'?

The current aims and objectives of Rotary rigorously exclude any reference to business advantage being derived by its members. In fact the *Rotary Guidebook* explicitly states:

Rotarians are not in Rotary to do business with each other. They are, indeed, specifically forbidden to use the privileges of Rotary membership for the purpose of commercial advantage, and the honour of the Movement in this respect is very jealously guarded by the general body of the members.[16]

But other statements are in direct conflict with this claim: for example, 'nowadays it is not expected that any Rotarian will use Rotary *deliberately* for the purpose of business advantage', or

That aspect of the Movement [business favouritism] has *largely* disappeared now, and no Rotarian is expected *necessarily* to trade with another Rotarian except insofar that members of a Club find it pleasant to do business with fellow members just for the sake of the friendly relationship which exists between them.'[17] (All emphasis added.)

It is this final phrase, 'friendly relations', which probably best describes the reality of Rotary and its business links today – and though more subtle than 'boosting' it is a powerful business asset. Gone is the secret black book of transactions between members: it is the more discreet way of deals between friends, mutual business confidence derived from making contacts socially, and the feeling of being part of a self-selected élite. It encourages trade between members and therefore discriminates against those in the same business who do not, in every sense, 'belong'.

But it is not merely these informal ties which lead to business advantage. It is also the institutional set-up of the Rotarians which encourages such activity. The single classification system, crucial to eliminating competition, still remains in force. Interestingly enough, the only exception allowed to this is where an Active Member proposes an 'Additional Acting Member' in his *own* business or profession, so allowing him to bring in a colleague whom he considers not to be in competition with him.

Each new member of the Rotarians is still encouraged to give a talk on 'My Job', recalling the old boosting days. Nor does it stop with one talk. Of one of the four branches of Rotary service – Vocational Service – the *Rotary Handbook* says, 'Because it encourages a man to talk about his job, it gives Rotarians the opportunity to understand some of the problems and responsibilities of other people's business and professional life.'

The leaflet *Rotary in Brief: Service above Self* explains that business and 'service' are, for Rotarians, one and the same:

To be a Rotarian implies the acceptance of the concept that a man's business or profession is not merely his livelihood, but his way of living; that a man is in business to serve his customers or clients, his employees, and all with whom he has to deal, in the fullest sense of the word 'SERVE'.

So the wheel comes full circle, and the idea of business men getting together to serve the community is translated into the community service functioning merely as an aspect of a way of life: the man's business.

Power

Rotary today is a powerful organisation. Its magazine and journals are full of the accounts of leading politicians visiting Rotary functions, or of Rotary representatives calling on the likes of Mrs Thatcher, President Reagan and other leaders almost as a matter of routine. At national level, in Britain, Rotary (together with the much smaller organisations) represents the business community and business interests. Unlike the big women's organisations such as the Women's Institute and National Council of Women, which have some access to Government policy formation at a lower level, there seems to be no system of consultation, debate and formal resolutions in Rotary to determine the policies its leaders put forward. While its leaders talk to the politicians, Rotary at the local or regional level is kept determinedly non-political, as a way of avoiding conflict between members which could disturb the friendly atmosphere of the business club.

It may be, though, that Rotary – in Britain and Ireland at any rate – is becoming *more* rather than less political, and very much in the direction of conservatism. Its increasing emphasis on private charity as opposed to public services is heavily political in tone, especially in the British organisation. Its *Rotary Guidebook* also talks of 'unmistakable harbingers of Rotary's involvement in local and national affairs' and highlights in particular 'the Movement's expressed anxiety over what it judges the anarchic dismemberment of previously accepted standards of behaviour in the family, the community and the nation' – which is all the more striking because of the organisation's tradition of *not* taking sides on this kind of issue.[18] One could perhaps hazard a guess that an important element in the Rotarians' dislike of the changes of modern 'family' life is the uppity behaviour of women – now starting to stake a claim to the Rotarians' private business preserve. For British Rotary at least, women's interests (including business interests) are seen as a threat.

Women fight back

'If you can't beat 'em, join 'em' is the philosophy of the Soroptimists, an alternative though much smaller international organisation of business and professional women who organise on the same lines as Rotary complete with charitable work (arguably more imaginative and innovative than the men's) and the 'single classification' rule. The Soroptimists represent one response to the men-only rule of Rotary; the other is a full frontal assault on the men-only rule by means of court action. One could perhaps include a third response, but it is strictly one of damage limitation: the 'Inner Wheel' of women with husbands in Rotary. Some of them could perhaps be described as 'Rotary widows'.

It should not be surprising that the Inner Wheel as an organisation (quite separate from Rotary, and in fact hardly ever mentioned in Rotary publications – a reflection of its importance?) is fiercely opposed to the idea that Rotary should admit women. They themselves would not qualify for membership, having been placed in the full-time occupation of business *wife*, by definition of their membership. It may not be much fun being a Rotary wife but at least they have the other women in the same position to meet and organise with. For most of them, it would be out of the question to set up in business in their own right (although it is a reasonable bet that many of them are involved in their husbands' businesses and some may well be the power behind the throne and the real reason for the man being in Rotary in the first place).

The Soroptimists would not go so far as to oppose the opening up of Rotary to women; many individual members would be among the first to be invited to join Rotary. They are a classic case of women setting up a mirror-image organisation when they find themselves excluded by the men, and they face the dilemmas that would follow from any erosion of that policy.

I suspect, though, that the Soroptimists would carry on proudly with their own loyalties and traditions intact. There has to be a strong element of feminism in such an organisation, even though many members would probably not call themselves feminists. The objective, from the foundation of Soroptimism in California in 1921, has been 'to strive for human rights for all people and in particular to advance the status of women' – which is far more radical than the Rotary notions of service on the old 'noblesse oblige' charity ethic. Soroptimists are deeply involved, too, in the international network of women's organisations, and are part of the round of negotiations and development projects arising out of the UN Decade for Women. Ailsa Stanley, press officer of the Great Britain and Ireland Federation, recently told *Everywoman* magazine: 'We think women do things differently. We're not all that happy with the world men created.'[19]

The Soroptimists, then, have a strong ethos of their own which could make it difficult to envisage them all defecting to the Rotarians at the first opportunity even if they were invited. Under Rotary procedures, of course, only those few who were in a business not already represented would get the invitation anyway. If discriminating in business clubs on grounds of sex were to be made illegal in Britain then obviously the Soroptimists, offering similar if smaller benefits of mutual business advantage to the Rotarians, would have to become an 'open' organisation. But this is somehow easier to imagine them doing with a good grace than their Rotary brothers.

Rotary as an organisation has been so keen to stick to its men-only rules that it is prepared to deny its own business heritage and character in open court, claiming to be merely a 'private club' in order to defend the exclusiveness principle.

In 1977, the Rotary Club of Duarte, California, admitted three women into its membership. The Rotary International

Board of Directors withdrew the Club's charter. The Duarte club applied to the Superior Court of the State of California to have its charter restored, claiming that the 'male-only' rule is discriminatory under California civil rights law which bans all discrimination against sex, race, religion or ethnic origin in business establishments. In February 1983 the court ruled in favour of Rotary International and its men-only rules. One of its findings, which was crucial to the verdict, was that Rotary was not a business establishment.

But on 17 March 1986, California's Court of Appeal reversed the lower court's judgement. Judge Eugene McClosky, in outlining the court's decision, concluded:

While fellowship and service to the community play a very important part in the Rotary organisation, the business benefits and commercial advantages to be gained are also clearly an inducement for the business and professional leaders of the community to join.

Disagreeing with the initial finding that the business advantages of membership are merely incidental, he continued:

By limiting membership in local clubs to business and professional leaders in the community, [Rotary] has in effect provided a forum which encourages business to grow and which enhances the commercial advantage of its members.

The RI Board of Directors hit back with a statement which said:

We find it incredible that a voluntary organisation such as Rotary which each year provides more than $300 million worth of services to improve communities, which sends each year 10,000 young people on international exchanges, and which is immunising the world's children against polio – all done without regard to race, sex, creed, or nationality – be likened to commercial business establishments.

However, at the end of their statement, which threatened expulsion for any other club which emulated Duarte, the

Board promised a 'study' of the question and reconsideration at its next Council on Legislation in 1989.

Meanwhile it was appealing to the Supreme Court to quash the verdict. But in May 1987, in a unanimous verdict, the court ruled that States were entitled to force Rotary and other all-male clubs to admit women. Justice Lewis F. Powell said that the evidence 'indicates that the relationship among Rotary Club members is not the kind of intimate or private relation that warrants constitutional protection' taking into account the size of the club, its purposes, the way it selected members, and other policies.

Women who see Rotary and other all-male business clubs are on the attack, not because they want to join in the bread-throwing and the silly songs but because they see these as important areas of making business contacts and doing business deals: especially as employees of large companies, their ability to join a relevant business club could make the difference between meeting sales targets and not, and therefore between getting promotion or not – or even keeping the job. In a smaller business, belonging to Rotary or something similar could mean the difference between survival and expansion, or failure and liquidation.

This is the reason for the massive legal challenge in the Duarte case, which could be followed by others if Rotary in the US does not shape up. Lynn Hecht Schafran, who was involved in the case as a lawyer for the National Organisation of Women, commented after the Supreme Court's decision that 'no issue generates this type of intense resistance as much as men-only clubs'. But it is now looking as though Rotary could be opened up only in the US, birthplace of the men-only Rotary movement, while everywhere else the doors remain firmly closed to women because of weaker anti-discrimination laws.

The Sex Discrimination Act in Britain, for example, would not apply to Rotary even if it was proved to be a business club, and therefore an important business and employment asset, according to the Equal Opportunites Commission. It illustrates a major weakness in our legislation.

Voices are now being raised within Rotary for the admission of women – in the organisation's own interests. Over a period Rotary's image as a white, increasingly elderly men's organisation has been compounded by a high turnover of membership as business men find alternative ways of seeking business contacts or simply find Rotary too time-consuming. The 1986 Council on Legislation which met in Chicago in February heard a speech by John Ruger of New York, a previous opponent of female membership. He had changed his mind because, he said

. . . times change and so must Rotary. Today in the business world, more and more women have assumed positions of authority and management. As a result, many Rotary Clubs are suffering membership loss because there are no eligible males who hold these classifications.

However, as he pointed out, 'this proposal does not mean that Clubs must admit women because they are women, but only if they meet the qualifications'. It would mean in effect using a relatively small number of women to fill the gaps and give Rotary itself (and its mainly male members) a boost.

Rotary magazine summed up the arguments in the following way.

For:

● Business itself is adopting policies against the exclusion of women.
● From the viewpoint of a developing country, women are active in business and government. Similarly they are active in Rotaract. Why, then, are they excluded as Rotary club members?
● Rotary denies itself the talents of many excellent business and professional people – simply because of their sex.

Against:

● Admitting women will 'split' Rotary, destroying its unity and damaging its work. 'The future,' said a delegate from Britain, 'can take care of itself.'

● In some countries, customs and culture do not allow women the full participation in society they have achieved elsewhere. It is unfair that the 'liberal' customs of some countries should be imposed on more 'traditional' cultures.

● There are already many worthy organisations that women can join, such as Zonta or chambers of commerce.

The argument about the unevenness of cultures between the 'under developed' (Britain) and the 'more advanced' countries (the US and Canada) is a favourite amongst all Rotary hardliners. So is the idea – familiar also in Church of England debates – that admitting women will split the organisation in Britain since some men could not bear to be in an organisation that was *not* men-only. As one correspondent in *Rotary* (June 1986) put it, speaking for the Windsor and Eton club: keeping the organisation men-only is 'a legitimate tradition and way of life to be preserved' and added that many men joined Rotary 'because it *is* a men's organisation'. He added the novel twist that many men would resign if women were invited in – because their *own* wives would not be eligible. And in any case, 'If there be ladies to whom Rotary is "an object of suspicion" such persons if they exist would hardly make good Rotarians.' It is the kind of argument we used to use when we were 8 or 9: 'Those that ask don't get. Those that don't ask don't want.'

The expectation, though, is that the discriminatory policy will be reversed, if only for the US, because the legal expenses of keeping women out will start to outstrip even its huge financial resources. They console themselves with the fact that it is unlikely to make a dramatic impact, given the continuation of the 'single classification' rule and the principle of admission by invitation only (which of course permits all kinds of discrimination – under the table, so to speak). There is also the weight of eighty years of discrimination which means that men would in any case control the organisation far into the future by force of tenure and seniority in the past. Rotary is starting to move from the strictly men-only rule to a more 'normal' arrangement of an ostensibly open organisation with unofficial *apartheid* to preserve male supremacy.

In this chapter I have concentrated on Rotary as by far the biggest and most influential business organisation at every level – but the trend for the future may well be for it to decline slowly, becoming ever more ageing in membership and outlook as it goes along. Some women may decide to join it, if their local circumstances suggest some advantage in that; many more will continue to be excluded, and may in any case find more congenial surroundings in mixed or women's organisations which are perhaps more closely specialised in their particular profession or business.

This is in fact the growth area for business and professional women in the United States – Women in Law, Women in Journalism, and the rest. In Britain, where business woman Lynda Longbottom has been studying how women's business associations are working, she had found a very fluid situation of women joining national bodies and dropping out when they don't seem right. 'What's really taking off,' she told me, 'is an informal network of local associations covering women from all kinds of business, some of them not affiliatied to any national organisation.' They are open to all women in business, a complete contrast to the Rotarians with their exclusion of possible competitors, and even the Soroptimists with the same rule. The move is to go the opposite way to the men, not to copy their exclusiveness.

There are of course Chambers of Commerce, and other open forums for both women and men in business, and they too will play a role. But what is disturbing here is the fact that men who know each other intimately, through Rotary or the Lions (or the local golf club, come to that) will be able to use more open structures much more easily than women who do not already know many people. In the face of such inequality, it is not surprising that women in business want to meet together as women only, to find their own network of contacts and to start working towards a more equal business world.

If you can't join 'em, beat 'em. But even though men-only Rotary and other business clubs look like declining and slightly sad organisations, we should not underestimate the commercial and political clout they still enjoy, and will continue to do for a long time to come. Not until the local bank manager and those who run the major local companies, large and small, withdraw from men-only associations will there be a move towards real equality of opportunity for women in business.

PART THREE

Male Powers behind the (Establishment) Throne

6
SPEAKING THE RIGHT LANGUAGE
The Education of Very Important Men

A lecturer at a London teaching hospital, St Thomas's, greeted the 1985 intake of new medical students with the instructions: 'Hands up those who went to comprehensive school.' One hand went up. He then asked who had been to grammar school. A second hand went up. 'Ah, good,' he told the rows of privately educated students. 'At least most of us speak the same language.'[1]

This is perhaps the key to élite private education: it is not merely a matter of the 'school-approved' accent and mannerisms, but expectations, ways of relating to 'superiors', equals and 'inferiors', shared topics of conversation, shared knowledge of certain sports or certain people, shared likes and dislikes . . . a shared culture. One insider with a sharp eye for his own people and how they operate is Harry Huff, a retired civil servant formerly involved in civil service recruitment, who observed that selectors at all levels who go for the people most like themselves are fairly unaware of what they are doing, and not nearly as calculating as critics of the Oxbridge/public office connection think. 'It just comes to them like the air they breathe – the air they first breathed in Oxford?' When he was interviewing, he found that Oxford candidates in particular simply expected to succeed. 'Very Oxford,' was the comment when a very self-confident young man went out – 'especially if it wasn't justified.'[2] But as those who lack self-confidence know only to well, this is an almost priceless asset in itself regardless of whether it is 'justified'.

There is much talk in these insider circles of 'two cultures', meaning the arts and the sciences. But an outsider might be more struck by the two cultures (or more) of élites and . . . others. The confident though unassuming culture of the top men comes almost entirely from the top private schools and Oxbridge (although it *can* be acquired by outsiders, especially men, if they join the élite at a later stage).

Both the private schools and Oxbridge colleges are starting to admit girls and women – the schools into the sixth forms, the colleges into the system as a whole (at the price of women's colleges being almost wiped out). At both levels, the men remain a very large majority and seem set to continue that way indefinitely. It is a very interesting case of men-only institutions admitting women – on the men's terms – and becoming more secure as a result.

There is a vast literature on the fee-paying schools, especially the élite ones that until recently have called themselves 'public schools'. The Headmasters' Conference (HMC), which represents almost all of them, decided in September 1986 to drop the term as 'misleading and provocative'. Bruce McGowan, of Haberdasher's Aske's School and Chair of the HMC, told its annual meeting that the name 'public school' had 'unwelcome and undeserved overtones of social exclusivity'.[3] The schools' critics would not agree that these overtones were exactly undeserved. They include an apparently endless supply of former pupils writing of the misery of their schooldays, as well as educational sociologists for whom these schools represent a crucial element in British educational development and the basis of a class-based social hierarchy (there are few if any mentions, incidentally, of the fact that these are predominantly male institutions).

Rather than attempt yet another thesis on these schools, which I shall call private schools (everyone, it seems, has their own term), I shall make the introductions and try to sort out how important these 'boys-only' schools are, how they relate to the universities – especially Oxford and Cambridge – and how they seem to be adapting in ways that will preserve or perhaps increase their importance.

A lifetime of connections

Let's start with some comments from those directly involved. A boy at Winchester who was interviewed recently for a television programme talked about language and class at the school:

'If anyone did have a particularly, um, fringe accent – who was right on the borders – he would first of all be sort of persuaded gradually to conform with everybody else. And if he didn't he would be ostracised, put out, and people would go out of their way to be unpleasant to him.'[4]

A proud father, himself a product of private schooling, Cambridge and the Stock Exchange, speaks of his plans for his two sons starting with a boarding 'prep' school from the ages of 7 or 8, valuable for instilling 'a degree of male discipline', away from 'mother's apron strings'.[5]

Schools may be rated on the basis of the useful friendships they create for later use. Roddy Llewellyn, former friend of Princess Margaret, failed the entrance exam for Eton: 'It was a shame because at Eton you make a network of friends to last the rest of your life, whereas I have only a couple from Shrewsbury. That place was so priggish, humourless and uncivilised.'[6] Professor Max Beloff claims that 'it is obvious that personal contacts will, on the whole, be easier between those who have shared the formative experiences of early life. It is then that people make friends, rarely later.'[7] This is true, it seems, of private-school boys, though hardly of women or even of men in general. The idea of keeping in touch with your old schoolmates throughout your life is very much part of the private education system.

These schools are very varied, and a boy can love or hate his school – but its influence lasts a lifetime with an intensity that is quite different from most people's memories of school, let alone any continuing association with it and its other 'old boys'. You could say that the whole point of a private school is really the relationship a man has with it and with the whole experience once he has left. Not to mention, of course, the likelihood of his wanting his sons, if any, to go to that or something similar and so come through into the father's world. They can literally, then, speak the same language.

Sending a boy to a private school, even one of the self-styled 'Great Schools', does not guarantee an automatic top job for life, or the lifestyle that goes with that. What many of them do offer is a formal education and coaching carefully tuned to these jobs in terms of the best possible qualifications – sometimes directly but much more now via Oxford and Cambridge. At the same time they offer an informal but powerful indoctrination into the culture of what you could loosely call the old boys' network (and this can be seen in a very literal sense with the 'production line' effect from these schools into the clubs). The old boy network itself can be seen a kind of club, where you have no obligation to pay your dues and return to the club's headquarters but there are all kinds of advantages on offer if you do. And there is of course the club badge, otherwise known as the old school tie.

Don't suppose for a moment that this all 'just happens' without thought or careful planning. The literature is thick with claims from those who are its biggest beneficiaries that the old boy network is a thing of the past (often unblushingly followed by the statement that it'll get you an interview but 'you' have to get the job). If there's no such thing as old boys preferring each other to outsiders, then why bother with the pretentious stripey neck-gear, and why the tight-lipped disapproval if a man is suspected of wearing it 'fraudulently'? The behavioural subtleties by which old boys recognise each other usually ensure that only the 'real thing' actually gets the job. Tim Heald has a typical story of one applicant, apparently too good to be true for an important job, being unmasked by the selection panel asking him about obscure people and places he could only have known if he'd been through the school of which he was claiming to be an old boy.[8] Another lower-class impostor bites the dust.

Speaking of interviews, there are of course right and wrong ways of doing things right down to the initial handshake, which they would teach you if you were a boy in a private school and you are unlikely to find out, otherwise, until it's too late to get the early highflyer job (if indeed you ever find out, and you really have to be a man to do it right anyway). It seems that the old-boy equivalent of the masonic grip is like this: shake hands firmly, looking the person whose hand you're holding steadily in the eyes. Practice a steady handshake, neither limp nor over-hearty. If your palms sweat, dry them surreptitiously on a handkerchief first. Don't say 'Pleased to meet you', but 'How do you do?' or 'It's good of you to see me.' Cribbed for you from the standard headmaster's homily and codified in the Independent Schools Careers Organisation's *How to Apply for a Job*. It doesn't really work, though, unless you have the smooth self-assurance these gestures symbolise. If I tried it after reading the advice I'd probably laugh, and they wouldn't give me the job.

The observer of all this is Clive Griggs, in his *Private Education in Britain*. He comments that the affinity which exists among old boys – whether or not they knew each other at school – has to do with a similar social background which they all find impressive, which derives partly from the school itself and partly of course from the similar home backgrounds of many of the boys: middle- to upper-middle (there isn't enough aristocracy to go round, despite the image). He suggests that the 'invented traditions' of the schools reinforce the general feeling of being different and a bit superior to everyone else who doesn't know them. Some of these pseudo-traditions are common to most if not all private schools (like accents which sound like parodies of our own dear Queen, a way of speaking which appeared only about a century ago). Others are special to the school, usually emerging for no particular reason except to be different. There may be a special language such as the school name for things, passed on from older to younger boys to learn and be tested on. At Cradleigh bread is 'toque' and ketchup 'shog', at Radley new boys are 'pups', and those who play cricket 'dry bobs'. And so it goes, with grown men trading their special boy-names for things when they meet.[9] If you find it tedious, you're obviously not an old boy.

There are also, incidentally, very elaborate rules and regulations, especially on the pecking order *within* the school which is dear to much of the system and which you would know intimately if you were a true old boy. They regulate who can use what buttons on their jackets, put their hands in their pockets or carry different kinds of umbrellas.[10] All of these are signs of status or membership of exclusive clubs or organisations *within* the school. One old boy described Harrow's 'Phil' Society as important for boys with social ambitions. 'Extreme prowess on the rugger field [sic] and general "good chapness" seem to be essential prerequisites.'[11] All this is carried over into the rules about when and where you should wear your old school tie. Never wear you Old Etonian tie in town, by the way. If you're on your way to the country you should change it at the Chiswick roundabout. The rules tend to vary from time to time, too, so you'd better keep in touch. Just another little trick for demonstrating who's a real old boy and who's not (though you, my dear, would *never* get away with it).

I can't really resist a couple of tie stories. A certain Hugh Montgomery-Massingberd told Tim Heald that he had never

worn his Old Harrovian (Harrow, you know) tie since that
time at Lord's when the man sitting next to him, seeing his
tie, asked: 'What years were you at Monkton Combe?'[12]
You'd need a smattering of old boy language to know that
this is the most dreadful insult to an Old Harrovian. But it's
nothing compared to the shock and horror displayed by the
Tory benches when the immaculately dressed George
Thomas entered the House of Commons for the first time,
wearing the nice new tie he'd just bought at the Co-op in
Tonypandy. The Tories were 'going frantic', and when he
reached his seat he asked neighbouring Jo Grimond what the
matter was. 'I think it's the way you're dressed,' was the
reply. Naturally, he looked first to his flies but they were
all buttoned up. He looked up to see the Tory Chief Whip
beckoning him out of the chamber. The back-benchers on
that side were cheering and baying. 'Are you aware,' said the
trembling Whip, 'that you are wearing an Old Etonian tie?'
It appears that the headmaster of Eton wrote indignantly to
the Co-op about it. I would like to think the Co-op bought
another lot of them and cashed in on all the fuss. But George
Thomas gave his tie away, to another yokel who didn't
know what it was.[13] If you ever see it – black with a thin
diagonal stripe of light blue – be sure to buy a few for any
men you know, and wear one yourself of course.

Why should ties be so important? Mainly because they are
the most noticeable accompaniment to men's formal suits.
The schools and their clubs have tried producing striped or
crested cufflinks, but the problem is nobody's really going
to see them: too hit and miss, and that will never do.
They've also tried car badges but you can't really start an
old boy or cricket conversation when you're travelling in
opposite directions along the motorway. Ties do the job just
fine, and you can choose whether to wear your old boy job
or not depending on the occasion and what you want to get
out of it. Besides, ties are such men-only things. They are
even seen as phallic by some observers. I have a private
theory that a major reason why men continue to insist on
these otherwise useless items of formal clothing is precisely

so they can signal to each other across a crowded room in old-boy language.

On the other hand, the schools do not rely on chance meetings or anything so haphazard to introduce their school-leavers to influential old boys. Tim Heald has an illuminating explanation of the procedure which was being developed at his old school, Sherborne, which seems to be along the lines of many others as well. Every year, potentially useful old boys were invited to a Careers Convention for Sixth Formers to give an inside view of the different areas of work they were involved in, covering an enormous range. The mixture on offer would vary according to which old boys were available, and obviously not all the boys would be inspired in any particular direction. For those who were, though, they had not only a rare glimpse of the field from a privileged insider – which is hard to get at that stage of the game – but also an influential contact with that subtle old boy connection, possibly leading on to other old boys in the same field and providing a head start on others who entered 'from cold' and having to start from scratch.

Other connections might be organised by the school on a one-off basis outside the Conventions: for example, a boy who suddenly decided he wanted to be a Fleet Street journalist would be put in touch with an old boy in a position to help and advise him on Fleet Street, which otherwise is of course very difficult to get into. A further development was that of a school profession 'speciality' – in this case chartered surveying; once there were enough 'old Shirburnian' old boys in the profession it became an easy job for school-leavers to aim for as well. Heald comments: 'This looks like a coming network, fortified by regular formal dinners for OS Chartered Surveyors in Sherborne and London.'[14] They are rivalled only by old-boy chartered surveyors from Marlborough, doing the same thing. One of our own informants told us of a 'production line' from Dulwich College to accountancy – the same principle.

Winners and also-rans

How important are the private schools, and are they heading forwards or backwards? It has been estimated that even excluding those over retirement age, there are at any given time about one and a half million men in Britain who are old boys of a private school.[15] Geoffrey Walford, who estimates that the number of pupils in private schools in England and Wales in 1982 was about 522,000, in about 2,400 schools, stresses that this represents less than 6 per cent of the total school population, which is a smaller percentage in private schooling than most other industrialised countries. However, far from making this an unimportant or marginal sector, 'in some ways, it is the smallness of the numbers involved and the associated élite nature of some of the schools that is at the root of the controversy about the desirability of their continued existence'.[16]

If it is the élite character of the schools that counts, then we are looking in fact at a pyramid structure with little-known, contemptuously named 'minor public schools' at the base, the also-rans in the middle and a few very grand ones at the top with Eton presiding over the whole edifice. The different ranks are represented in different associations: there are a few special schools for children with disabilities (which are a quite different phenomenon); schools registered with the Department of Education and Science but no other organisation; the 200-odd belonging to the Independent Schools' Association; the 234 girls' schools which have their own associations (and we'll get back to those later); twenty-two schools belonging only to the Governing Bodies Association; moving up slightly, forty schools of 'lower academic standing' associated with the Society of Headmasters of Independent Schools; just over 200 in the Headmasters' Conference, which includes all private schools with any pretensions to social and academic advantage, although it covers a range from the well known to the extremely obscure; and finally the schools generally accepted as 'leading schools' (all of them boys' schools),

Ampleforth (the top Catholic boys' school), Charterhouse, Eton, Harrow, Marlborough, Rugby, Shrewsbury, Westminster and Winchester.[17] Somewhere in those categories are to be found seventy-four which were formerly direct-grant schools, part of the State system but with private school attachments which are now completely private, together with a number of choir schools run by the Church of England, providing private education heavily laced with Church music and also strictly for boys only.

The subtle ranking of boys' private schools is expressed graphically by Evelyn Waugh, himself an old boy of 'minor' Lancing College, in *Decline and Fall*. 'We class schools, you see, into four grades,' says one of his characters from a thinly disguised Gabbitas-Thring, the private education agency, 'Leading School, First-Rate School, Good School and School. Frankly, School is pretty bad.' And equally frankly, it is the leading and almost-leading boys' schools which really count if you sincerely want to join an old boys' club that really works for you.

So let's see how it is working. At the time Anthony Sampson last surveyed the scene in 1982 the Chair of the BBC, the Editor of *The Times*, the Foreign Secretary, the heads of both Foreign and Home Civil Services and half the Chairs of the big four banks came from just one school: Eton. Meanwhile the Home Secretary, the Chancellor, the Director-General of the BBC, 'a bevy of judges' and the other two big bank Chairs came from one other: Winchester. 'Such a lasting duopoly,' Sampson suggests, 'must surely have some significance in Britain's anatomy.' Well, yes. These two, he adds, 'have advanced into new areas of influence; and their success is more marked than in Macmillan's time' seen by many as the heyday of the old boys — 'or (as far as I can trace) than in any earlier time'. He recalls another commentator, Anthony Hartley, who wrote twenty years previously that 'Eton and Winchester sometimes seem to be conspiracies rather than educational establishments'. If they are conspiracies, they are making big advances, involving old boys with no prior connections with great wealth or aristocratic names. 'It is their political skill, their confidence and flexibility which accounts for their rise much more than their wealth or family connections.'[18] It is the devotion to the political games, as taught in these two schools (Eton boys in particular are constantly electing each other to positions) that Sampson sees as the key to their predominance – very much a culture of superiority, manipulative technique and self-confidence, overlaid on a degree of academic achievement which is also an increasing feature of the leading old boys.

And what does this culture look like? A poll at Eton in 1980 showed that 74 per cent of the boys agreed with the idea that 'Etonians could be said to have certain features that for whatever reason set them apart from others.'[19] Outsiders speak simply of the arrogance displayed by many of them, an upsurge – in the rather surprising view of Eric Anderson, head teacher at Eton (and he should know) – of a snobbish 'Brideshead syndrome' which is also affecting Oxford and Cambridge.[20] Sampson tells us that 'the most obvious asset of Etonians remains social confidence, based on a fixed belief in their own superiority, which can quietly demoralise others'. The old criticism of them, he adds, was that they were confident, stupid and out of touch with the lives and needs of most of the country. As Eton becomes more of an academic forcing-house with stringent entrance exams, and of course increasingly expensive, Etonians become confident, clever – but still out of touch and out of sympathy with most of the country. And of the old Winchester boys (Wykehamists) the saying is that, once given a ladder, they will climb to the top of it without questioning its purpose.[21] Heald is of the opinion that the 'boundless self-confidence' fostered by both these schools is more 'shamelessly displayed' by Wykehamists, while Etonians are usually much smoother.[22] Of such are our famous men and many of our national leaders made up.

Let's take a look at some statistics about the advancement of the old boys, especially from these two schools. A major study of élite positions by Boyd shows that in

1970/71, 62 per cent of top-rank civil servants, 83 per cent of ambassadors, 83 per cent of High Court judges or above and 67 per cent of top-rank clergy in the Church of England had been educated in private schools, mainly the very well-known ones.[23] A more recent survey in 1982 of top positions in the army, the judiciary and business showed a very similar pattern.[24]

This extremely high proportion of top jobs going to old boys of private schools has been maintained consistently since the end of the last century despite the opening up of public secondary education free of charge after the 1944 Education Act — with a whole sector of élite grammar schools, modelled very much on the private-school ethos, providing excellent academic training on a similar level to that of the private schools. It simply made no impact on the private school boys' dominance of the top jobs. An important comparative study of private and public schooling published in 1980 looked at the hypothesis that the private schools were a 'meritocracy' producing boys of higher IQ than the state sector. It concluded: 'IQ itself was surprisingly unimportant.' It was the school, and above all the family or origin (with the wealthier and better-connected ones sending boys mainly to private schools) that really counted when it came to achievement, rather than intelligence. In fact, this same study has shown, the private sector is far *less* meritocratic in its selection than the old grammar schools were.[25]

A very interesting element to emerge from another study was the finding that old boys of private schools reached senior positions faster than their state-educated counterparts. They were simply promoted at a more rapid rate, on a 'highflyer' system of assessment which is also very important in the Civil Service.[26] Courtaulds' records, for instance, showed that its company directors from private schools had an average age of 50 while the others averaged 56 — meaning of course less time to become fully effective at the top, or to move still higher. It is a syndrome well known to women in hierarchies, of course — with the added problems of career breaks and a lower retirement age.

'Private school background' alone, it seems, counts for many top jobs. Boyd describes the advantages of old boys as seen from the banks:

A major cause of the large public school population is the kind of career experience which a bank board values. The men selected to serve on the boards usually come from families who can afford fee-paying education. Lloyds seek to have land-owners, industrialists, and financiers represented on its board. Such men are selected not merely because they lend prestige to the bank; rather they are chosen because they possess knowledge of people with whom the bank deals.[27]

Incidentally, what happens to the 'not very bright' boy whom even the most dedicated of private school teachers cannot make into top civil servant material? He probably does not become a refuse worker or lorry driver, you may be pleased to hear. The advice to parents of these boys, offered in the Careers Bulletin of the Independent Schools Careers Organisations, is further private tuition at college level, perhaps for a private pilot's licence. 'Failing all this the leaver can look for a job. If he does not himself soon talk someone into employing him . . . his father should not hesitate to do a little place-seeking in the eighteenth-century style on the golf course or at his club. It still works . . .'[28] This reminds me of an old boy-friend who asked me if I could find a job for a school-leaver whose father he'd known well at school and all that. 'Can he type?' I asked innocently. Collapse of stout party.

But let's get back to the high-flyers, and especially their role in politics and Government. A count of all members of Parliament in 1982 showed that at least 42 per cent (not all listed their schools) were privately educated, with 20 per cent of these being old boys of Eton.[29] Obviously not all the parties showed the same pattern of private-school background – although surprisingly the Labour Party, which had only 10 per cent of its parliamentary party from private schools in 1935 (when there was far less alternative in the public sector) now has about 25 per cent old boys –

a symptom of the trend for the party to go increasingly for male 'intellectuals' as candidates (including those sponsored by the trade unions) which has accompanied the virtual freeze on women's entry into the parliamentary party during that time. The last Labour Cabinet, incidentally, had about 33 per cent old boys of private schools.[30] It was a tradition set on its way by Clement Attlee, who was a fervent Old Haileyburian. 'Other things being equal, I didn't see why I should not select someone from my own school,' Attlee is reported as saying – and he did. Christopher Mayhew, one of his appointees at the Foreign Office, told Heald that 'he made a joke that he enjoyed promoting Haileyburians – mentioning Geoffrey de Freitas and an air marshal. But it was, of course, just a joke.'[31] In fairness, though, it must be said, that Labour's Shadow Cabinet in the late 1980s contained nobody who was sending any of their children to a private school.

The real political affiliation of private-school old boys is of course the Conservative Party. Clive Griggs in fact suggests that both in the last century and this one, 'private education has been the Tory party at school'. Between 1886 and 1916 just over 80 per cent of Conservative Cabinet ministers had been to private schools; in the post-war period, 1945–79, the proportion was 73 per cent when in office and 78 per cent when in opposition. The concentration, as with the Labour Cabinet, becomes intensified at ministerial level, fluctuating between 81 per cent and 94 per cent since 1925. Stanley Baldwin, as Prime Minister, told a Harrow speech day in the 1920s:

When the call came for me to form a government, one of my first thoughts was that it should be a government of which Harrow should not be ashamed. I remember how in the previous government there had been four, or perhaps five, Harrovians, and I determined to have six.[32]

In the second Thatcher Cabinet the proportion of old boys went down to 81 per cent as compared to 90 per cent for her first,[33] but this group includes a few such as Cecil Parkinson who can put on a good act 'as to the manner born'. She herself, indeed, was at grammar school, though she is no slouch with the public school accent and manner. Norman Tebbit, on the other hand, doesn't bother. There are those in the Tory Party who see all this as a dreadful mistake and plan to get back to normal (over 90 per cent old boys) as soon as they can. Mrs T., incidentally, sent young Mark to Harrow, and *every* member of her Cabinet has sent their children to private schools according to Jack Straw's survey in September 1986.[34]

Purchasing privilege

Current trends in eduction, not least because of a favourable Conservative Government attitude, suggest that private schools will expand at the expense of the State sector and that old boys will consolidate their grip on top jobs in the private and public sector alike, as well as the Government itself. The spirit of opportunism that lies behind this resurgence in boys' private schools is expressed by George Gale in the *Sunday Express*

A public school education is a cheap way of purchasing privilege. For between £10,000 and £15,000 you can pay your child's entrance fee and life subscription into the upper classes. . . . It is a marvellously British racket. The Mafia and Freemasons are kids' stuff compared with the protection racket of the old school tie. It's legal. Anyone can join in, provided he's got the cash. It's a great bargain.[35]

It is a bargain which is now increasingly being taken up by those parents who *can* afford it, helped by tax cuts for upper income-earners, tax and rates concessions for private schools and fee-payers on the grounds of 'charity' and a direct subsidy in terms of the assisted places scheme (effectively 5,500 State scholarships a year to the private schools which go mainly to boys and almost entirely to those who would have had private or grammer-type schooling in any case).[36] The

State also provide free teacher training, and the payment of fees for the children of diplomats and senior military officers. The total subsidy was estimated by Neil Kinnock in 1981 to be over £450m.[37] At the same time central Government support for many local education authorities has been cut back with the largest, the Inner London Education Authority, now getting nothing at all.

As the State secondary schools in particular have become a political battleground, with long wars of attrition over merging the sub-élite grammar schools with secondary moderns to form comprehensives, and the bitter dispute with teachers over pay which has lagged behind most comparable occupations, many middle-class parents have been withdrawing their children at secondary level (though often taking full advantage of the primary schools and, in the case of girls, paying for sixth-form only). The payoff, cheap at the price, is getting their children and especially the boys a head start on others, both academically and in terms of the whole private school culture of self-confidence (or on arrogance), coaching in the right behaviour and introductions to future colleagues and mentors in the kind of positions that the parents want their children to aim at. In a private school they will be taught high expectations: that they will be 'leaders' in positions of authority over others. There is also what they unblushingly describe as 'educating the whole man' – not just academically but socially, culturally and politically as well, with values added which are consistent with taking responsibility, running things and giving orders. Ralph Miliband suggests that these values are 'a conservative philosophy whose themes remain tradition, religion, nationalism, authority, hierarchy and an exceedingly narrow view of the meaning of democracy . . .'[38]

Irene Fox, who interviewed 190 sets of parents from a sample of private schools, found that the same two benefits were mentioned consistently: firstly the ability to produce better academic results (through smaller classes and better provision of books and equipment – crucially important with the challenge of the new GCSE exam, and demand for computer skills) and secondly to 'develop the character through discipline'. Many parents claimed that they had been 'forced' out of the State sector in order to get the advantages for their children which used to be offered by the grammar schools[39] – for which, incidentally, these same parents would invest by paying for private 11-plus tuition especially for boys, if there was any doubt about the children passing the exam. It is for many parents a question of paying for key bits of education where that will provide a particular advantage, and using the State sector for the rest.

Although private schools are being promoted in the name of individual choice, it is in fact very much a matter of Government policy, combined with some astute adaptations made by the top private schools themselves in order to retain the old boy advantages that they can offer parents as an incentive. The political issue is not so much the *existence* of the private schools as the public funds, including tax concessions, which keep them going at the sumptuous level to which they have become accustomed. The Labour Party plans to remove the schools' 'charity' status and stop direct financial subsidies (although not in terms of teacher training). The Liberal and Social Democrats take a similar line, although this probably has less priority in their overall approach to education. It is the Conservative Party which promotes private schools and persistently under-funds State education. The Conservative Party *is* the old boys' party. As Lord Hailsham put it:

A man is as entitled to buy his wife the comfort of a hospital pay bed or his son a public school education as he is to buy his wife a dress or his son a bicycle. Socialists may call this privilege if they will; Conservatives call it economic democracy.[40]

The schools have played their part by adapting their systems to make them generally more pleasant for the boys, and more attractive to the parents. Many of the harshest aspects of private school life have been softened since a threatened revolt in the 1960s against fagging (young boys working as servants for the older ones), beatings, the dictatorial powers of prefects and the compulsory rugby and cricket. Boys can now enter many private schools at age 11 instead of the previous 13 – straight from State primary schools. Although the private schools are exempt from the new 'national curriculum' many of them will use it anyway so that boys can transfer easily from the State sector. Prep. schools and pre-prep. schools for the 5–13 age range have become less formal with a more 'family' atmosphere (although one teacher in such a school told us that there is little that can be done for a number of very unhappy small boys who are effectively being 'dumped' in boarding prep. schools by uncaring parents).

Meanwhile, abandoning the previous devotion to Latin and Greek there has been heavy investment at all schools in science laboratories and equipment, as well as computers, which provide an educational resource far beyond what the State sector can now offer. There is less emphasis on boarding than before, with dayschools and semi-boarding gaining ground. There is also a general move towards what Edward Blishen describes as 'the unspeakable pleasantness of Eton' offering 'the best of what is old with the shiniest of what is new'.[41] Expensive high-tech equipment and intensive tuition for A-levels and Oxbridge entrance are now the best guarantee that the new generation of old boys, at least from the 'leading' schools, will continue to get the best jobs and the fastest promotions, at the same or possibly even higher level than before. (Boys from the 'also-ran' schools may lose out, in the short term, because they have not kept up with educational trends and are woefully unprepared for the new GCSE exam.)

It is a highly competitive business. The 'leading' schools are in close touch with each other to work out, in what Heald describes as their 'gossipy inbred world' – which includes 'any number of informal clubs and liaisons' and some opulent dining clubs – the best ways of maintaining their privileged position in a rapidly changing society.[42] They also organise a formidable old boy lobby which works particularly on central Government. The main private school organisation, the Head Masters' Conference, was set up in 1869 to lobby the Government against attempts to integrate their schools with the then new, national State system. Since then there has been constant and very successful lobbying of Government, using the vast network of old boys in powerful positions. They managed to block a number of proposals, including those of the Fleming Committee in 1944 which had concluded that private schools promoted unwelcome social divisions ('Nothing could have been better devised to perpetuate them than this educational development').[43] Under Labour the HMC hired a public relations firm and formed their lobbying organisation, the Independent Schools Information Service (ISIS) to combat Labour proposals to abolish private schools. They even managed to block Labour's proposed abolition of their charitable privileges. Faced with a renewed determination within the opposition Labour Party in the mid-1980s to withdraw subsidies and charitable status, the schools are now recruiting parents at the reported rate of 300 a week into ISIS to help defend the private education to which they have now committed themselves. There is talk of action committees to influence the result in marginal seats, and using the courts if this tactic fails.[44]

Introducing girls

Before we leave the private schools we ought to take a look at the girls in them, an innovation which John Dancy at Marlborough, the pioneer of getting girls into the sixth form in the 1970s, saw partly as a way to 'consolidate the liberal position so that the changes were irreversible'. Girls were to perform a 'civilising' mission on the boys.[45]

Private schools for girls were established in Britain at the turn of the century or later, in imitation of the boys' but very different in many ways. The boys' schools, although some of them were medieval in origin, were also very much a nineteenth-century phenomenon, but from several decades earlier with the function of gentrifying the newly rich industrial class. Very little analysis has been written about the girls' schools, in stark contrast to the boys' ones – reflecting as well as anything else perhaps their much lower status in both education and career terms. Judith Okely has written a revealing account of one 'middle-ranking' boarding school for girls, based on her own experiences there in the 1950s, emphasising that 'the development of a distinct class consciousness is seen as more important than scholarship and achievement' since the girls, in sharp distinction to the boys of similar families from whom they were so rigidly segregated, were supposed to have no economic or political aspirations apart from the marriage to an old boy. So while the boys' schools were a preparation for independence and power, the girls' 'may be, invisibly, a preparation for dependence'. Academic achievement was very low in the list of priorities (she herself studied for her A-levels semi-secretly when no one was looking) and girls were fed into Swiss finishing schools or exclusive secretarial colleges while the boys' schools had their links with Oxford and Cambridge.

Discipline, she explains, was draconian with girls rarely allowed out and constantly watched inside the school grounds – their movements, activities and even conversations circumscribed by sets of rules which required total concentration, the almost inevitable lapses being punished by humiliation in front of the class or the whole school. Conformity was all; differences, for instance in the speech and behaviour of the few scholarship girls, 'were ridiculed and mimicked until repressed'. The girls' schools, in which 'obedience rather than authority is emphasised', complemented the authority system which characterised the boys', where senior boys could behave much like feudal overlords. The boys' and girls' private schools, in short, were exact opposites of each other in many ways, preparing the boys for 'leadership' and the girls for social climbing through conformity with the rules; marriage was the goal and very much the better of the two (mutually exclusive) choices presented to middle- and upper-class girls: marriage or a career.[46]

That was the 1950s: things are different now. But not necessarily any more equal, by a very long way. Girls now make up just under 12 per cent of the pupils in Head Masters' Conference school, where in the early 1960s none of the schools had any girls – the exceptions being a handful of 'experimental' schools outside the private mainstream.[47] About two-thirds of the HMC schools now have *some* girls, in the sixth form only, while about a quarter of the schools are co-educational throughout. However it is important to note that most of the big names, including Eton, Harrow and Winchester, remain boys-only, although with the occasional daughter of one of the teachers doing Oxbridge entrance only.[48] Most of the increase among girls is for boarders rather than daygirls, to recoup losses from the decline in boys' boarding. The main impact of these changes has been to weaken those girls' schools which rely on boarding fees, and there are predictions that many of them could be wiped out as the boys' schools take the most profitable part of the business.[49] There are fewer girls than boys in private schools in any case: 185,000 and 242,000 respectively in 1987. Fees at the girls' schools are lower, since many parents are not prepared to spend as much on daughters as on sons, and the amount spent per pupil on buildings and equipment is little more than half the average for HMC schools. As the emphasis in girls' education swings towards academic achievement and university entrance, boarding schools like the one described by Judith Okely – or even the more academic ones – are unable to compete. The girls in private schools will increasingly be second-class pupils at institutions run for the benefit of boys. The Sex Discrimination Act does not apply to the private sector.

Geoffrey Walford, one of the leading commentators on private schools, tells us that it is the middle-ranking boys' schools which are taking in girls, not the élite ones. 'The higher the status of the school the more likely that the school will be single sex.' Girls have been admitted, he suggests, on strictly regulated terms and only when there is a specific vacancy not taken up by a boy. So, for instance, the increase in the number of girls boarding at previously all-boys' schools is almost exactly the same as the decrease in the number of boys boarding. There was also a big advantage to be gained from taking some girls into the sixth form: preserving a large sixth form which could then offer a wider choice of A-level subjects (which the parents of boys were starting to demand); and the guarantee of a place in the prestigious HMC, which bases its judgement largely on the size and quality of the sixth form.

Taking girls was also seen by many boys' schools as the lesser of two evils in keeping up numbers and revenue, especially in the hard times of the mid-1970s. The options were 'females or foreigners', girls being easier to deal with and already sharing the basic language and culture of the school. Girls could also be hived off legitimately to separate buildings, and not be integrated into the house structure used for the boys – something they could hardly try to do with 'foreigners'.

Walford sees the whole system as being one of a 'dual labour market': just as women are hired and fired to meet the employers' needs, so the schools take or reject girls according to the schools', not the girls', best interests. For example, girls are often admitted to boys' schools to study for particular subjects which are not sufficiently popular with the boys that year, but where a teacher is being provided and has to be paid for. If that teacher or subject is dropped, girls are then turned away. In several schools, also, girls are only accepted after the boys in the school's fifth form have made their choice of A-level subjects, so 'only girls whose choices "fit" are accepted'. Generally speaking, girls are admitted to the low-status subjects, often the traditionally 'feminine' ones like languages and the arts generally.[50] In fact the proportion of girls taking science and maths subjects only in boys' schools is far less than among the boys in these schools, and slightly less than girls in the girls' private schools; this pattern is even more marked in terms of pupils going on to higher education to study science, engineering or technology.[51] Access to boys' schools, then, certainly does not mean automatic access to boys' subjects or career patterns. It is worth noting also that the girls would have to be much better academically than the boys, to get places allocated to them, since there is more competition for those. They are generally more successful in terms of exams, and thus further enhance the school's standing in the increasingly competitive commercial-academic stakes.[52]

Not much research has been done on how girls brought into boys' schools get on, or whether their presence has made any major difference to the predominantly masculine system of hierarchy and the values of male 'leadership' and competitiveness. Walford found, when he interviewed men and boys in a private school that had not yet admitted any girls, that the arguments in favour of it had very little to do with the benefits to the girls and everything to do with helping to 'civilise' the boys and give the school a higher moral tone as well as helping to pay the bills. 'Opportunites were offered to boys, and girls fitted into this framework by providing further opportunities for the boys' general education, rather than being offered opportunities for themselves.'[53] Going on to interview some girls who had entered this kind of scene, he observed:

Obviously all of the girls knew that the school they were entering would be male dominated, but to 'know' this was different from experiencing it and practically all of the girls expressed initial shock at the reality. Even the few girls who had experienced co-educational education before had difficulties with the male ethos of the school.[54]

Some girls in this situation have told us of their feelings of extreme isolation, and the need to be constantly on guard against sexual harassment and abuse.

A great deal of work has been done in the State sector to

show how co-education can 'batter' girls who become the target of boys' obsessive sexualisation of everything, while the quality of teaching they receive suffers from the boys' insistence on more attention, facilities and space for themselves.[55] It is difficult to think of a situation which is much worse than the one described in true co-education, where there are at least approximately equal numbers of girls and boys. As one writer reminds us, the boys' private schools have always made up 'a world devoid of women, who only feature as "a quacking bitch" or "solvent old maid". The talk is of "House Tarts" – "a coveted blond of fourteen" – "runty boys" . . .'[56] A few girls here or there are likely to make little difference to the boys-only culture. It seems likely that they may become merely the targets and excuses for some of its worst aspects.

Onward and upward

These days, although boys' private schools are still very closely linked with top jobs, it now works by their channelling pupils through Oxford and Cambridge rather than directly from school to work. As Tim Heald puts it, a public school background 'only really comes into its own when married to Oxbridge'.[57] Intense effort in the private schools goes into coaching the boys for university and this is seen as the objective for any boy who is remotely capable of following a degree course (although some of the Oxbridge courses are intellectually undemanding, just as some others are of a very high standard: most, as in any other university, are sort of average). Boys' expectations are geared to Oxbridge, as Greg Eglin found when he compared sixth-formers in four private schools in London with those in seven local comprehensives. Although roughly equal proportions wanted to enter higher education, the private school pupils were much more likely to be aiming at university while the others covered all other types of higher education, especially in science and engineering.[58]

The proportion of private-school leavers going to university has risen enormously in the last couple of decades, with the Independent Schools Careers Organisation, which represents 261 schools, estimating that 84 per cent of the boys went on to further education, predominantly to universities.[59]

In the private school contest to pack as many of their pupils as possible into Oxbridge, new devices are being thought up all the time as the Oxbridge colleges (whose own academic performance is very much in question now that these are just two of the dozens of universities in Britain) try to recruit some of the better students from *outside* the private sector. There used for instance to be substantial numbers of 'closed' scholarships which were for boys from a particular private school to go to a particular college, with admission guaranteed regardless of merit or otherwise.* These are now being phased out. The music scholarship for men only (to sing in the men's choir) still persist. Similarly, there has been a tradition of recruiting boys who were good at particular 'manly' sports played at the schools and colleges alike, with the emphasis on rugby, cricket and rowing. Heald mentions allegations that 'rowing mad dons would telephone headmasters of famous rowing schools like

* The historian Paul Johnson sees the Oxbridge colleges as having been 'taken over' by the upper classes after the English Civil War, a process that also undermined the rest of the school system on the grounds that it was too much education that had caused all the disturbances – 'the Bible under every weaver and chambermaid's arm hath done us much hurt', according to the Earl of Newcastle, and 'the universities abound with too many scholars'. With the banning of Dissenters from Oxford and Cambridge and exclusive concentration on a Latin and Greek-based education, the number of scholars fell off rapidly and the ruling class took over Oxbridge for the education of their sons. In 1577 William Harrison noted that at the two universities 'the poor men's children are commonly shut out, and the richer sort received (who in time past thought it dishonour to live as it were upon alms). . . . Besides this, being for the most part gentlemen or rich men's sons, they oft bring the universities into much slander.' The true history of the universities and schools, which is fascinating since it bears little resemblance to the changeless notions of unbroken 'tradition' claimed by the men of the Establishment today, can be found summarised in Paul Johnson's 'Education of an Establishment' in *The World of the Public School* (Weidenfeld & Nicolson, 1977).

Radley and Shrewsbury and offer to admit their eight en masse'.[60]

Now, though, it's all about passing the entrance exams and the interview – but the private schools have plenty of tricks up their sleeve there, too. The exams are easy: there isn't that much competition for places and you just coach or 'cram' the pupils to pass certain subjects on a certain day, using very small classes or even the 'tutorial' system of one-to-one teaching that prevails at Oxbridge itself. The fact that, until very recently, the exams required an extra term in school after A-levels, ignoring other opportunities for higher education and the several months afterwards with nothing much to do, meant that schools where this was seen as normal had a huge lead over the others.

To get over this, in 1985 both Oxford and Cambridge have abolished the extra-term exam and introduced a new one to fit into the A-level cycle. The Cambridge system is called STEP, the Sixth Term Examination. One admissions tutor, Dr Searby, told a reporter wistfully: 'We hope that schools won't believe it to be necessary to set up special STEP classes.'[61] The move coincided with a boom in private school entrants that year as two sets of pupils applied at the same time.[62]

Then of course there is the interview, which many tutors regard as the ultimate test of ability, although it is now well established in equal-opportunity research that this is a classic situation for people choosing those most like themselves rather than assessing candidates against genuine requirements. Or more down to earth, as one objector wrote to *The Guardian*:

'Well, thank you for coming to see us. How's your father, by the way?' 'Very well indeed, Sir. He asks to be remembered to you.' 'Yes, came up in '57. Ran a mile in 20 minutes, as I recall. We must see if we can put you on his staircase. Goodbye. Don't go without your gloves. Over there on the sofa on top of *Who's Who* and *Debrett*. No, that's a chair, the sofa's the long thing. That's it. Splendid.'[63]

The sophisticated private school leaves nothing to chance. Teachers use their network of old boys and other teachers to find out which are the best courses or tutors; then who the interviewers will be, what they have published and any special likes or dislikes. The candidates are briefed accordingly, and given the books published by the interviewers so that they can flatter them by their respect for their ideas. One (anonymous) specialist in such exercises told Heald: 'We play the system to the best of our collective knowledge and ability, and see it as our job to do so.'[64]

At this kind of level, it is a matter not merely of getting a boy into Oxbridge but of finding the 'fast stream' and certain influential teachers who can provide the best guarantee of a brilliant career afterwards. But of course there is plenty of inertia, too, which gets boys from a certain background into the institutions. Statistics quoted by Clive Griggs indicate that at the higher levels of A-level qualifications there is little difference in the success rate of private school pupils and others – but the difference becomes very marked as one moved down the grade scores: 'Those admitted from independent schools had, on average, lower grades than entrants from maintained schools.'[65]

Since Oxbridge is providing such a good launch pad for a lifetime of success, you have to be able to use those connections and that clublike atmosphere as if you belong there. Certainly some adaptable bluffers from not quite the right background can assimilate the club's culture, its language and its ways of operating – but as that serious bluffer Anton Gill explains, it's all so much easier, and you use that short time so much more effectively, if you can 'fit in' from the word go. 'It still certainly helps to have been to one of the dozen or so first and second rank public schools.'

There is no culture shock from the grand buildings, college servants, being away from home, wearing odd clothes, and freezing beds; it's just an extension of school. Unlike the ordinary student who is often desperately lonely and may take at least a year to get used to the place, 'the average Oxbridge fresher from Bedales or Repton or Marlborough is more likely to be going up in the company of some of his schoolfellows'. There are also older students from the same school, which means access to the trendies, the dining clubs and the prestigious societies. 'Thus it is that many people from ordinary schools are socially *grey*, and join the Tiddlywinks Society . . .'[66] Oxbridge men are nothing if not snobbish about those they do not want in their clubs.

To 'belong' at Oxbridge you need the right background (or be a very adept 'hack' – slang for social chambers who cultivate contacts to their own advantage for the future). You will also need money: dining clubs in particular do not come cheap. There is the expensive food and the even more expensive wine – which you also have to know well so you should be drinking the vintage varieties often. Even grander than the students' dining clubs are those of their teachers, who can draw on the cellars of their college for heavily subsidised vintage wines. The fifty members of the Saintsbury Club, half from Oxbridge and half from the wine trade, meet twice a year at Vintners' Hall in London and reckon that while the food is not as good as the élite equivalent in France, the Club des Cent, the wine is superior. Other clubs operate as a link between senior university staff and influential graduates, 'clubbable high achievers of the Robin Day, Peter Parker class' as Tim Heald describes them. He adds that both Oxford and Cambridge are 'positively riddled with such organisations' but that Cambridge has a reputation for higher living and a liking for interminable 'feasts' while Oxford 'probably has the edge for political intrigue'.[67] It is no accident that many of the young male politicians entering Parliament, especially on the Tory benches, already know each other: they have been in the same social and political cliques and clubs at Oxbridge.

In the case of Oxford they may well have come up through the debating society, the Oxford Union, which its historian David Walter describes fondly as catering for 'an inner élite, ambitious to shine in politics, the law, the church, diplomacy, the media and the arts'. What struck me most forcibly when I spoke there, apart from the ease with which elegant young men wore their expensive evening dress, was the naturalness and familiarity which they had already acquired about dealing with top politicians and other celebrities who are so happy to debate there.

With such privileged access, it can be a smooth transition into politics, and high political office, if you play your cards right. During the last decade each of the four main parties has been led by a former officer of the Oxford Union (Edward Heath, Michael Foot, Jeremy Thorpe, and Roy Jenkins in his SDP phase). The admired qualities here, we are told, are 'powers of persuasion, panache and wit. Knowledge is of much less consequence.' It has been accused of being pompous, mannered and outdated, or alternatively infantile. Membership is expensive, and Barbara Castle attacked it as 'the cadet class of the establishment'; she also commented that it was excellent training for Parliament because both institutions were dotty, out-of-date gentlemen's clubs. Harold Macmillan, on the other hand, who loved it, told the Union that in its debate 'there is something deeper: Oxford, Britain, everything we believe in.'[68]

Anthony Sampson inclines towards Barbara Castle's view, at least on the inner workings of Oxbridge if not in gentlemen's clubs in general.

The spells and enchantments which these universities cast on many of their graduates still (I believe) exact a high price. They encourage them to be preoccupied with the past, to assume that structures are permanent and unchanging, and they provide few links with the world of industry and the north . . . in an ex-imperial country which is constantly tempted to take refuge in its past such institutions can become like ballast to an overloaded ship.

And, he thinks, the 'seductions of Oxford and Cambridge' have been intensifying with the increasingly harsh climate of the last twenty years: 'their magnificent buildings, their endowments, libraries and new benefactions are immune from the [University Grants Committee] axe, and the colleges can add to their incomes by renting themselves to business conventions during vacations'. They are so firmly entrenched in the Establishment generally, he observes, that one of the ambitions of many Very Important Men is to return to their own college as something grand, complete with title, wine cellars and a whole style of living and the potential for influence at court to which they wish to become even more accustomed.[69]

'Some of our friends,' says the dying master of a Cambridge college in C. P. Snow's *The Masters*, 'show a singular instinct for preferring mediocrity. Like elects like, of course. Or between you and me . . . dull men elect dull men.' And they do, with a vengeance. A range of 'élite' positions were examined by Frances and John Wakeford in their major study in the early 1970s: while 13 per cent were held by Old Etonians and another 14 per cent by old boys of a further five élite schools, over half were held by graduates of Oxford or Cambridge. Many of them were contemporaries and likely to have known each other at university, if not before. The 'clusters' of men who had been to both an élite private school and Oxbridge were very prominent, particularly among Church of England bishops, the Vice Chancellors of all universities, and High Court judges; they also dominated Conservative politics, the High Street as well as merchant banks, the largest insurance companies, the highest ranks of the Civil Service and Bank of England – and they were also a high proportion of the wealthiest business men. All of these groups were composed of men only. The group of Vice Chancellors was interesting in that it had a high proportion of men who had not had élite private education, but *had* been to Oxbridge.[70] It is an important group because at the national level its members chair Royal Commissions on key current issues, and are members of specialist committees, research councils and boards of trustees. They are often very influential locally, as well, frequently being on the governing bodies of private as well as State schools, and of course exerting considerable power over their own university. In this way many of the new universities have been cast in the 'traditional' mould of

Cambridge or Oxford, but without the rule-bending which is often a characteristic of the genuine article – with stultifying results, which must be due largely to this wholesale transplant of dull Oxbridge men on to new and potentially very different institutions. East Anglia's apeing of Cambridge comes particularly to mind: it has imported Cambridge procedures and traditions, written them into 'rules' and now has a very rigid and even anti-intellectual system. For instance, where Cambridge gives advanced degrees for published work, East Anglia requires theses according to a rigid (and unreadable) formula and has penalised students for publishing their work.

Like goes on electing like. Dr Herbert Eisener found in 1982 that Fellowships of the Royal Society, the most prestigious scientific institution, go out of all proportion to Cambridge men – a pattern which had been well established over many years. This applied even more to the very young Fellows who were elected while still under 40. The explanation, quite simply, was that candidates had to be personally known to at least three of the six proposers required.[71] It is a classic case of 'who you know' counting far more than what you know, what you have done or even what you have published.

One interesting area, where critics have complained for years about favouritism shown to Oxbridge graduates, is the senior ranks of the Civil Service where the interview plays a decisive role and where there is a pervasive system of selecting 'highflyers' virtually from day One, who are programmed to reach the top ranks. Oxbridge graduates are also concentrated in the more powerful and prestigious departments in Whitehall, particularly the Treasury, Foreign Office, Employment and Energy. The present generation of top-ranking permanent secretaries are almost exclusively from Oxbridge, several of them from top private schools as well. But this near-monopoly is beginning to slacken: in 1986, for the first time since competitive exams began over a hundred years ago, more than half the entrants at the highest level came from universities other than Oxbridge; 32 per cent were women. A breakthrough? With morale and the status of the Civil Service having been under sustained attack from the Thatcher Cabinet, many bright young men had been leaving for the City, so more graduates were being taken on. And ambitious Oxbridge leavers were going for the private sector.[72] The apparent breakthrough, it seems, could mean simply that the Civil Service was no longer the route to a top job.

One Oxford student in his final year, at the same time, was describing private-sector companies wooing him and his colleagues with champagne, caviar and astronomical salary offers. In times of record unemployment and dislocation in the country as a whole, he wrote, Oxbridge students were on the make. There was almost no interest in 'alternative', socially constructive careers but the theme was: 'wise up' – and go for where the money is.[73] This could now mean advertising, PR or computers as well as finance. And, of course, the ever-popular media, to which 'arts Oxbrites flock like lemmings to a cliff', where they form a formidable 'mafia' according to Anton Gill.[74] This is 'where social confidence and smoothness are at a premium' in Anthony Sampson's judgement.[75]

The last word on the influence of post-Oxbridge ('Poxbridge') will have to go to Gill, its bitchy but accurate chronicler.

The Oxbrite nearly always finds that 'the friends you make in life are all, by some remarkable coincidence, from Oxbridge (more or less).' 'Other people just don't seem quite so reliable, somehow . . . Knock an Oxbridge Man and it's like knocking a piece of solid English oak: *solid*, through and through. But not, of course, as thick.'[76]

Oxbridge men 'mix'

Oxbridge has gone 'mixed', as they call it: up to a point. It seems to have been more to do with keeping lavish Government funding than a genuine enthusiasm for equal opportunities. The men at Christ Church College, Oxford, admitted women in 1980 protesting that 'the single-sex colleges, evolved first in the conditions of the Middle Ages and then of the 1870s, were a unique and successful venture.'[77] In other words, *we* can be a big success by keeping *you* out.

The only exceptions to the new 'mixing' (the last men-only college, Oxford's Magdalene, decided to go mixed in 1986) are the two women-only colleges in each place: New Hall and Newnham at Cambridge, St Hilda's and Somerville at Oxford. They have now become the focus for many women's concerns as the hope of genuine equality in the mixed colleges has turned to rather bitter disappointment. Several women's colleges went mixed in the name of equality, only to find that virtually all their new teaching jobs went to men while the former men's colleges continued to appoint almost all men, with a few isolated women in junior positions. There seem in fact to be fewer women employed in senior positions, at least at Cambridge, than in the days of segregated colleges when the larger number of women-only colleges could appoint only women.[78] Where women are used now it is often as permanent 'outsiders', 'a pool of cheap labour' formed by women who are highly qualified academics forced to live in Cambridge, often because of husbands who have tenure there. It has even been suggested that these semi-official 'casuals' do most of the teaching in some subject areas without ever being employed by the university or even one of the colleges.[79]

'The 1970s and early 1980s will be recalled by the women of Oxford and Cambridge universities as a period of most deceptive revolution,' as one (male) commentator summed up his review of the progres of women into appointments as Fellows, the junior teaching grade. Although the number of women coming in as students had tripled (from an extremely low base to about 30 per cent of the students in 1985) only 15 per cent of Fellows were women and half of these were in the shrinking number of women's colleges. Admitting women was still a poor second to the universities' concern to get male students from State schools, though. Nor was there any sign of improvement in the former men's colleges which had been 'mixed' for longer than the others: it looked like stalemate, or even a move backwards. Many disenchanted Oxbridge women, it seemed, were commenting that 'mixing' had only improved the lot of the already advantaged men. A separatist movement is the result, seeing single-sex institutions as the only way that women's influence can be brought to bear on these two universities – but with the loss of most of the women's colleges already a *fait accompli*.[80]

One issue to emerge from the few studies that have been done is the striking difference between the women and men who arrive at Oxbridge as school-leavers. Kate Pretty's review of the situation of women in Cambridge indicates that as a group they are mid-way between the Oxbridge men and women at all other universities in Britain in terms of the proportion coming from private schools, and the proportion from London and the South East. Most noticeable, though, is that they enter Oxbridge at a big academic disadvantage as measured in grades achieved at A- and S-level – which Kate Pretty does not explain but I would suggest is because academically inclined young women, together with their teachers and parents, do not see Oxbridge as the high-flyer route to fame and fortune which it is for the men. The higher-achieving women are therefore more likely to go to other universities. ('I just felt very strongly that it wasn't for me' was the comment of one objector.) Interestingly, though, whereas the Cambridge women do rather badly in the early exams compared to the men they have moved up considerably by the end, although not enough to achieve the same proportion of first and 2:1 degrees which are the route to postgraduate study and an academic career.[81] The three-year intensive course is simply too short for students who are not already on an inside curve to catch up academically. This applies even more on a social and political level, in terms of getting to know people and developing ways of operating that will mean a classy job and being marked as a 'highflyer' from the moment they start their careers.

The women who invest a lot of time in social mixing with

the 'right' men are less likely to achieve; those who concentrate on improving their academic scores are hardly likely to have the time (or inclination) for such 'hacking'. As Kate Pretty observes, many of the young women 'lack the confidence and the formal academic training which are so natural to many of the men who are their contemporaries', a problem going back into their school experience which has after all, for many of them, been in mixed schools run on male lines which reinforce stereotypes about what girls can and can't do. And 'at Cambridge they are competing in a traditionally male world for traditional male rewards but without the advantages of a traditional male social and academic education'.

Virginia Woolf, in her 1938 essay *Three Guineas*, has much to say about the exclusive male education which the grander private schools and Oxbridge provided, and the exclusive male culture of effortless superiority which they taught:

As long as the Church of England refuses our services – long may she exclude us! – and the ancient schools and colleges refuse to admit us to a share of their endowments and privileges [bought, as she points out, at the expense of women's education and financial independence over many generations] we shall be immune without any trouble on our part from the particular loyalties and fealties which such endowments and privileges engender.[82]

As financial advantage dictates a partial 'mixing' with girls or women where it suits the men and the institutions they control, there is less clarity perhaps about our being immune to their exclusive loyalties. But it would be a mistake, I suggest, for women to offer any loyalty to the 'ancient schools and colleges', certainly not until they become genuinely equal-opportunity institutions, in all senses, which would in any case destroy them as forcing-houses for privilege. Good luck to women who have got something out of them – but let us not condone the infinitely greater advantages they give all those men who turn that into a brilliant career for themselves, and power and privilege over everyone else.

'There they go, our brothers who have been educated at public schools and universities, mounting those steps, passing in and out of those doors, ascending those pulpits, preaching, teaching, administering justice, practising medicine, transacting business, making money . . .' as Virginia Woolf describes them.[83] And, we may add, watching cricket, joining the men-only clubs, sitting in all-male officers' messes or ecclesiastical offices . . . for that is the world, a men's world, of Who You Know (and how you behave) for which the very important boys are being prepared in those exclusive schools and universities of theirs.

7
VERY IMPORTANT MEN'S CLUBS

'It's not what you know, it's who you know that counts.' How do you get introduced to the right people, if you don't already know them? In the club, that's where. And for the élite that means one or more of the men's clubs in London's West End and the City. Membership costs hundreds of pounds a year, the surroundings are often very grand in the marble and oak panelling style, and access is by personal recommendation only.

The 'club atmosphere' makes possible the kind of frank and open exchange which Very Important Men associate with excluding anyone who is not 'one of us'. This was brought home to me when I attended a meeting stuffed with VIMs, one of the annual Anglo-American Parliamentary Conferences on Africa. It contained selected top people from Government and Parliament or Congress in the United States, Canada and Britain. But surely, you might ask, from Africa too since that is what it was all about? Not at all: 'It would spoil the club atmosphere,' the British participants responded, to a man, when I asked. Their Canadian counterparts clearly understood and agreed, and the Americans had no objection either. The fact that some of the conversation might have been seen as misguided from an African point of view reinforced the point: they wanted to speak freely to each other and so kept the Africans (and most other people interested and well informed on the issues) outside the club doors.

Exactly the same applies to the clubmen's discussions about public policy in Britain, discussion which can have major implications for those of us who are on the outside. Top judges and lawyers meet in clubs. So do civil servants and business executives, police chiefs, senior armed forces personnel, academics, bishops, Lords, Members of Parliament . . . in short, virtually the whole of the Old Boys' Network is channelled into VIM clubs. They enormously reinforce the network itself, especially when it comes to top jobs and important positions in both public and private spheres. It is a strange anomaly that positions of major public importance are decided in this intensely private sphere. Public accountability does not enter into it (nor, with a few exceptions, do women).

Despite a few changes, these clubs remain very much a man's world: VIMs, not VIPs – but they help to ensure that the two are almost the same. The Carlton club accidentally acquired a token woman because of its tradition that the Prime Minister is automatically an honorary member. The Athenaeum has women in the basement (which will be explained in due course). The Oxford and Cambridge has some women, since accidentally voting in a Hilary they'd assumed to be male. The Reform club is mixed, since a few years ago – but as Glyn Worship reported from his little club crawl in 1986,[1] there is still only a small handful of women and since one of the first was Sara Keays, who became a target for the Establishment in her own right,[2] this has seemed to 'discredit' the idea of letting women in. The scandal 'was considered by gleeful glimpse suitable comeuppance and proof positive that a woman's place was not in the club'. Of course there's always the ladies' annexe, to help pay for the men's club itself, and a few (very few) women's clubs, which are now on the endangered species list.

For an institution which is well known to be central to the whole British Establishment, the men's clubs are striking for their absence from any of the normal sources of information; books by independent observers, analyses of their influence and how they work. Some have their own, highly favourable official histories publicising the glories of a bygone age when Victorian novelists wrote their books in the club, hardly the basis for understanding the real role of the club today. I had to piece together scraps of information from a trawl of press cuttings (going back to World War Two, some observations from clubmen in writing on other topics) but obviously, we also needed to penetrate the clubs from the inside. This is one area where you need a man, and volunteer Peter Watson agreed to try.

Club men are there because they are well connected: and they are even more well connected because they are there. Which means top jobs and public appointments that merit space in *Who's Who* (perhaps most accurately described as *Who Belongs to What*). They all seem to be proud of their club membership and list their clubs in detail in their entries, so this was clearly the place to start. Peter approached a cross-section of Very Important Men: politicians, journalists, architects, lobbyists, Harley Street doctors. . . . Many of them were surprisingly forthcoming about the joys of their clubs: they seemed to be trying to persuade Peter to join them.

'One feels enormously at home'

Let's start with a right-wing Conservative MP, long established and a member of White's, the Beefsteak, Buck's and the Carlton club – all very exclusive and expensive. 'I'm quite a clubby person,' he explained.

'Usually I go to White's for an extended lunch – it's one of the most exclusive clubs and an exciting set of people. The Beefsteak is a connoisseur's club. The membership is one of excellence in character, I find – very entertaining. I'm often in the Carlton with friends, other MPs, colleagues and so on, it's our own Tory club. One feels enormously at home there, there's no danger of undesirable ears being on the premises.

'I don't think you can differentiate between business and pleasure. I'm always doing both when I'm at the Carlton. It's entirely random whom you meet at the Beefsteak. It doesn't matter if I don't know the person sitting to my left, as I know he's a decent chap and we can talk amiably about anything under the sun.'

Another club man, a 25-year-old member of the Stock Exchange, told us how he uses the East India Club: quite a contrast.

'I go about four times a month, or four times a week when I'm feeling brash. I go with people from work or the City that I know, basically for a piss-up. Drinks are cheaper than in pubs and you can stay the night if you want. I wouldn't, because the rooms are so expensive.'

He had been banned twice, once for damaging a marble bust and the second time for 'even worse behaviour' which he did not explain.

'It's like a glorified pub which you have all to yourself. It's a great building though, sadly wasted!' This club has a connection with Dulwich College, one of the private schools, and he had got the head teacher there to recommend him for membership. It was useful, too: he could meet other City men in the club who 'could potentially be useful'. 'It's like a continuation of public school in a way, the same old standards being lived and breathed. It's all a bit of joke sometimes . . .'

What about the atmosphere in the club?

'Boring, dull, snotty, very dry, that sort of place. Lots of old men sleeping under newspapers. The atmosphere is quite businesslike in a way, as if the club is run like a business, almost, instead of a recreational place. It's full of accountants in the evenings – any accountant who's anyone will go there. It's a middle-class club essentially which is trying to top-notch but hasn't made it and knows it hasn't.'

Did he feel that was part of an old boy network?

'The old boy network is fine as far as it goes. I've met a few Old Alleynians [ex-Dulwich] in there, you meet them everywhere. I would guess that 30 per cent of our school-leavers go into the City and some of them become accountants. There's certainly a conveyor-belt effect. This club does have some influence, too, in the business world. I've had a quiet word with a few people I've met in there about business deals, to get information I couldn't get at work, or other people's perspectives on things. The impression I get is that people do go there and talk business sometimes, but they have to keep it quiet.'

(There is a rule in most of the clubs that you don't do business in the club – more honoured in the breach than in the observance, as a club man would say.)

'I'm quite right-wing, but some of the people in there are more extreme and blinkered than anyone I've met anywhere else. It's a pretty right-wing place generally.' What about the exclusion of women? 'It's just an old-fashioned, anti-quated anachronism. Doesn't bother me, mind you, but . . .'

A heavyweight political journalist works for an equally heavyweight newspaper, with contacts and influence to match. Where does this come from? According to him, it all has a lot to do with his membership of the Garrick Club.

'I go at least once a week, it's a great place. Sometimes in the political season I'm there every day. If I don't go at lunch-time I'll go after work. I often go with a small group of friends I have at work, on the paper. We go there to talk about things it would be unwise to discuss at the office, or anywhere where you don't know who's around, listening. On the occasions I have been there alone I've always met someone I know, such as a lawyer, so you can't really be there "on your own" as it were.'

What about his wife? 'My wife doesn't like it, she's a bit of a feminist and disapproves of the whole thing. I sometimes persuade her to come in the evenings as a guest but she doesn't go often.' (Since the discussions were con-fidential we could not ask his wife for her comments but we are fairly sure his report of her 'disapproval' is putting it too mildly.)

And what about organising formal functions at the club?

'I have done that sort of thing, more often at lunch I think. I've taken people there who I've had to write about and it helps, you can get a lot more out of someone in the club than in an office. It butters them up! You can say absolutely anything you like in the Garrick without fear of being quoted, fortunately. It gives us a chance to have a go at our colleagues and criticise people in an atmosphere where it doesn't matter. In any other place you might create controversy by doing so. The gossip is fantastic. I think that's a great asset to the club. The unusual mixture of the law people and arts people helps: neither group knows too much about the other, it helps to keep you in touch. Everybody talks in the Garrick, there's a club tradition that you should talk to complete strangers.

'It's a very good place to go and relax and let off steam. I also do quite a lot of underhand business there: for instance, we might be having a meeting or discussion about something at work, and we'll go and complete the meeting in the Garrick. It's a very free and easy place.'

Did he feel proud to be a member? 'Yes, it's great to belong to such a famous and prestigious institution with so many talented people and such a long waiting list. I feel quite privileged. You meet all sorts of interesting people.' What influence did the club have?

'There's quite a lot of influence in the arts – I think a lot of projects, and financial support for various things originate in the Garrick. Especially among the lawyer fraternity. It's like a big family. You meet people from different professions, and from your own, in an informal way. Sometimes I meet a few old friends there and it's interesting to see what they're up to.'

So how did he feel about women being excluded from membership?

'Oh, I don't mind about that. I don't feel very strongly about it one way or the other. On principle I suppose women should be admitted fully, they're allowed into most parts of the club anyway, I think [as "lady associates"] but this doesn't bother me a great deal.'

On to a top architect, a member of Brooks's. He goes less frequently, about once a month on average: 'usually on my own, occasionally I take a guest'. It's a convenient place for lunch.

'The atmosphere is congenial. I play bridge there sometimes. There's a good library, where I sometimes do research. I have a good sense of belonging: it's like having a second home to go to. There's a diversity of members, which I enjoy. You can talk about things you can't discuss with the wife, like football and cricket. The club is a good cross-section politically and there's also a wide range of people from business-related aspects of life such as trustees, writers, people from the arts and especially from Christie's and Sothebys, whom I meet regularly.

'There's no business that really goes on at Brooks's but it's a good place to start fund-raising schemes off, like one I did recently for the Museum. You really just have to be a nice bloke to get in. . . . [What about the ban on women?] I don't mind about the restrictions about ladies entering the club – only allowed in during the evenings, aren't they? – no, it's just a fact of life.'

Next we have a solicitor and board member of an important public authority. He belongs to the City of London Club and goes two or three times a month for lunch there, usually entertaining people he has invited for a private party. This is a 'quasi-business arrangement' which includes charity-related work and 'plans for political lobbying in an informal way'. How about the atmosphere?

'It's friendly and peaceful. It's a social club with a business background, so the geriatric element is not as obvious as it used to be. Quite properly one is not allowed to transact business on the premises, though. Typically, I would take someone there who is not a partner in business or on the fringes of the business world, as the atmosphere is more relaxed than the firm's own catering and entertainment facilities and one can also talk privately. The membership seems class-ridden in the sense that it maintains its own exclusivity and standards. One would not take a junior employee there if there was a chance that his boss would be in the club as this could prove embarrassing. There is I suppose a certain subtlety in behaviour which is there, but it's difficult to put a finger on it.

'I have indirect links with the political world and many international contacts. I've taken ministers and MPs there. Visiting American lawyers love going to the club: this is the greatest compliment, second to being invited to someone's house and a degree better than being invited to a restaurant. For overseas entertaining the club is very useful: it gives prestige to the British and to the City, a very valuable purpose. I had lunch with three eminent Chileans from Valparaiso today and I'm sure it does a lot of good entertaining people in this grand fashion: they were very flattered. . . . [And what about the women?] I don't think there is any logic against having lady members but I've never bothered to enquire about club rules on this.'

Another club man who uses his membership for political lobbying is the 42-year-old Director of an environmental pressure group, a member of the Reform club (one of the most expensive).

'I go at least once a week, any time of day. In my business – political lobbying – I don't keep regular hours like people with standard jobs and I find it advantageous to have somewhere close to the office where I can go at any time.

'I always go with someone connected in some way, directly or indirectly, with my business. It's a nice environment, physically speaking, to carry out political lobbying. I feel it's my territory, so to speak – but it can also act as a compliment to whoever I might be dealing with. I also go with fellow members to discuss topics of mutual interest.

'I like the building and the way it is looked after. The Reform has a fairly open-minded atmosphere which I like, not as stuffy as the Athenaeum. The surroundings are quite imposing and conducive to a quiet atmosphere, but not a sleepy one. I enjoy having a piece of the finest real-estate in London at my disposal. It's rare nowadays to be able to live in such style and I'm glad to have the opportunity to do so.

'Obviously the nature of the membership ensures that influential people can be met there, although I'm not aware of the club having a voice of its own. We're having a Reform Club debate soon, something which hasn't happened for many years, so this question of influence may change if the debates are to be held on a regular basis – which I hope they will.'

The Reform now has a small group of women as full members. What did he think about that?

'I'm all for it. I don't have any passionately held views on the subject, though. I'm not an ardent feminist or anything like that. It's certainly an asset, now that there are women in most professions which make up the membership of the Reform.'

Although most clubs are very 'English' and white, one of our interviewees was an Indian doctor with a flourishing Harley Street business – which had prospered greatly as a result of his membership of the Oriental club. He visits it very frequently, perhaps three or four times a week when he is entertaining friends or relatives from abroad. He had been introduced by a Pakistani diplomat. 'I was amazed by the place. I didn't realise that in the heart of London there existed a place like this. It's like a piece of India.' But there was 'a kind of familiarity that isn't oppressive'.

He got his first break as a Harley Street doctor from connections made at the club, and finds occasional clients there as well. It now provides a prestigious place ('my club') to meet representatives from the Gulf States who send patients to him. Perhaps equally important is the non-medical contact.

'When I needed some financial advice, I know a chap from the City (quite high up) who goes there and I asked the club secretary, 'Can you arrange for me to meet so-and-so?' 'Oh yes, he'd be delighted,' said the secretary. The next time I went there the head waiter had obviously been informed and had arranged dinner for us, and this chap was very helpful.'

He had been able to raise a million pounds in a hurry for a hospital venture on the strength of that.

What did the club mean to him and especially the guests he brought in to it?

'It tells him that he is part of the Establishment somehow – I don't like using that word, but perhaps it is to be used – it opens a number of doors which would otherwise not be opened. I found it exceedingly useful to break into upmarket medical practice. It has tradition, it has atmosphere, it has a certain class. Most of the people who attend my club have a certain style, style which is reminiscent of Old England, aristocracy, traditionalists, with a culture and a background. I am a snob in that way . . . a Brahmin, I started with privilege and bundles of self-confidence.'

And what about the men-only rule? 'I'm an old-fashioned man. I think I rather like it. I'd be sorry if ladies were admitted on an equal basis. Don't get me wrong – I like ladies very much . . .'

'Snobbish middle-class boy makes good'

Our next interviewee was much more of a 'fringe clubbiste' as he calls himself: he uses clubs erratically, but keeps up his membership where it could be useful. He is a professor at the University of London.

'I'm not a clubby person. I resigned from the Athenaeum when I was feeling broke fifteen years ago and I hardly ever go to the Beefsteak. My motives for joining both were mainly snobbish middle-class boy makes good. The club life I enjoy is – apart from the Dilettanti which I try never to miss – of a lunch or dining-society sort and the Oxford and Cambridge Club: groups of old friends absorbing new ones.

'I always go alone, my purpose is pleasurable off-duty stimulation. I feel very much at home. I am very much aware of personal and old-boy networks without either feeling this oppressive or trying to take advantage of it. But the high-table habit, as realised for a whole year as a young bachelor don at Oxford, the charm of

informal ceremony and the easiness of talk based on the assump-
tion that everyone has something of interest to offer, keep me a
fringe clubbiste.'

Another infrequent attender is a Savile club member and
senior civil servant posted to Wales: before his move there
from London he used to attend much more often. 'Being a
professional person, I like meeting other professionals from
different areas of life; there is always an exciting mixture of
individuals in the club, a "different" atmosphere.' He too
said he did not 'feel strongly' about the absence of women.
'I think it is just a fact of life. I suppose it might change in
the future but I don't think it would make much difference
to me.' On second thoughts though, he added, he would like
to be able to take his wife (this is one of the few clubs
without even 'lady associates' or female guests allowed
through the doors). He could take his wife to the local working men's club for the entertainments, he argued; he, at
least, enjoyed that experience.

A young Conservative MP told us more about the Carlton
club. It had, he found,

'a unique atmosphere, having such a powerful tradition of Conservative politics which is of course unique in itself. I often go there
with parliamentary colleagues for lunch or an evening meal – for
pleasure, really, but there's always the chance that something
could come up in conversation that it would be undesirable to talk
about outside. Quite a lot of business goes on, mainly of the
political sort. I go there for an evening meal sometimes when we
have to prepare a lobby. There's a pleasant atmosphere, good for
relaxing as well as talking privately about sometimes high-level
political matters. Yes, I know of several policies which have been
forged in the Carlton. Of course, you can invite who you like for
a meal there and do your business privately without the wrong type
of people being around. There's an old boy network, I suppose, like
the Brass Monkey Club . . . I think it goes on quite a bit, and yes,
I like it.'

The Brass Monkey Club? That one wasn't on any official
list.

'When I was a student we decided to get together as a faction, if you like. It's an evolution from student politics and at the moment it's got three members. We were all active in student politics together at Oxford and when my friend put down 'Brass Monkey Club' on his *Who's Who* entry I followed suit. We like to discuss non-traditional Conservative politics together. We don't have any premises so we can meet virtually anywhere.'

A similar little club was mentioned by a senior medical administrator in the NHS. He belongs to the Chasers Club, which meets once every six weeks and has no premises of its own yet. 'It often meets at one of the members' bases, home or film première. A member's company might put on a wine-tasting evening at their base. We have a private dinner twice a year.' There were twenty-four members, mostly from companies (he did not tell us whether they were companies from which he made purchases for hospitals in his region). There are elements of the Rotary ethic:

'It's really a charity business organisation. The club was started by a small group of people, old school friends in fact: there's a beneficial reason for the meetings. They are good for fundraising and we finance clubs like the Westminister Boys' Club, Ilkley Activity Centre, a drug addiction centre.'

Influence? 'Yes, the club does have some influence unofficially. We influence decision-making, for example in social policy and drug addiction policy – and some input into industry.' All the members were from the same school, and in fact there was a rule to exclude anyone who had not been there.

Another informant who agreed that many of his friends from school were in the same club was a prominent chartered accountant and member of Brooks's. 'Lots of them are Brooks's members,' he said. He goes there about four times a year, and to the City Livery Club about twice a month – usually with colleagues, to 'get away from the City atmosphere'. He also hires club rooms for private parties 'so that business work can be done in a different atmosphere'. No pretence here at not doing business in the club. Firm dinners and parties were laid on at Brooks's, with him as the host.

'The club is designed for feeling at home,' he told us, echoing a popular theme. 'There is a close atmosphere in which you can discuss private matters if you want to. It isn't a lively atmosphere like a pub. The waiters aren't too interfering and you can pour your own wine.' He accused others of manipulating the situation in clubs.

'The City clubs are helpful contacts for communication, access to information for work – or anything is possible. I think networks are a fact of life. They tend to be manipulated by certain people, of course, but for me they're a harmless, essentially social matter. There are also a lot of people who join clubs and get themselves into networks for the sake of nostalgia and escapism. I think these people are really rather lonely and pathetic. . . . Yet, of course networks are a potential source of influence or power, which is why some try and use them to their advantage.'

He had his very own theory about them, as well: 'If this country was invaded by a foreign power, the clubs would form the centre of a resistance movement. A lot of resistance or underground activity would go on in clubs.' The idea of VIMs strolling into their clubs under hostile occupation and plotting the resistance as they poured their own wine is a little startling, but he seemed quite serious. Perhaps he was projecting what he saw around him in these clubs: men making decisions without reference to the outside world, but which could have a powerful impact on that world.

There are, indeed, some unlikely views circulating among our interviewees. Take the senior archaeologist who claimed to be a socialist – and finding his own private haven in the Athenaeum Club. He visited about three or four times a month, he told us, usually for lunch. He sometimes took his wife in the evenings. 'The library is splendid. I also use it for entertaining people from abroad, fellow archaeologists.' There was a tradition, too, that you talked to your neighbour at mealtimes. 'It's considered very bad form not to.'

'I'm very proud to be a member of a club which has had, and still has, a great many men, distinguished and famous men who have made a contribution to society in the arts, sciences, learning . . . it's the only club where I feel at ease and conscience-free as a lifelong, committed socialist.'

He could also meet many other men in the academic world and in Government, in his field, who he would not necessarily see often outside, and

'I find it very useful to see them in that atmosphere, away from our respective offices. In an informal setting you can get quite a lot of business done.

'I think the Athenaeum is probably one of the more notable clubs for this. The mixture of people is important. For the sciences, senior civil servants and bishops especially, the club serves this function – not so much for the arts, which is geared towards the Garrick. But then you can meet unusual groups of people, like a fellow academic, a university professor, a bishop and a senior civil servant. I've had meetings like that here, with a diverse array of people. Of course in my area, as in any other academic or university or medical area, some of us might get together in the club and reach an important decision about the direction of future research, for instance.

'It's amusing to go into the club and spot the different groups sitting together: you wonder what they're up to! I think it's a very valuable function of the club because one's meeting in an informal social atmosphere, you can't take briefcases or papers: it's an unwritten rule. You're not sitting round a committee table. You might call it an invisible college. I think I prefer that phrase to "the Establishment" applied to the Athenaeum.'

Did he see the club as part of the old boy network? He certainly did:

'That's how the club gets its members, of course. I've nominated a publisher who was a contemporary of mine at university, two professors of archaeology who are contacts of mine through work, one journalist – all contacts at some stage of my career. It's not democratic, but nobody ever thought that clubs were. I see it as a group of like-minded people, recruiting all the time.'

And how did it work for him personally?

'There's no doubt that there's a certain cachet about being a member of the Athenaeum. You get slotted into a definite group of people who have achieved a certain eminence in their field, creative or administrative. It also gives me this opportunity of meeting people I'd meet officially on a certain level, in a different atmosphere – and it gives you a different relationship with that person. There's also the side-effect of meeting people from outside your own field which it's possible to exploit, which I know can be immensely valuable.'

One man he knew had used the club to get a job he was after as a top museum director: he'd sat facing the door in the coffee room so he could see everyone who came in. Important people, like trustees of the museum he was interested in, would be invited to come over and sit down. 'If someone wasn't much use to him he'd just nod to you!' Mostly, though, the more ambitious members operated a little more discreetly than this.

'Where it *does* help and is certainly used a good deal is for sizing people up for honorific jobs, usually any posts that are going in No. 10 Downing Street, members of Royal Commissions, Civil Service posts, universities – members of their Senate – or whatever. People thought suitable for such posts will be invited into the Athenaeum.'

These 'public' appointments, organised privately, are precisely the ones from which women are most comprehensively excluded.

He was, personally, '100 per cent in favour of the admission of ladies on an absolutely equal basis as members'. It would be an asset to the club, he thought.

'One of the things about the place is that the criteria for membership do not cover political, social or religious distinctions; the sole criterion is eminence in the arts, learning and so on. As a lifelong socialist this is the only type of establishment I'm prepared to associate myself with.'

But he was not risking his own position by insisting on equal access for women.

A similar view of the Athenaeum came from a senior civil servant, although he did not see his own career as being involved. He too used the club extensively for 'contacts' related to his work, including a number of overseas visitors.

'In my case – I have a pretty heavy diary schedule at the office – lunch gives you an opportunity to have an off-the-record chat, a bit of gossip, bit of brain-storming and do some business on the side. The majority of lunches I've had have been business in the sense that they've been connected with some of the work I've been involved with, but it hasn't been straight hard graft all the time.'

The idea of 'the Establishment', he thought, was pretty old-fashioned but, as he put it, 'there is a sort of group of people'. In his case it was other senior civil servants (who among other things are responsible for getting people onto the 'public' bodies) and 'a fair number of people who were at Oxford with me who I've bumped into in other spheres. I usually meet three or four people like this when I'm there.'

On the general atmosphere and feel of the place, he observed: 'There tend to be fairly large numbers of elderly and distinguished people hanging around, so it's hardly like a disco or a rave-up – a definite skew towards the *crumblies*.' This nasty word, it seems, is a favourite among those who see the club as a place for wheeling and dealing.

'You will get people meeting in the Athenaeum in groups, exchanging ideas and concerns about issues of the day, and that can feed through. It would be fair to say that people don't necessarily go to the Athenaeum with the intention of getting involved in decision-taking, but may get round to making plans or whatever through having common interests.'

Like most of those interviewed, he was not bothered by the exclusion of women: 'I don't regard this as intolerable injustice or a gross blot or anything like that!' He described it as 'silly' and old-fashioned, and to the extent that the club was geared to professional work and public service it was 'a bit restricted' not to be able to deal with women in that area, when at work (he claimed) they had 'absolute equality'. Excluding women was, from his point of view, 'marginally inconvenient'.

Charity and politics were the focus of the next man, a top official in the St John Ambulance who belongs to the Carlton club and goes there at least once a week.

'I go because I like the members and the club itself. I also do quite a lot of straightfoward charity-orientated work which I am involved with there. The Carlton is an extremely sociable place: naturally most members know each other very well. You *can* catch the place when it's full of crumblies, but there's always a very interesting atmosphere there as senior Tory MPs, retired MPs and prospective MPs can be seen there at once.

'Well, of course the Carlton has the potential of influence. It's a place where Tory MPs can talk freely about subjects they would not like members of other political parties, or certain undesirable individuals in the Tory party, to hear. I think an awful lot of policy discussions go on there, but perhaps not so much in a strictly practical sense. Contrast this with the St Stephen's Constitutional Club, where I'm sure Conservatives who man Central Office make policy in a regular fashion.'

Finally, we talked to another very influential journalist, a member of the Travellers' club, who goes three or four times a week – 'more often in winter'. When he went with people connected with his work it was a mixture of business and pleasure ('the two overlap in my occupation') and he could discuss work-related topics. 'The Travellers' is the best pub in London.'

And the women? This man saw himself as family-orientated, and although he had been a club member for thirty years he liked it more now that his wife and daughter could go to certain parts of the club at certain times, as associates.

'It's more convenient. However, I'd like it to remain as it is now, male members only, though I don't feel passionately about this. I like the club atmosphere – the very relaxed, quite intimate inter-relationship between a small number of people in a physically quiet environment, away from London noises and so on – and I think this is preserved best in a one-sex community. Please note, [he added seriously] that although I think there should be no lady members this view is not necessarily anti-female.'

Club atmosphere

There is, perhaps mercifully, no space in a single chapter to provide a complete guided tour of VIM clubland: members of this club or that, as we have seen in the interviews, are always ready to claim superiority for 'my club'. They are as varied as they are numerous, but what concerns us – the outsiders – is how their operations affect *us* by providing a secluded haven for privileged discussion and decision-making, and also how they act as recruitment grounds for senior jobs in private industry and in public appointments. The increasing importance of the clubs as places to 'wheel and deal' in terms of business contacts and insider information is also an element we need to be aware of.

This increasing use of clubs for business purposes is something that has emerged strongly from my survey of reports in the press over the last few decades. After World War Two there was general fluttering in the gentlemen's dovecotes: would the clubs survive? With the passing of the gentleman of leisure and limitless private income, the rising costs of the magnificent but decaying buildings and the need to pay club servants real money, it looked like the beginning of the end. Forty years on, it is clear that it was more like the beginning of a new and even more prosperous era for many clubs with company expense accounts replacing the private income as the main source of funds.

Club membership and entertainment have become part of the job for many top men. One sign of this is the clubs' catering, which has moved from school dinners to the posh restaurant style almost in a single bound. Male managers, solicitors, advertising executives, sales reps – all have found the clubs an excellent place to operate and an incomparable status symbol. The clubs, as the Establishment chronicler Anthony Sampson has put it, 'have maintained an aura of exclusiveness while welcoming almost any new member' (although, as he thought too insignificant to mention, this only applies if the member is a male one). Very few clubs, he was reporting in the early 1960s, actually had waiting-lists and not many had black-balls (the system whereby one member can member can exclude another – as Thackeray was by a man in one club: 'We don't want any writing fellows here'). 'But all of them convey an atmosphere full of black-balls.' 'In all clubs, perhaps,' he observes, 'there is an element of imposture. Everyone, as he ushers his guests through those mahogany doors, becomes a slightly less real person, talks a bit louder, shakes hands a bit more heartily.'[3] The splendid surroundings, reeking of Regency rakes and gamblers or Victorian landowners and empire-builders, are now being put to an essentially commercial use. It comes down to who can afford the fees, or whose company will cough up for the club along with the company Daimler. Sampson's description of the Arts Club is particularly graphic: 'It is now also concerned with the art of advertising and the science of public relations, and from the bar can be heard the baying sound of admen on the move.'

A little story told by another insider, Tim Heald, illustrated how the olde-worlde grandeur and snobbery of the clubs can coexist with pure financial gain. The setting is White's, 'grand in the old manner', as Heald puts it – grand enough, too, to have a long waiting-list *and* frequent black-balls. In case you're interested, Prince Charles held his stag night at White's. One man (not a member) together with his partner (who was) were about to embark on a business trip

to Texas. They had never been there before and had no contacts at all. A day at White's spent chatting up anyone who
happened to be there gave them enough Texas millionaires
for a schedule of three a day for the whole two-week trip.[4]

Perhaps the most important thing for us to know is not so
much where all these clubs originate or even who belongs
to what, but how they are now used for specific purposes.
If you are trying to find work as a barrister, for instance, you
need to know that large numbers of senior male barristers
and judges hang out at the Garrick Club where they get their
kicks from being with actors (they say that both groups are
involved in high drama) but do plenty of wheeling and dealing among themselves as well: who gets which brief, a word
in the judge's ear, and general gossip – boosting and
denigrating legal reputations. Anthony Sampson describes
the importance of having a secluded meeting place:

. . . the barristers remain more individualist than any other profession, and by their own decree they cannot share the risks. . .
Moving between their chambers and the courtroom, they can
develop an odd mixture of scholarship and showmanship which
cuts them off still further from ordinary people

but makes it particularly important that they have the Garrick in which to get together.[5] Some high-flying barristers
are moving out of their legal chambers into the City or industry (banks are particularly lucrative areas of work for
them) and obviously being a member of the 'right' club and
knowing the 'right' people is crucial to this kind of move.
Many judges and barristers will of course obviously belong
to more than one club, since after all you can often pick up
business from men in other areas of activity than your own.

If clubs are particularly important to the independent
operators – the wheeler-dealers who know how to use contacts and pull strings – this applies not just to self-
employed professionals like the lawyers but also to those
who are after the favours of public bodies and the Civil Service. Senior civil servants (the men) are often, as they say,

very 'clubbable'. Academic and scientific deals are particularly likely to be done in the clubs, as our own informants have already made clear. Anthony Sampson, who should know, confirms the importance of the Athenaeum in particular:

Members have complained that they could hardly hear themselves talk above the noise of lobbying – particularly for university grants: the Athenaeum is the favourite meeting-place for vice-chancellors. It is also a centre for a very unclubbable breed – the scientists (the Royal Society Dining Club assembles here) who use it as a base for manoeuvre and fundraising.

(You can also lobby Jimmy Savile, while you're at it, for a slot on his show.) One scientist told Sampson that the last war had been run by the scientists and civil servants in the Athenaeum and the military top brass in the United Services Club facing it: 'since they all talked very loudly, it wasn't difficult to discover what was going on.'[6] Senior military men are *very* clubbable, with several clubs of their own. So much for clubs as a centre for resistance to enemy occupation; they are more like the perfect vantage point for enemy spies.

But let's get back to day-to-day realities. If you want to lobby Government officials you need to know that the 'Foreign Office canteen' is the Travellers' club, that the Reform club is where Treasury civil servants discuss the economy, and the Economists' Tuesday Club debates all the reasons why planning is impossible. It was in a private room at the Reform, incidentally, that a group of mega-lobbyists successfully plotted how they would persuade the Government to accept commercial television and so make them a fortune. They only had to step outside the room to find many of the people they need to influence, in the receptive kind of mood brought on by good food and even better wine.

Church men, too, are not above a little influence-peddling, very important in a hierarchy where promotion is based on your 'reputation' and jobs are not advertised. The Athenaeum is becoming boring but has to be mentioned in this connection as well. Many observers see the bishops as doing important wheeling and dealing there (they can join without the usual fee, under a special club rule, although you'd have to be a rich or dedicated episcopal climber to afford the other expenses and find it all worthwhile). As Sampson puts it, 'the club is never without episcopal activity on a Trollopean scale'.[7] Anthony Trollope did in fact write his novels in the club.

And speaking of writing books, it seems that large numbers of them are conceived, discussed, commissioned, written and publicised within the walls of the Garrick, which is where publishing men hang out with each other, with the (male) reviewers and of course with the (male) authors. Tim Heald tells us that he got his book *Networks* commissioned in this way and proceeded to use the club's members and their contacts to research it. This results in some interesting information – but put together with a slavish admiration for many of the institutions he talks about (including the VIM clubs, although he would not be so disrespectful as to call them anything like that). In particular, he is full of admiration for the institutions to which he himself has belonged, including Sherborne School and Balliol College, Oxford, as well as the Garrick Club, which he describes admiringly as

a market place for books and book ideas. Some books never go outside the Garrick until they are actually published and it has certainly been known for a very famous Garrick author to use his Garrick agent to – in effect – auction his unwritten manuscript among the various Garrick pubishers.[8]

And you thought there was a free market in ideas . . .

Similarly in journalism: as our two senior and very influential journalist informants told us, their club membership is a great advantage to them in plying their trade. Many women, of course, are trying to make their way in journalism and may well belong to what they fondly perceive as close-knit little mixed clubs or cliques of their own. The experience of Katherine

Whitehorn is worth thinking about, though: she was at *The Spectator* in the late 1950s in a jolly little team who all got along very well both professionally and personally. She was very much one of the gang, although the only woman: there were weekly lunches in the office where they invited prominent people. Then there was a party to celebrate Bernard Levin's departure for pastures new (and more lucrative). She got dressed up and joined the pre-lunch drinks, assuming they were going to lunch together somewhere. At one o'clock the new editor announced lunch – from which she was automatically excluded – at the famous Garrick.[9] So much for being one of the boys! The shock, hurt and outrage she expressed is exactly what women in the City feel when they suddenly discover that they were never seriously in the running for a deal that was done behind closed masonic doors, or women in large companies who find that hard work and loyalty to the firm just don't count when the jobs get handed out in cosy conversations over the club's after-dinner port. Perhaps we should all be a bit less shocked and surprised when it happens to us, and see this as a major factor in all our lives even if we just don't see it most of the time.

The Savage affair

Another woman who suddenly got a nasty shock after her male colleagues went round VIM clubland talking about her was Dr Wendy Savage. She herself observed after her sudden suspension, trial and subsequent triumph over malicious accusations made against her professionalism in obstetrics, that men who are Members or Fellows of the Royal College of Obstetricians and Gynaecologists – and she herself received the accolade of a Fellowship in the middle of the controversy – are invited to join two men's clubs, the Travellers' and the Gynaecological Club. The rumour, she reported, was that in the 'cosy male get-togethers all the consultant posts are "fixed" '. The same goes for positions

of power in the Royal College itself. Although there are
many women practising in this speciality and they make up
11.5 per cent of consultants in England and Wales and 10 per
cent of RCOG committee members, all but one of the
twenty-six committees is chaired by a man (automatically
a member of one or both clubs) and the ruling Council is all-
male except for one woman. She observed wryly: 'The in-
congruity of a specialty devoted to women being almost
totally controlled by men has always struck me forcefully.'

It did indeed strike her, and in a particularly brutal way:
one member of the clubs was honest enough to reveal what
had happened after keeping a diary of the items of 'information' offered to him or passed in his presence. The campaign
of malicious gossip launched by her male colleagues,
medical correspondent Michael O'Donnell revealed,

included allegations about Ms Savage's sexual and marital history
which, if the doctors who uttered them had bothered to make but
the simplest of inquiries, would have been found to be untrue. Yet
these nasty smears were passed on by some of the most senior people in medicine and accepted, unquestioned, by others as evidence
for the prosecution in the court of gossip.

There were also damaging professional allegations about
dangerous procedures they were claiming she had carried
out, and which were being repeated unquestioningly by 'a
professor of obstetrics I'd expected to be a Savage supporter'.

It was a damaging accusation and, when I returned with evidence
that it was false, he told me that he too had investigated it and
found it untrue. He also told me that the allegation had been widely circulated as fact among the obstetrical establishment.[10]

Wendy Savage had the courage, and the support in the
community she served, to challenge the gossip in public —
and she won with the support of women right across the
board. Her accusers had in fact tried their best to keep the
hearings out of the public eye, imposing heavy 'club rules'
-type reporting restrictions. It was only after she had been

cleared and reinstated that, as another medical correspondent reported, 'the tide of opinion in the common rooms and wards flowed in her favour'.[11] If important men's reputations are formed in the clubs, how much more is this true of the few women who make it to comparable positions but who are not allowed into the inner sanctums where that much-valued 'gossip' which many of our own informants referred to (and which many men would claim to be the preserve of women) is passed around. And of course the brave man who challenges the truth of it, or the integrity of the gossiper, could be at risk of alienating another man whom he would prefer to cultivate for the benefit of his *own* career. Mustn't spoil the club atmosphere . . .

The political club

In British politics the club atmosphere and club gossip are of central importance. There is a famous story about the Beefsteak, a rather dingy place from the outside which is also away from the West End's clubland area of St James's and Paul Mall in a seedy side-street off Leicester Square. Before the war the police, having observed rather well-to-do old men emerging every evening having apparently had a good time, decided to raid it one evening. They found four men sitting round the long table: the first three said they were the Lord Chancellor, the Archbishop of Canterbury and the Governor of the Bank of England. 'And I suppose,' one policeman said to the fourth, 'that you're the Prime Minister?' 'As a matter of fact I am,' said Arthur Balfour. And he was.[12]

Political manoeuvring, on the Conservative and Liberal Party side at least, has always been carried on largely in the VIM clubs. The political atmosphere in virtually all of them is conservative and complacent – 'I'm all right' – as many observers, including our own informants, report. In many cases, they would have to be described as very right-wing.

The Carlton club was founded in 1832 as a centre for the

Tories. The Reform club was a parallel organisation for Liberals, who supported the Reform Bills to widen the franchise (although as several observers note, any radical instincts have 'long since disappeared' from the Reform). Party organisation at the time was rudimentary and the clubs were crucial not only as centres for discussion of policy and as meeting places, but also as part of the party machinery itself. They were often responsible for selecting the relevant party's candidates.[13] The tradition continues: for example, it was at a meeting of Conservatives at the Carlton club in 1922 that it was decided to take the party out of Lloyd George's coalition Government. Most Tory MPs still belong to both the Carlton and the 1922 Committee of Tory backbenchers.

These days Liberals (and most recently SDP and Democrat men – who joined enthusiastically) hang out at the National Liberal club (although this too is credited by insiders with being a 'small-c' conservative place). One club story is about Winston Churchill who started as a Conservative, became a Liberal and then crossed the floor back to the Conservatives again. Challenged about this at the Liberal club, he explained: 'Any fool can rat, but it takes a man of courage to re-rat.' The club became known in the late 1970s for what reporter Glyn Worsnip describes as 'nocturnal gentlemanly rudery and other unsavoury doings, including financial mismanagement'. It was then that the management was cleaned up and SDP men invited in to save the club's finances.[14] More recently, the Liberal club has been opened up to full membership by women.

A few Labour Party men, too, have started to come into the clubs, although not on such a massive scale. Roy Jenkins in particular joined a number of VIM clubs, with their famous wine cellars, but then left the Labour Party. Aneurin Bevan got his bottom kicked in 1950 when he went as a guest to the far-right Tory stronghold of White's.[15]

They are a fearsome phenomenon, the massive philistines of White's whose 'arrogance still fascinates the Tory Party, and the prospects of White's backbenchers baying for vengeance can still intimidate a Cabinet Minister', according to Sampson.[16] There is also the more serious meeting place of the Carlton club, whose security matches that of central Government offices because of the high concentration of Cabinet Ministers;[17] the Junior Carlton, the Constitutional, and all the 'super-élite' clubs such as Brooks's – which has had thirteen Prime Ministers as members, and been labelled by Trevelyan as 'the most famous political club that will ever have existed in England'.[18] But let us not forget the RAC club, forever famous as the meeting place of Burgess and Maclean who met there to plan their quick exit to Moscow when they were discovered to be spies.[19] The RAC club is more like a big hotel than a club, 'founded by hearty motoring men in 1897' and now has 12,000 members. Unlike most clubs, 'no one at the RAC appears to know anyone else',[20] so it is handy for a little cloak and dagger.

All this, you might think, would be quite enough. But not so at all: men's political habits mean the creation of a steady stream of *new* clubs. The rationale behind political dining clubs is explained by one of the men interviewed by Anna Ford in her book, *Men*. He relished his all-male dining clubs for discussing politics, he told her: 'the same sort of conversation that you get after dinner when the girls are gone.'[21] The specially created dining clubs also have a cliquish element which even Pratt's or White's cannot match; members are all of one political persuasion, or have strong political interests in common.

Nearly all of them, incidentally, are Conservative cliques. Labour politicians of a certain kind, as well as SDP, Liberal and Democrats, go to town on dinner parties – which are a one-off version of the dining club, with women (though often they are not the women who are directly involved in the issues and alliances being discussed). Labour's parliamentary cliques or factions, and the interminable caucusing on the right (which invented it) and the left (which cannot now do without it) are of the deadly serious meeting type rather than the more convivial arrangement of the Tory dining clubs.

So what are they? Well, first there's the 'One Nation' which meets every Wednesday evening for dinner. It was founded by a group of MPs including Edward Heath, Iain Macleod and Enoch Powell, who all entered Parliament at the same time, and still includes the principal Conservative liberals or 'wets'. Members leave if they get appointed to a Ministry, and rejoin when they are sacked. A leading member, Lord Alport, explained the objective:

We sought to wean the Conservative Party, post 1945, away from the image of the party of 'hard-faced business men who had done well out of the first and second world wars'. We sought to capture and hold the middle ground of politics.[22]

On the other wing of the party is the '92' club, headed by the ultra-right Patrick Wall. Then there's 'Nick's Diner', named after Nicholas Scott ('mainly men who were trendy and popular in the early '70s and are starting to look a bit fly-blown', as one critic put it) and the 'Guy Fawkes', which has younger men. The smartest of all – according to Tim Heald, anyway – are the 'Blue Chips' who dine every other Thursday at the home of Tristan Garel-Jones. Ideologically it is similar to 'One Nation' but is much superior socially. Many of them are Lords or have strong aristocratic connections as well as belonging to political 'dynasties' – their fathers and perhaps grandfathers were MPs and diners before them. They weekend together also, in their often splendid houses, and provide each other with godparents for their children.[23] All *very* cosy and cliquey. Less cosy, and nastier, is the 'Currie Club', a group of Tory MPs who make fun of Edwina Currie, Minister of Health, by meeting at regular intervals to scoff dumplings, chips and pudding and smoke after each course.[24] You don't have to be a fan of Mrs Currie to find the 'joke' offensive.

Dining clubs would not be complete without a mention of 'The Other Club', which meets every other Thursday during the parliamentary session in a private room at the Savoy. Members include many of the senior male members of the

Conservative Government and, perhaps surprisingly, the Labour opposition as well: Labour's James Callaghan is Secretary at the time of writing. Needless to say, it is for men only.

It was the senior woman in French politics, Simone Veil, who summed up best for me the relationship between VIM clubs and politics – and not just in Britain, either. 'Politics,' she told me, '*is* a club. And the men don't like women in their club.'[25]

But how then do we explain the rise of Margaret Thatcher, in a Conservative Party dominated by discussions in men-only clubs such as the Carlton? This seems to me to be no mystery: although she had no right to use these clubs herself, she was the candidate of a right-wing, almost all-male faction which most certainly did. Men like Airey Neave, it is generally known, were of crucial importance in manoeuvring Mrs Thatcher into the leadership against the more middle-class, less 'clubbable' man Edward Heath. And if now Mrs Thatcher *still* does not go to the men's clubs (she is careful not to use the Carlton as a man would, despite the honorary membership) she has devised for herself a devastating alternative and a very satisfying form of revenge on all those clubbable wets who have made no move to challenge the 'men-only' rules: she has used her personal power of patronage to control her Cabinet, and indeed the whole of the Government including the Civil Service, in a ruthless way which goes far beyond what any other British Prime Minister in history has felt able to do. She has ridden roughshod over those sacred clubbable cows of the Establishment like the BBC, the Church of England, the club-nominated quangos . . . it is the ultimate revenge of the outsider. Like Edward Heath, and other liberal 'wets' sacked by her, they can always go back to the 'One Nation' men's club for mutual consolation with some rather good port, if no actual power.

Letting in the ladies

Before we leave the glittering world of VIM clubland, we
need to take a look at the institution of 'lady associates' and
the situation of the small women's clubs. Women can be
full members, we should remember, at very few of the VIM
clubs, including the National Liberal Club, a vast building
where not much happens; the Oxford and Cambridge
(which between you and me is not one of the grander ones
and could do with the money); and the Reform. The latter
just happens to be one of the two most expensive clubs in
terms of entry and subscription fees: women were invited to
join when the fees were put up very steeply and there were
fears that men would drop out and the club itself might not
pay its way. It was self-interest, not the principle of equality, that dictated this move. The number of women involved is very small and likely to remain so; nor do they seem
about to feel completely at home. Lesley Bygraves, one of
the few women in the Reform Club and a director of a public
relations company, told a reporter that she planned to use
the club strictly for business. 'I don't think it will change
much now with women members. Women should be pleased
that they have been admitted. But it would be a bit of a cheek
if we immediately changed things.'[26]

In most of the other clubs there are women with associate
membership, or allowed in at certain times and in certain
parts of the building as guests of the men – usually in the
evenings when the club is pretty dead anyway, and extra
visitors help keep the club open by buying meals and drinks.
In some clubs this means wives and daughters of the male
members, in others women can become associate members
in their own right. At the Carlton, for example, women who
manage to become MPs, MEPs or Conservative peers –
hardly a large number – can become 'Associates'. Even
they, incidentally, are allowed only into two of the rooms,
and cannot vote or hold office.[27] The Carlton at least
allows women to enter through the front door. Elsewhere,
for instance at the Travellers' and Buck's, there is a 'lady's

annexe' which is virtually cut off from the club itself and where the men can go with a woman or in some cases women can go on their own.[28]

Perhaps the most illuminating comment on the humiliation of being a 'lady associate' in a VIM club comes from Elizabeth Parsons, Chairman of the University Women's club who had previously been a 'lady associate' of a men's club. 'My contemporaries, when we joined in the mid/late '70s, rejected the men's clubs which we were entitled to join . . . we came here because we were blowed if were were being treated as second-class citizens.' The women have men as Dining Members, and take care to treat them fairly.

'Our men members don't have quite the same horrible things imposed on them that you get – revolting treatment you get – in the men's clubs. I mean, here we do allow them into the library and the bar, they can buy their own drinks with pleasure. They can buy their own meals, they can sit anywhere they like in the dining room. They can do what they like. We don't dislike men.'

This is in sharp contrast, apparently, to the men's attitude to women – particularly when her previous club, the Oxford and Cambridge Women's, had merged with the United University and the men then set up a system where women had to dive down into the basement to get to their bit of the building. They also lost their own bar, and found the waiters ignoring their orders in favour of the men's squash bar. 'The final straw was when they combined the libraries of the two clubs, and the books they put in the ladies' wing were all Victorian novels.'[29]

In normal life taking valuable books without consent would count as theft, but it seems that in clubs anything goes. In fact it seems to be standard practice for men's clubs to take over the assets of women's clubs in what is meant to be a merger of equals, and then restrict the women to 'associate' status with a long list of humiliating restrictions on where they can go and when – which always seems to come as a big surprise to the women. Isn't it time women recognised this as the normal pattern of men's club behaviour?

This was certainly the case in the merger of the Cowdray club, the most prominent of the women's clubs, with the Naval and Military ('In and Out' to club men). After paying a 'dowry' of £250,000 from the proceeds of their own building to the men of the N and M, the women suddenly found themselves 'associates' with large parts of the club and even the main entrance put 'out of bounds' by the men. There was particular anger among the women at being barred from taking their male guests into a buttery rebuilt largely with their money, meaning in effect that they could not use their own club for the business entertaining which they had intended as its principal function. Meanwhile, most of the women's money is being used 'for the benefit of the Naval and Military'. One woman said: 'I think we've been sold down the river. What we wanted was a club we could take our friends to without being treated as inferiors.'[30] They had been well and truly had. The 'In and Out', incidentally, quickly dropped its race bar on men who were not 'of European descent' when a protest was made about this in 1972 – as did White's in 1985 when one of Mrs Thatcher's political friends in the Asian (male) community wanted to join.[31] Mrs T. herself, of course, remains ineligible.

So the Cowdray, practically the last of the half-dozen women's clubs that flourished between the wars, has disappeared and its members relegated to second-class status in the men's clubs. They just could not afford to keep going on their own since women do not spend the amounts of (expense-account) money on food and drink that keep the men's clubs prosperous. Far from women advancing into men's clubland, VIM clubs had advanced on the women leaving nothing but a bunch of 'lady associates'.

All that is left are the University Women's club; the Soroptimists' Residential club, which is linked obviously to that organisation; the New Cavendish club, said to be mainly for widows living in the Home Counties; the Parrot club in the hotel behind Harvey Nichols and within spitting distance of Harrods, started by the manager for wealthy out-of-town shoppers and now also a popular venue for public relations parties in the evenings. And then, of course, there is the mixed Groucho club, started by two women as a pricey 'literary' club to challenge the Garrick.

And does it? The Groucho, in London's Soho, is obviously a big success: club snob Craig Brown described it disgustedly as 'a roaring, simpering, barking success'. Whether it is a club in the Garrick sense is far less clear: its atmosphere is apparently like a nightly launch party for some unspeakably boring product with people there to be be seen rather than to discuss anything they are really interested in. Brown's (biased) verdict:

Strange to say, when the media write about the Groucho, of which they are all members, they describe it as some sort of paradise on earth, a cross between the Algonquin Round Table and the Bloomsbury Group, when it actually resembles nothing so much as the Radio One staff canteen.[32]

Bitchy stuff, but confirmed by others. You may well sell something at the Groucho, hear about a job, make an impression – but the 'club atmosphere' so crucial to the discreet dealings of the upper bourgeoisie, dispensing real power, is a million miles away from the Groucho.

The name comes from Groucho Marx and his famous joke: 'Please accept my resignation. I don't want to belong to any club that will accept me as a member.' As club historian Anthony Lejeune put it, the 'best' clubs must 'provide at least a semblance of exclusivity. A club, after all, is a place where a man goes to be among his own kind . . . a refuge from the bustle and vulgarity of' – no, not Groucho's – 'the outside world, a reassuringly fixed point, the echo of a more civilised way of living . . .'[33]

If Groucho's is the answer to all this, heaven help us all. There are of course the new professional women's networks which use some of the conventions of clubs, notably exclusivity and lunch: there's the City Women's Network, for instance, and the Women's Advertising Club (limited to fifty members). They have major weaknesses as any kind of alternative to the men's clubs, though. By including women in the same line of business they lose the enormous advantage that can be gained by meeting others in complementary activities, who can be of more practical use to you; and by lacking the large number of very senior and well-connected individuals from the public sector as well as the business world, the opportunity for highflying deals and jobs is absent.

Perhaps the most successful of these organisations is 'Network', which issues a list to its 400 members of 'women to watch': women in the media, it seems, use this to decide which token woman to put on *Any Questions* and the like. It's a self-consciously clique-forming exercise; as Claire Rayner put it, 'London is full of interlocking circles, love: get into one or die!' Many of us, love, would rather die.

Ann Hills, who investigated the workings of these professional women's organisations, reports them as very businesslike and geared to acquiring skills. 'Networking for women is a highly practical activity, with precious little time spent lounging about or consuming port – the organizing career woman hasn't the time.'[34] But as Heald points out, referring to dining clubs but equally applicable to VIM clubs in general:

Food and drink are essential but so too is conversation and conversation among members of such exclusive little groups is bound to lead to the exchange of more or less privileged information, the creation of mutually shared confidences and to links and prejudices which provide the means, at least potentially, of doing what networks are all about, which is bypassing the usual channels.[35]

As the club woman Elizabeth Parsons put it, describing the way in which her women's club was fundamentally different from the men's, it is not 'competitive, secretive, scheming, plotting and pompous. I don't think I have ever heard anyone plot to take over the Government here.'[36] But then, that is precisely how these men *have* taken over the Government, and continue to control it – despite the revenge of outsider Mrs T., which will end when normality is restored and a club man put in her place.

If women are to have an equal say in politics and public administration, as well as equal access to the top jobs and the big business and financial deals which are on offer to members of the men's clubs, some kind of revolution will be necessary. While 'barking, simpering' clubs like the Groucho, or the exclusive variety of professional women's networks, may be useful to the women involved in them they also exclude *most* women and perpetuate the élitism and exclusivity which the men have made into a fine art: 'the unfair advantage in life', as Heald aptly describes it.[37]

Becoming a 'lady associate' to a men's club is to submit yourself to humiliation and open discrimination. There may not be white lines painted on the floor, but there are invisible barriers to the use of certain rooms and certain times of day, or even instructions to keep away from the main entrance. Waiting for equal access to all facilities, from the kind of men who repeatedly told us that excluding women 'doesn't bother me' is futile. And where the only concessions to us are prompted by a financial crisis, why *should* women bail them out?

We can and should acknowledge the seductiveness of being invited into a club, the excitement of becoming a privileged 'insider'. But to the people still on the outside, the snobbish exclusivity of a women's club or clique, or a mixed club, is every bit as sickening as that of the men. Let us show the world a different way by staying out even if we are invited in, inviting men who claim to support equality to leave, and declaring war on clubs of any kind where the whole point is the 'unfair advantage in life' to be gained from them.

8
CROOK AND GUN
Men of the Church of England and armed forces

There are of course many denominations in Britain, but the Church men who really count for the Establishment are those of the 'official' Church, the Church of England, with their links with boys' private schools, Oxbridge, the VIM clubs and (via the bishops who are active as Lords in the House of Lords) the Government . . . not to mention the Freemasons, the Army and in fact practically every aspect of the men's club world covered in this book. The Establishment connections have been built up by leading Church men ever since Henry VIII decided to have his own tame national Church.

We are indebted to men on the inside of the C of E for giving us an overview of what is happening. It is a vast subject which we can only glance at here: the history of Church and State; the influence of bishops on the Government, and of the Government on the Church; and the increasing distance between the life of the Church as a genuine community and the formal links of the top men with a remote and distinctly unspiritual government. The claims of women to a more human liturgy, recognising women's as well as men's values, are part of the new life of the Church of England as a living religious community – which of course includes the movement for ordaining women as priests, but also includes a drive towards openness about homosexuality; many priests are gay, and increasingly dissatisfied with the pretence and hypocrisy which the Church has forced on them. There is also a 'grass-roots' move towards much greater co-operation between churches at a local level and a more honest involvement with the whole community. There are many in the Church, who are part of this new movement, who see the insistence on 'tradition' by many of the men at the top of the hierarchy as being a reaction to the forces for change within the Church: an intensification of opposition to any threat to their own beliefs and ways of working which has at times erupted into threats to wreck the Church itself by splits and lawsuits, in the struggle for power to be held by men only.

We can already speak of a major rift in the Church of England – two cultures, in effect: the powerful and the powerless. The first, the Established Church hierarchy, is composed of the Church Commissioners who control the investments and property of the C of E (sometimes in defiance of members' wishes, especially over investment in South Africa and property speculation at the expense of church tenants). This group is all-male, with just a few women in junior or middle-ranking administrative posts. The second is all the people of the Church, women and men: its congregations dwindling, resources thinly stretched, becoming very much a minority in the community and increasingly aware of the tensions in society – racism, prejudices against women and ethnic minorities, injustice and poverty. As a religious community, it is stronger and more in touch with its spirituality as well as the community than when the C of E was genuinely the national Church and ordinary members had to behave according to the conventions. Only in the affluent suburbs does that tradition survive. As one informant explained: 'A lot of decision-making types live in suburbia,' and these parishes also raise considerable amounts of money with which they can continue in the style to which they are accustomed.

The Church Establishment, this insider added, provides 'the ritual and the justification for unchanging patterns of power and prestige'. The Archbishop of Canterbury in full fancy dress (clothing which had recognisable symbolic importance when it was adopted, but not now) is, he suggested, 'an icon' used to give an odour of sanctity to prestigious ceremonial and tourist events like royal weddings.

'This sort of thing is used by people who *don't* go to church. It's reassuring to people who need symbols and want to see the Church participating at a national level. If you are of a traditional temperament, it gives evidence of stability and a continuing sense of Englishness.'

One example, among many, of the 'two churches' within the C of E is the tensions over disposal of redundant church buildings in the inner cities. The policy of the Church as a whole is to seek first of all another Christian church that wants the buildings; then to look for community uses, including adaptation for housing association flats; and finally to sell the buildings to the highest bidder, which may be for its value as a site for demolition and rebuilding for luxury flats or offices. Within one London borough alone, within a couple of years, I came across three cases of the policy being breached by the men in charge of disposing of the buildings for the Church. One case involved repeated requests from black-led churches, formed after attempts to join white churches were spurned, for a church – which fell on deaf C of E ears until complaints had to be made via the local Council which got one of the empty churches handed over. Another involved repeated applications by a housing association, which had already drawn up detailed plans and obtained planning permission but which never succeeded in getting its bid accepted and finally saw the church sold off to developers for high-cost luxury flats. The third involved the church's trustees demolishing an important listed church with the promise to rebuild the façade as part of an office development, only to renege on the agreement and sell the cleared site to developers. The 'official' church representatives repeated throughout that they needed to get as much money out of the buildings as possible, as the excuse for disregarding policy set out by the 'real' Church.

It is important to recognise the schism in the C of E between official and real churches, but at the same time it has to be said that many of the men on the 'official' side, the bishops especially, can see only too clearly the dangers of what is happening. They often align themselves with the 'real' Church and its point of view, which is now categorically anti-Establishment, certainly anti-Conservative (although many of them would want to draw a veil over that), opposed to privilege (including that of the 'official' Church) and on the side of the poor and the disadvantaged who most certainly don't belong to West End clubs or send their sons to private schools. We have the irony of twenty-six C of E bishops sitting in the House of Lords as representatives of the 'officials', but also participating in the controversial 'Faith in the City' report which severely criticised the Conservative Government – and regularly speaking and voting against the Government in the House of Lords itself.

There are 'real' Church men who argue – and they have a strong case – that they should belong to privileged clubs and Freemasonry, and become bishops, in order to raise money and use their influence on behalf of the underprivileged. The problem with this argument is that generations of this kind of activity have done nothing to weaken the system of privilege itself. There have always been philanthropists and Lord Bountifuls, but inequalities in society are not challenged and the system based on the men-only principle carries on with, if anything, even greater force for having a few liberals involved. The acid test for these benevolent priests is, I suggest, the question of giving women equal opportunities and access. Progressive lines of argument in the Lords do not extend to the bishops taking up sex equality issues, for instance – quite the reverse, as

Bishop Montefiore's 1987 anti-abortion Bill, introduced without consultation with women's organisations, would seem to indicate. These men are not representing even those women who belong to their own church.

Very few bishops are prepared, either, to take a stand against the 'Man'-based liturgy and theology of the Church, its fascination with the male and insistence on the male representing all of humanity. The Archbishop of York is an exception: following the decision in 1987 to ordain women as deacons as well as 'deaconesses' he suggested that during the time of waiting until 1991 for the final decision on admitting women to the priesthood, new ways of doing theology through reflection on the experience of women themselves would be 'a proper development'.[1] The whole weight of the official Church has been pitted against action to carry out the full ordination of women, despite the decision by the 1975 Synod that there were 'no fundamental objections' to this. Archbishop Runcie, claiming to be a supporter of equality, was saying at the 1978 Synod: 'I believe this is one of those cases where to do nothing is correct.'[2]

Some inside observers see the 'official' Church as making only the most grudging concessions to the existence and membership of women, let alone their claims to a priestly vocation. One told us: 'The concessions that are being wrung from the Establishment are only a tiny change in the equilibrium of power – and in many cases simply give more power to men by increasing their sphere of influence.' There is still talk of a financial settlement, and giving bishops opposed to women a veto over their participation in 'their' dioceses. Archbishop Runcie, after ordaining the first women deacons, claimed that they were not 'ambitious' about rising higher in the Church – as if this was a qualification for women to be ordained, while the exact opposite was obviously true of *him* as well as other Church men.

Some extremely offensive statements about women have been repeated loud and long in the Church's debates about ordination. One Synod speaker in 1987 claimed that women priests would be 'of the Devil' while another complained that 'they will be in the bloodstream'. Margaret Webster, a former executive secretary of the Movement for the Ordination of Women, has argued that there is a deep fear and dread of women as 'The Flesh' – a temptation to males – which is instilled by many theological colleges so that even marriage is seen as a fall from grace. She reflected that she and other women entering theological college had 'colluded with this to some extent, believing – at any rate on and off – that we were lesser citizens of the Kingdom of God'.[3] It is a powerful belief, and one that still lies behind official C of E attitudes – despite the Church's reliance on women to keep going at all as a viable national organisation. Without women, there would be no Church.

The situation facing the women most deeply committed to the Church of England, the religious wing of the men-only Establishment in Britain which also manages to lend an air of sanctity to discrimination generally, is a uniquely painful one. Since 1987 women can be deacons in Holy Orders, like the men – except for the bar on promotion to priest which is almost automatic for men after about a year. They are also forbidden to celebrate Communion or pronounce Absolution for sins, the two central acts carried out by men in Holy Orders. It is yet another example, perhaps, of being allowed into 'the club' but only so that the men who control it can draw lines on the floor of the club house that women must not pass: you're here, and you will do everything you can to keep the club going, but you are not One of Us.

To one of the leading campaigners for women in the Church, Monica Furlong, this approach is idolatrous – making up God in one's own image. She has the strongest feeling, she says, that 'we are dealing with a hierarchy which has made the Church in its own image – white, male, British, public school, and middle-class.'

Old boy bishops

So let's go back to the 'official' system which gives the men power in the first place. We tend to take it for granted as part of the British Establishment itself, but it needs some further investigation. And what do we find? Only that the men running the C of E come from the same group of boys that are running everything else in sight, from the Government downwards. They have been to the same schools, the same universities, and belong to the same clubs. They control a number of Church schools in the State system, and run their own private schools, including the choir schools (for boys only – or else the girls are excluded from the choir itself, the focus of attention for the whole school – for no good musical reason). And they have schools, colleges and clubs which are exclusively for the men of the Church.

Kenneth Thompson, who studied C of E bishops as an élite group, observes that they are only too easily categorised in this way, being one of the most 'annotated' groups of men in the world and appearing in a wealth of reference books. In 1969/70, 88 per cent of the bishops had been to Oxford or Cambridge, a proportion unchanged since the 1920s. Most (85 per cent) had also been at private schools, and Thompson found them 'highly integrated compared with most other élite groups' with very similar ideas and ways of thinking and behaving. This had much to do with the type of religion taught and 'imbibed' in the schools and colleges they attended, 'a traditional faith bound up with classical learning and stressing the responsibilities of leadership and service' which 'fits smoothly into an ideology which stresses traditional leadership, and a process of education which is concerned with role allocation among the upper classes'. This is reinforced still further by the fact that almost all the bishops went to one of only four theological colleges near Oxford and Cambridge.[4] As one of our informants put it, 'It's very easy to use friendships made at theological college and renew them at strategic points on the career ladder.'

If anything, Thompson tells us, the bishops have become even more of a type recently since the previous connections with the aristocracy have been largely replaced by a common educational background. They are also increasingly likely to be the sons of clergy men (54 per cent of bishops in 1960). Even more rapid, though, is the rate at which the bishops are becoming divorced from the 'lower' clergy in terms of background and experience. Most of the latter are State-educated, from non-clergy families (92 per cent) and increasingly without any university education but trained at one of the non-élite theological colleges. And as the Church faces greater and greater problems in recruiting enough men for its priestly jobs, it has increasingly taken on part-timers and mature entrants, who further increase the social gulf between parish priests and chaplains on the one hand, and the highflying career bishops on the other.[5]

Anything less like an equal opportunity procedure than C of E promotions would be hard to find. In theory, bishops are appointed by the Crown Appointments Commission presenting a first and second choice to the Queen, who is told whom to choose by the Prime Minister. In practice, we are reliably informed, the first choice is automatically the one chosen – even in the controversial appointment of the ultra-conservative Graham Leonard to be Bishop of London, when it was widely reported that Mrs Thatcher had insisted on him even though he was the second choice. It may not really matter, anyway. 'The boot is put in at a much earlier stage,' said our informant. 'Over lunch the Archbishop's and the PM's appointments secretaries will discuss possible candidates and many would be discounted before the process proper had even begun.' It is a process of exclusion, then, of anyone 'unreliable' either in the eyes of the Government of the day or for the official Church's representative. The Prime Minister's Office has full-time Patronage Secretaries whose job is to 'sift out' unsuitable candidates.

When it comes to appointments a little lower down the ladder, including the assignment of 'livings' in local parishes, there is very little advertising of posts. The old boy network comes into play, together with a collection of institutions which all have rights over certain parishes: the local landowner, Oxbridge colleges, the armed services, and various trusts which want to see clergy of a particular theological or political persuasion appointed. The parishioners have little or no say, and can be landed with someone wildly inappropriate – which is unhealthy for the real Church although apparently of little concern to the official one which makes the appointments. Most commonly, it will be a 'high' man fond of incense and processions who can impose his personal régime on a 'low church' congregation to whom these are anathema.

If this seems undemocratic, not to say faintly East European, consider the system of 'electing' bishops under the previous system: the Dean and Chapter would get a 'congé d'élire' from the Crown giving them permission to elect a new bishop, but including a letter missive giving the name of the man they had to 'elect'. If they refused to do so, the Crown could appoint by letter patent instead.[6]

It is very much a pyramid, the official Church. It has two Archbishops, with Canterbury senior to York because it controls more parishes. Next come the Bishops of Durham, Winchester and London. All three sit as of right in the House of Lords, as do the archbishops. There are then forty-four diocesan bishops, who between them have twenty-one seats in the Lords which are passed down according to seniority (the length of time served as a bishop). An extra nine suffragan bishops look after particular areas within dioceses, and there are assistant bishops who are usually retired bishops with official positions. Then come the sixteen provosts and deans of cathedrals, forty-three archdeacons, and below them the proctors, rectors, priests-in-charge and curates. All, needless to say, are men; and the top men effectively nominate the middle men, who nominate the lower ones. It is top-down and no nonsense about democracy, accountability, equal opportunities, or the real Church (including the women) getting involved in the selection of official appointments.

The way policy decisions get made, too, is in a cosy club atmosphere to which the real Church, women and men alike, is not admitted. One forum is a dining club of about sixty members (in 1980), half clerical and half not and including the heads of some C of E private schools, known as 'Nobody's Friends', which meets three times a year at the Archbishop of Canterbury's Lambeth Palace, organised by the Archbishop's assistant. One bishop has described the club's name as 'the very worst form of English inverted snobbery' and they are regarded as being very influential within the official Church. The founder, William Stevens, set it up in 1800 as a place for men 'of sound principles in Church and State' to meet and keep up a network of personal contact. There is also provision for up to thirty 'extra-members' to include privy councillors, bishops, judges and 'other persons deemed to have qualified on the grounds of special service to Church and Queen'. There is a waiting-list for applicants, who can be easily black-balled by just four of the existing members if they wish to exclude someone. Notes compiled by the secretary of the club in 1941 specify that

when a new Member is elected he is expected, in the words of one of the earliest rules, to make an *éloge* [praise] on himself at the first meeting he attends: in other words to justify his presence. If the justification is regarded as satisfactory by Members – and there has been no case in which it has not been so regarded – the health of the new Member is drunk and he becomes thereupon entitled to all the privileges, amenities and, I will venture to add, the pleasure and happiness of being one of Nobody's Friends.[7]

The bishops have their own private and 'informal' organisation where they can discuss Church issues and politics out of the public eye, which is known simply as the Bishops' Meeting. The bishops, although in theory the C of E's leaders, operate very much under the shadow of the growing Church bureaucracy. The increasing stress within the official Church on the 'apostolic succession' (the all-male line of bishops since Christ – they ignore the

210 · *Male powers*

medieval stories about Pope Joan who at one stage got herself pregnant) seems to be part of the reaction to this.[8] It has also become the main argument against ordaining women, especially among the junior men. It could well mean that even when women eventually become priests, they are likely to be blocked from the position of bishop or archbishop.

The Bishops' Meeting has no public or legal standing in the Church, and its agendas and discussions are not communicated to the Church generally. The wide range of its business, however, has been traced by Kenneth Thompson from the letters and papers of recent archbishops and bishops, which showed that it was concerned with important policy issues for the official Church itself – but hardly touched on more basic questions like the relation of the Church to society as a whole. Thompson quotes a former Bishop of Sheffield as commenting in 1966 that he had attended more than a hundred of the meetings:

I cannot recall many occasions when we really faced the revolution in English society since the Book of Common Prayer was promulgated in 1662, or the radical change in thought and belief and in the pattern of life since the industrial and scientific revolutions; and in the light of these changes, the need for a new policy of engagement and penetration.

But as a meeting-place and social club, another participant said that they had left 'a happy memory of friendly association'.[9] These are associations which, as we have already seen, can be kept up also at the VIM clubs in London's West End, particularly the Athenaeum where the bishops can also meet senior academics, civil servants and other influential men. One well-known vicar we met, for instance, had just come back from lunch at the Athenaeum with a friend whom he 'hoped to pump for money at some later date' (for a very good cause, of course).

There is another important link between men in the C of E and outside networks, one which is under challenge in the Church at the moment: the masonic connection. Stephen

Knight, in his investigation of 'the brotherhood', concluded that 'the Church of England has been a stronghold of Freemasonry for more than two hundred years. Traditionally, joining the Brotherhood and advancing within it has always been the key to preferment in the Church,' although he conceded that the masons' influence had diminished over the last two decades with fewer masonic priests although still a very large number. Knight argues that Freemasonry, with its strong element of the occult and worship of Baal ('the devil') and Osiris ('death') as well as Jehovah, is a religion in its own right even though few masons know or will admit this – and one which is completely incompatible with Christianity. He particularly emphasises 'the double-speak of Masonry', the basic hypocrisy of its claim to co-exist without any strain with worship of a Christian God, and he gives a number of examples of masonic networks influencing the Church through its 'official' structures.

One case was that of a vicar in the home counties, not named, who came under enormous pressure to allow the annual Freemasons' Service to be held in his church, without him being present and with no assurances offered about the form of worship. Once he started to recognise masonic symbols, he started seeing them all over the church and began to suspect that it was really more of a pagan temple than a Christian church. In the course of the battle that ensued he discovered that the previous owner of the local estate, who would have had a strong say in the running of the church and appointment of its priest, had been a top mason.

To some of those in the official conformist Church, perhaps, one clue to the attraction of Freemasonry is that it offers a missing 'real' element which is only to be found, in the C of E, in the real Church. As the City banker and former mason, Andrew Arbuthnot, told Knight:

It induces a sense of brotherhood and togetherness by means of a secret society, which always gives that sense, but it leads people towards the thought of a Supreme Being, to the transcendental. It is at least as much a religion as the average, dry Church of England conventional matins service.

But the vicar with the masonic church said he had come to realise that 'the fellowship of Masonry was a counterfeit of the fellowship of the Holy Spirit'.[10]

Freemasonry within the official Church, and among influential contacts outside the Church itself, is an extremely contentious issue for many in the real Church, with people there 'screaming out for masonry to be outlawed' according to several of our informants. An official inquiry strongly criticised Freemasonry in a 1987 report to the Synod. Meanwhile, though, the connections remain extremely strong at points where the official Church makes contact with other male networks – particularly in London's 'City churches' which seem to be in a category of their own and which, we are told, gain money and prestige through hosting the ceremonies of the Livery Societies as well as masonic Lodges of the City. As one of those involved told us,

There are so many rich, undemocratic, interlinked organisations in the City that – leaving aside the question of masons helping each other into jobs – a masonic priest might be preferred for a post in the City because he would be able to get the most out of those organisations.

So there you have it: masons are in, women are kept out of the priesthood and the positions of influence in the official Church (and many masons, incidentally, would be among those blocking the women). It is in sharp contrast to many other Anglican churches all over the world, which are more like real churches throughout and which have in many cases ordained women as priests. Many of the most committed C of E women in Britain are now working on the margins of the official Church or beyond it, like Sister Joyce of the Community of St Francis who told us she sees the institutional Church as being tied up with a lot of irrelevancies and who works instead with 'women who want a spirituality which is authentic for them'. She is excited by completely new kinds of ceremonies, like those for women after they have been raped or sexually assaulted to help them deal with their pain.

The whole emphasis on maleness in the Church, she feels, and the imagery of a masculine God who is a father and authority figure over women, has proved so alienating to many that they feel excluded from services and do not attend. Or as Graham Leonard, now Bishop of London, put it in 1977: 'Women can hold positions of importance . . . but they hold them under the authority of Christ. That authority can only be represented at the altar by a man.'

Another man, Kennedy Thom of the Gay Christian Movement, has summed up the increasing gulf between the official and real Church, the privileged and the outsiders, hypocrisy and honesty, the empty shell and the living community.

Too often Christian doctrine has been allowed to become an ideology and membership of the Body of Christ an imprisonment in a totalitarian system. Where, as in the West, the Church has become the parent and partner of the secular culture, it needs help to rediscover the pain and importance of standing against received truths, standards and norms.[11]

It is ironic that while he and others are campaigning with women for a real church, many other men – including many 'closet' gay priests and bishops – are determined to keep it 'official – women keep out'.

For Queen and country (and men)

If the official Church is closely connected with the men's clubs and organisations of the Establishment, so too are the upper reaches of the armed forces – and especially certain regiments in the Army. The official Church and the armed forces are of course closely connected in their own right through the official chaplains, whose chiefs (Chaplain of the Fleet, Chaplain General of the Army and Chaplain-in-Chief) all work in the Ministry of Defence. They are represented as of right, also, on the C of E's General Synod. They are in charge of chaplains of all denominations except the Catholics. As the C of E's List of Organisations puts it: 'The religious training of the Army is an integral part of military life.' In the Navy, a chaplain is 'given particular opportunity to teach the Christian faith to young people in Training Establishment' and 'Christian Leadership Courses for all Naval ranks are provided at the [RAF Chaplains'] School during the year.' It is very much the official, men's version that is involved here, a religion of leadership and authority.

There is an anecdote which is regularly quoted by Army men, especially when they are arguing that 'it's not like this any more,' which goes something like this:

It was the end of a long interview. The young man was thick, but well-connected. As a last resort, the man interviewing him said: 'Now think carefully about this question. How would you pronounce A-I-R?'
Hesitation.
'Air,' at last.
'Very good. What about H-A-I-R?' 'Hair?'
'Excellent. And now L-A-I-R.' 'Lair,' is the more confident response.
'Now say them all together.' 'Air—Hair—Lair.'
'Air-Hair-Lair! Welcome to the regiment, my boy!'

Of course it's not really like that: they just manage to give that impression. As an officer of the Regular Commissions Board told Dennis Barker, who was invited in to write a detailed book on the Army: 'It is virtually impossible for even the most well-connected man to become an officer in the British Army today unless he also has brains and ability.'[12] It is very much the same line as the schools and other elements in the old boy network take: not that all have equal access on merit, but that privilege only works these days for a man who is also reasonably intelligent. But privilege and rank are themselves guiding principles of the British armed forces, and especially the Army; the old order of those born and educated to rule as officers, and the 'other ranks' of those born to serve, or be promoted to a level just below where the officer class starts. It is a world of male authority and machismo, both justified in military terms.

This is not the place to examine how valid this kind of British military culture is for defence itself – although many critics see it as inappropriate and extremely wasteful of public money, contrasting it with less rigid systems in other East European countries. The armed forces are strangely invisible these days from the ordinary civilian world in Britain, and especially for most women, but they remain an important element in society and especially in the men-only networks of power and influence that lie behind the Government and major public institutions.

Among Army officers about half are from private schools, mainly the ones derisively referred to as 'minor public schools' – although Eton has strong links with the élite Guards regiments. Most officers come straight from school rather than via universities. The strength of the connections, paralleled by the tradition of boys following their fathers into particular regiments, is explained by Clive Griggs partly in terms of the links set up when wealthy families actually *purchased* commissions to allow their sons to enter the Army as officers. He also points out that many private boys' schools have had compulsory officer training for all boys since 1863 (followed in 1870 by military drill practice in elementary schools to prepare the lower-class boys to fill the lower ranks – that one now discontinued). The private schools' cadet training system, often advertised as an important element in the vital task of instilling 'leadership' in the boys, introduces military concepts and loyalties in the boys – something of which many girls are unaware – while preparing some of them to go on and join the armed forces themselves. The Combined Cadet Force, which is predominantly a private school operation although a few State schools participate, is subsidised via the Ministry of Defence: in 1984 the total subsidy was £3.6 million.[13]

This system, together with the youth programme of the
Territorial Army (mainly for boys) involves considerable
numbers of boys and men in team activities, discipline,
military and technical skills, and a habit of operating in all-
male units which is completely foreign to the experience of
most girls and which serves to increase the cultural divide
between women and men in our society much as the male
character of school and commercial sport does. Indeed, a
man's involvement in the TA at weekends and holidays has
much the same effect on the family as single-minded pursuit of football or cricket does. TA members in fact are often
much keener on playing soldiers or sailors than the full-time
professionals are.[14] A recent ad for the Royal Naval Reserve
spelt out the attraction: 'After a week of taking orders, why
not give out a few?' 'Why not be a boss this weekend?' 'As
a Seaman Officer (male), you can . . . eventually command
your own Minesweeper or Patrol Craft.'

The connections between the armed forces and the
private schools work both ways, since not only do the
schools provide the officers but the officers' children are
sent (at public expense) to those same schools, reinforcing
the shared culture and expectations which already exist.
'It's not a snobbish matter to send one's children to a public
school,' one officer told Dennis Barker. 'Frankly, boarding
school, where you have to be self-reliant and do your
homework, is a better grounding for someone who wants to
be an officer in the British Army.'[15] It is no secret that the
Conservative inclinations of the private schools, their
emphasis on teaching 'leadership' and authority (both
vested in men) and their dislike of opposition to the left of
them are all echoed very strongly in the forces as well. And
the concept of women's rights is pretty alien to this way of
thinking.

There is an element, too, of extreme-right ideas at different levels. Among the lower ranks, National Front and
other fascist publications circulate (including, in Northern
Ireland, extreme Unionist papers).[16] Among the top brass
there has been talk of action against a Labour Government

that went 'too far'. The Army's peacetime role is in fact increasingly linked with strike-breaking and providing reinforcements for the police in controlling demonstrations and civil disturbances, and all ranks are well aware that it is 'the lefties' that are going to be the enemy here. Dennis Barker's inquiries about all this made it clear that such an idea is definitely not part of the official curriculum – and the idea of acting against the Government definitely not spoken about on the record – but that it is most certainly a topic of conversation while hostility to organisations seen as 'subversive' is a matter of shared conviction. One major told Barker:

If a militant picket got between us and an ambulance or some other necessary public utility and refused to get out of the way, and it was our orders to go through, then if a violent picket insisted on a rifle butt over the head, they would get it. Would my men go along with that? Are you kidding? It would be them who would be pushing me to give them the order.[17]

A Company Commander in the upper-crust Guards commented languidly: 'Could the military stage a coup in Britain? Quite impossible, my dear chap. Could you imagine the Grenadiers and The Blues and Royals combining in anything, let alone a coup?'[18] Well, the general idea (and despite the fancy trimmings, all the training is devoted to this) is that they can combine, very effectively, to fight wars. Otherwise we really *are* wasting our money. At the higher ranks they also combine a great deal: socially, in the various élite Service clubs in London's West End, and clandestinely in the brotherhood of the Freemasons to which the 'brother officers' seem to be strangely attracted.

Stephen Knight found that senior military men were particularly prevalent in the ultra-secret Higher Degrees, which are unknown to the majority of Freemasons and organised from the Supreme Council at 10 Duke Street, St James's, in the heart of VIM clubland – while the rest of the organisation is run from the United Grand Lodge. There are overtones of terror and torture, according to Knight's description of the house with its Black Room, Red Room and Chamber of Death. The armed forces, Knight tells us, are already represented strongly in ordinary Freemasonry but even more so in the higher degrees. Membership of the Supreme Council has included 'scores' of the top men from the armed forces, with particular emphasis on the Army. The Most Puissant Sovereign Grand Commander, the actual head of Freemasonry (as opposed to the nominal head, the Duke of Kent) was until 1982 Major-General Ralph Hone, a former Army man who went on to senior office in the Government with special reference to colonial and foreign affairs.[19] If it's a conspiracy theory you're after, with plans for a coup or other intervention against the will of a democratically elected Government, it's the top military men meeting in their Chamber of Death in Duke Street you'd be interested in.

A culture of humiliation

But let's get back to the observable world, and especially the way in which the Army keeps notions of rigid hierarchy going both within *and* outside its ranks. This is a constant theme running through all the writing about the Army, from Peter Tatchell on the left to Dennis Barker and Anthony Sampson who, if not of the right, certainly report from the officer's rather than the poor bloody infantry's point of view. Tatchell emphasises the Army's objective of breaking the man in order to create the soldier, quoting Brigadier-General Crozier in 1915:

The process of 'seeing red' which has to be carefully cultured if the effect is to be lasting, is elaborately grafted into the make-up of even the meek and mild. . . . The British soldier is a kindly fellow . . . it is necessary to corrode his mentality.[20]

Tatchell goes on to emphasise the humiliating and absurd Army regulations collectively known as 'bull' (yes, really)

– like the hours of polishing to make ordinary boots look like patent leather, or the deliberate issue of narrow ties that have to be stretched by several hours of work to make them the correct width. Some of this is very expensive and wasteful, like the constant repainting of barracks. The wasted hours also come pretty expensive at the rates of pay now current in the professional armed forces. Then there is the segregation of different ranks, with personal service from the lower ranks to the commissioned officers: 'The officers' mess . . . has the appearance of a well kept stately home. Inside, there is the atmosphere of an exclusive gentlemen's club with thick pile carpets, leather-bound chairs, and silver trophies and battle honours adorning the walls.' On some field excursions (though not under battle conditions) the officers' tents may come with white linen tablecloths and silverware with lower ranks serving a fine meal, while ordinary soldiers queue outside for a mess tin of stew with bread, and nowhere dry to sit down.

Beneath the veneer of control, Tatchell suggests, there is in fact extraordinary indiscipline, with racism and vicious anti-gay feeling expressed through 'unofficial' physical assault and humiliation of misfits or racial minorities, together with extremely harsh punishments for the slightest breach of regulations. While the officers in their own mess disapprove of what goes on, he says, few take any positive steps to eradicate it.[21] This is borne out by a number of recent scandals involving 'humiliating and degrading' treatment of young recruits in Colchester and West Berlin, which included stripping them, forcing them to bugger each other, and a variety of assaults. It all means an intense pressure to conform if you can – and then take out your frustrations on someone else who can't (like a woman). There is said to be a very high incidence of battering in the families of service men. Barker reports soldiers, absent for months and finding their young children unwilling to approach them, *ordering* them to show affection and getting only fear from the children and resentment from their wives. 'He fights back in the way he knows – with an attempt at dominance.'[22]

If the military style can have a strong impact on men's relationships with their own families, ordinary observation would suggest that it also affects their attitudes to women generally. Many of us would remember that men we have encountered unhappily have had some kind of military background, at school or in the forces, which gave them authoritarian language and behaviour if not convictions. The more of a 'leader' and the more boss-y the man is, the more likely that he will have passed that way.

The organisation 'At Ease', which is campaigning for reform in the services, makes out a strong case for saying that the present system of inducting recruits is criminalising hundreds of young men who have had no previous brushes with the law. Many of them sign up in their teens without realising how difficult it will be to get out; if they decide they want to leave, and discover they cannot do so for several years, many become desperate enough to go absent without leave and, faced with the certainty of a military prison, cannot then give themselves up. They live as illegal immigrants in their own country, unable to claim social security or get a regular paid job. Some live under false names, others resort to theft in order to get any money at all. The organisation is campaigning for an amnesty for those who give themselves up, and an end to long-term binding contracts signed before the age of 18.[23] They also want the bullying and brutalising that occurs in the services to be dealt with firmly, and more humane punishments and a more rational set of regulations. It could well be in the interests of all of us for service life to be made more humane: who needs more disturbed, brutalised and criminal young men in our society?

Connections

The military world is not a self-contained one. It is linked with the world of employment and public life at all levels. 'The way of life of Guards officers,' as Anthony Sampson summarises it, 'remains interlocked with horsey occasions, debutante dances and State rituals; and many heirs to big estates still remain Guards officers until they inherit.'[24] There are about 400 of these, and they are closely linked with the upper reaches of society and the monarchy; during the Suez operation and even now in Northern Ireland, their polo ponies got shipped out for them. When they move on they appear in the highest places (six in Mrs Thatcher's first Cabinet, for instance). Tim Heald gives the example of John Buchanan, who joined the Grenadier Guards during World War Two on the strength of being 'Tiny's boy'; in 1946 he was looking for a job and met a fellow Grenadier in the Guards Club who told him there was a job going at the United Nations as private secretary to the UK Permanent Representative. It was not being advertised. 'If Buchanan would like the job it was his. He did and it was.'[25]

The system works also for many of the men in the lower ranks, who have a considerable number of jobs reserved for them as commissionaires, security guards, drivers, butlers, ceremonial officers and so on, if they can get the necessary recommendation from their senior officers. Heald gives us a number of examples of this from a not particularly grand regiment, the Devon and Dorsets, which has managed to line up some plum jobs for 'their' men when they retire (much earlier than their civilian counterparts). Heald observes,

Jobs like these do not come about through 'the usual channels'. They happen because people 'have a word' with people. They happen because someone recommends someone. And if you have served with the right regiment that becomes, in the right circles, recommendation in itself.

He quotes the Colonel, Michael Bullock: 'For many men, be they officers or soldiers, once they have served in the Regiment, they are committed to a brotherhood, club, freemasonry for life and this extends throughout their lives, long after they have left the Regiment.'[26]

On a more prosaic level, the men also get – from all the

forces, but the Air Force and Navy more than the Army –
a skill for life ranging from a manual trade to high-tech
expertise. The technical training provided in the armed
forces, mostly for boys and men only, is an important element in the job segregation of women and men in society
generally, and the lack of women in engineering and
technology in particular. Technical skills are much more
marketable than the kind of skills women and girls are most
likely to be offered in the forces – shorthand and typing,
hairdressing, tailoring, cookery – and although high
unemployment has meant that not every trade can
guarantee a job, it puts you in a privileged position in relation to those with none at all. Air Force recruiting literature
places particularly heavy emphasis on the trades on offer,
each one with a final section in each trade group's leaflet on
its 'value in Civil Life'. Some of the training could be
acquired outside the Forces only at great cost: pilot training
is a case in point, where a private pilot's licence costs up-
wards of £30,000 in flying lessons whereas in the Air Force
it is free of charge and they also pay trainees handsomely
while they are learning. It is an important reason for the
male near-monopoly of the highly-paid pilots' jobs in commercial aviation.[27]

There is two-way traffic, too. The Army's Royal
Engineers, for instance, often keep their 'best men' away
from purely regimental duties and allow them to study for
civilian professional qualifications. Men are seconded to
private industry for specific contracts, obviously an excellent way for them to negotiate the 'right' job when they
leave.

Segregation

And the women? There are relatively few women in the
forces, compared to the men: women are 5 per cent, men 95
per cent. They are organised in separate units like the
Women's Royal Army Corps, Women's Royal Naval Service

and Women's Royal Air Force – although in the Air Force and parts of the Army they work alongside the men. The women have a different set of tasks and most of the trades offered to men are closed to them, especially in the Army and Navy – often for no apparent reason. In the Air Force for instance women cannot be musicians and men cannot train as 'kennel maids', among other restrictions. The forces are specifically excluded from employment legislation, the Equal Pay Act 1970 and the Sex Discrimination Act 1975. The kinds of jobs offered to the women are an extension of domestic work: nursing, catering, cleaning, driving, secretarial and administrative jobs. There are some women working as mechanics or tank instructors, or aircraft maintenance personnel, but they are a small number in relation to the total. The key role of women during World War Two in these kinds of jobs, and in flying transport aircraft, has passed into folk memory.

It is an ironic twist that the clippings files on women in the forces are littered with headlines about 'firsts': the first woman mechanic to work on the Battle of Britain Memorial Flight collection, the first woman bomb disposal expert, the first woman to have pilot training, in August 1984 (although the impact of this suffers when you read the story: it was only in a little single-engine Chipmunk, and so that she could understand the men's problems when she became the senior medical officer on a helicopter base). The stories make an unpleasant read, too, because of the tone in which they are written, one which seems to come at least partly from the attitudes of the men in the forces. On the WRNS: 'for most of them though it is very much a career – not just a marriage bureau. But that doesn't mean that Wrens are spinsterish and thick-ankled'; 'Dishy officer Maggie drills her lucky lads'; 'Snapped one bushy-eyebrowed commander [male]: "Wrens don't have traditions, only habits – most of them bad".'

Despite the ambivalent 'firsts', the structure of the armed forces ensures that women cannot become important either in basic trades which will be useful for outside employment, or as commanders. The numbers of women in the forces as a whole is restricted by law to 5 per cent, and this limit also applies to each of the separate units within the force. It particularly affects the Air Force, which is very popular with women wanting to learn a particular trade there: some wait two or three years for a 'women's quota' vacancy.[28] The ratio of applicants to jobs is much higher for women than men throughout the forces, and a woman generally has to be better qualified already, to get in. Since promotion is also linked directly to the number of people under your command, and women work mainly in segregated units, the 5 per cent Rule severely restricts women's promotion prospects beyond a certain point.

Women are not allowed to serve in any 'offensive' capacity although the distinction between defence and offence is far from clear – except in the regulations excluding women from certain jobs. This was a very big issue in the US armed forces a few years ago, since the 'combat roles' had little to do with actual fighting but provided higher rates of pay for the often more desirable jobs – so it was quite possible for a male cook, for instance, to get a 'combat' designation and higher pay than a woman working alongside him. The fight for women to take combat roles was a long and bitter one, but eventually won, and the women now take the same training and the same jobs as the men. There has been a similar trend towards integration in many of the armed forces of other NATO countries, prompted mainly by shortages of suitably qualified men as well as the pressure for greater equality.

In Britain the segregation remains very rigid, making it the only NATO country which does not give equal pay and which also discharges women if they are pregnant. Exclusion from 'offensive' exercises bars women from the top jobs, while the 5 per cent Rule restricts the number in middle ranks. Only men receive extra pay in terms of the 'X factor' for being officially in a combat role. The pay for the job is also lower if a woman manages to get a command. The first woman to command a NATO defence base earned less because the men could claim high overtime rates for flying exercises. (The pretext for excluding women from pilot training is that it is aimed initially at fighter jets, and men get 'weeded out' later for transport, reconnaissance, helicopters and so on – which otherwise women could train for.) But there has been a relaxation as regards weapons training. Since 1984 all women may be armed officially 'for defensive purposes' and there are now armed control points staffed by women: hardly non-combatants. To this cynical outsider this looks very much like putting women in the front line, while refusing to integrate them on the grounds they can't be in the front line. The distinction between the front line and the rear is, in any case, largely irrelevant to modern warfare. The new SA 80 rifle is to be issued without distinction to women and men, incidentally.

Perhaps the most absurd aspect of the situation is the simultaneous use of women for dirty jobs *and* the heavy-handed insistence on their 'femininity'. In the Army Air Corps, for instance, the men have the glamour of flying the helicopters while the women pull them in and out of hangars, refuel and clean them – so the men don't have to get their hands dirty.[29] But at the same time the women wear impractical skirts, sheer tights and court shoes (leading to headlines like 'Down to the sea in skirts'). At Sandhurst a few women have been admitted for parts of the training and the passing out parade – but 'only part of it, for the width of their skirts limits the size of their stride and prevents them keeping pace with the men's brisk marching'.[30] Who decides on the ludicrous rule that physically hobbles these women? It is the top (men-only) brass.

The insistence on women in the forces being 'feminine' or 'surprisingly un-military' is extraordinary. Elaborate courtesy rules are observed: at officer level, men open doors for the women. At the Air Force academy at Camberley, female cadets get taught subjects like flower-arranging (I kid you not). As one Army recruiting leaflet puts it, the job for women is: 'paper work, people, technical problems and adding the feminine touch!' (their exclamation mark, not mine). It's the feminine touch OR ELSE.

If playing the 'statutory feminine' in a military context, where the culture and values for the men are very much on the macho side, is a bit strange for a society where women are rejecting stereotypes and seeking to define themselves . . . then just think of the crude stereotyping of 'the wives' married to men in the forces. Perhaps most restricting of all is the difficulty of getting a reasonable job, since you are whisked around the world or else left on your own for months with children or other dependants. In areas around the major camps, too, there is strong prejudice against employing married women living inside or known to be married to a man in the forces, because of the military discipline which can be imposed directly on *her*.

It all helps to reinforce a now outmoded set of military assumptions about women's essentially 'domestic' or 'family' role which coexists very easily with a derogatory view of women as objects for sex. Dennis Barker reported from one Army outpost in Northern Ireland: 'Their accommodation block was covered in do-it-yourself shelves, old steel locker cabinets and new pin-ups – a decor consisting almost entirely of sheet metal and pubic hairs.'[31] Pornography is staple reading and viewing matter – as reports of the violent hard-core videos shown on ships bound for the Falklands battles made clear. It is a closed, men-only culture hardly touched by the presence of a few women in some units. One reporter observed: 'In groups, servicemen are conventionally disparaging about the women who now work alongside or even command them.'[32] And some of the officers' messes, notably in some of the Guards regiments, are still rigidly men-only.

To be married to this system is to be an appendage without needs or aspirations of your own beyond the marriage, something which is constantly dinned into you when you go for medical treatment or other services and are asked automatically for your husband's name and rank. The petty humiliations and segregation of the hierarchical system are much more rigid for the women than their husbands – who work closely with men of higher or lower rank as a matter of routine, especially on exercises away from the base.[33] There is legal discrimination, particularly in social security benefits, against 'service wives'. No wonder that women in the forces who marry male colleagues, and decide to resign and be 'a wife', find the reduction in their status and autonomy a shattering experience. As one of them put it:

'It was awful. From being known by my own rank, in my own right, I became simply the "wife of". The other men's wives had never been out to work. Suddenly I was being treated as a second-class citizen – I couldn't stand having to ask my husband for money.'[34]

If the armed forces' attitudes and treatment of women strike you as anachronistic and undermining, you may feel cheered by one little anecdote recounted by Dennis Barker about the Guards who supposedly guard Buckingham Palace – but from *inside* the railings. The reason, it seems, is that the sentries used to stand outside to provide pretty pictures for the tourists and look as if they were guarding something until the 1950s when a (female) tourist started touching up one of the Guards who was standing rigidly to attention. It almost seems worth it, despite the fact that on the third occasion the Guard broke regulations and hit her – but then retreated with his mates inside the railings, complete with two-way radios in case of further incursions.[35] The rigidities of military men's treatment of women, the anti-women culture of barrack room and officers' mess alike, and the statutory discrimination which backs up the whole system do indeed look like a legitimate target: let them retreat behind the railings!

Crook and gun

Anachronistic they may often seem, but the Church of England and the armed forces as sanctifiers and defenders of the established order in Britain are far more powerful than we usually think. Both have rigid hierarchies, with the key positions reserved for men only. Both have strong connections at the top levels with the other men-only elements in our Establishment such as the private schools for boys, élite colleges of their own, the VIM clubs and the Freemasons. Both are specifically exempted from sex discrimination legislation in their employment practices as well as in their 'private' world of clubs and officers' mess.

Women are in practice vitally important to both the Church of England and the armed forces – in the latter case they are likely to become increasingly so as the number of men available declines, and skill becomes increasingly important. Cynthia Enloe, in a survey of women and the military generally, stresses military dependence on women through the ages – and the denial of the dependence as well as the inevitable presence of women at the front line (especially as nurses) although the 'front line' is tortuously defined as the place with no women. She argues that there is a 'mutuality of interest between men and the military' in defining masculinity as 'not female' and combat as its justification, which women ought to oppose strenuously, resisting military efforts to enlist women to suit its alien needs. While the armed forces may seem 'simplistically hierarchical', she points out, 'in reality most military institutions are like that of Victorian Britain in so far as male bonding cuts through and often contradicts the more formal concepts of the chain of command.'[36]

All of this, it seems to me, is borne out by the information I have surveyed for this chapter (and is largely true, incidentally, for the Church as well). But the fact remains that many women do want to join the armed forces – particularly technical trades in the Air Force – and are prevented from doing so; the women already in the forces are looking for an equal chance within the existing structure, while the unfortunate 'wives', trapped in their husbands' rank only more so, are desperate too for improvements within the system as it stands. If we want to abolish discrimination against women in society generally, we are obliged to tackle that which exists so powerfully in the forces, it seems to me, as well as in the official Church. These are not segregated institutions (although they segregate women, in a way which is often gratuitously humiliating) – they are central to the employment structure and Establishment networks of this country, and while many of us may oppose the very existence of one or perhaps both, we cannot ignore their continuing and pervasive influence throughout Britain, via the men-only networks with which they are so powerfully connected.

9
INSIDER DEALING
Finance and the City

'There's Freemasonry in the City,' one informant told researchers for this book,

'But it's only among the top men. They don't like anyone in who's not very senior and very well-informed. If you've been in the City for a long time and you're on your way up in a financial institution or a broker's, you're useful: senior partners or directors get approached, nobody lower than that. Information is passed around, inside information. The traders and investors can meet the men in the institutions, who also sit on company boards of directors, or in some cases they chair the Board. It's quite incestuous. It opens a whole new world of contacts, so the brokers and senior banking people get inside information on what's happening in the companies that will affect their value. A financial analyst can often go to his boss and say some company's shares are looking too expensive for the return, so they ought to sell. The boss says no. Then you realize that he went to the Lodge last night and already knows about the takeover bid that you hear about the next day when the share value rockets.'

There has been great anxiety recently, in Britain as well as the US, about insider trading – buying and selling shares for personal gain on the basis of information which is not available to other investors. A few privileged people make very large profits at the expense of everybody else. This is nothing new – indeed malpractice, fraud, and what is euphemistically called 'over-enthusiasm' among speculators has been the major problem for the financial system in Britain since its origins in the City of London coffee-houses of the eighteenth century. For many years, in fact, many of those involved could see nothing wrong in it; it was what made the financial world go round. But the City itself, in the form of the Takeover Panel and the Stock Exchange, has long been officially hostile to insider trading and after many attempts to get legislation making it a criminal offence, this was finally achieved in 1980.

Since that time, though, little seems to have changed. A parliamentary question from the Labour Party's Robin Cook in November 1986 revealed that the Department of Trade and Industry had no clear idea even of the number of insider deals reported to it since 1980 but thought it was 'about 100', of which only nine, mainly trivial cases, were prosecuted. Meanwhile, a study of share prices in the first half of 1986 by *Acquisitions Monthly* concluded that in seventy-eight takeover bids the share price of the targeted company rose on average by a quarter in the three months before the bid was announced – a clear indication of early buying by insiders tipped off early about the impending deals, which would raise the price even further once they became known.[1] The spate of mergers and takeover bids have enormously increased the importance and the impact of the old practice of insider trading, both before and since the 'Big Bang' in the City in 1986 when dealing was computerised and many traditional restrictions lifted.

The nature of dishonesty goes beyond insider trading in the securities market. There have been successive disasters, affecting in some cases several million people in financial losses: they include unsafe insurance, a string of failures in 'fringe' banks and later the Johnson Matthey Bank (rescued at enormous public expense by the Bank of England) and the collapse of large insurance syndicates at Lloyds. Several of these incidents, and those of direct deception and fraud, meant several leading figures having to leave the country rather abruptly when the losses became evident. There has been legislation after each successive disaster, akin to locking the stable door after the golden horse has bolted. But the unofficial meeting-places where these kinds of deals are done – the masonic Lodges, the livery companies and the clubs – carry on quite happily with no hint that perhaps their involvement should be investigated along with the criminal or marginal activities of the leading individuals in each case.

For this chapter we were able to draw on a considerable amount of documentation, in book form as well as reporting in the financial press. For the insider view on what it all means, of course, we went to some key insiders who agreed to speak only on condition of strict confidentiality.

City masonry

Let us start, then, with the Freemasons since we have already been formally introduced by our informants. The masons operate on a far higher and more exclusive level in the City than elsewhere. Next time you see the Lord Mayor's procession, for example, remember that it is effectively arranged – as is the choice of Lord Mayor – by the brotherhood.

Stephen Knight managed to get a fascinating account of the Guildhall Lodge in operation. Since its inception in 1905 at the Guildhall – the official residence of the Lord Mayor of London and seat of the City's governing body, the Corporation of London – the Lodge has included members and officers of the Corporation together with very senior men in finance, public companies, insurance, the London Metal Exchange, the City police, law, City planning and international trade, as well as having sixty-two different Lord Mayors as its Grand Master.

The new Worshipful Master, Brother Richard Coward

(already a senior mason) duly took the 'sign of fidelity' and various oaths, and learned the secret sign of the Installed Master, the secret grip, secret word and an elaborate Sign of Salutation. Coward was being made Worshipful Master in the place of one of the few Lord Mayors who was not a mason, Christopher Leaver. Following this elaborate ritual, Coward then invested the officers of the Lodge for that year – men who between them were running practically all aspect of the Corporation, which is the local government body running the City of London's square mile.[2]

Stephen Knight's researches in the City led him to the conclusion that not only were the Mayor and Corporation strongly masonic (with a few exceptions) but the senior officers of the Corporation, who run it on a daily basis (and among other things work on planning applications which can be worth hundreds of millions for property developers) were virtually all masons:

Indeed, it is virtually impossible to reach a high position in Guildhall without being an active Brother, as three senior officers currently serving and two past officers have informed me. The subject of Masonry is spoken about openly in interviews for high posts.

He himself found that a masonic handshake suddenly reversed the previously hostile attitude of the Guildhall's doorkeeper who suddenly started to treat him, literally, as a brother.[3] So much for the ideal of public service.

Citing confidential statistics from masonic headquarters in Queen Street, Knight tells us that of the 1,677 masonic Lodges in London, hundreds were in the City – for the top men among the 345,000 people working there each day (only about 4,000 people actually live in its area). There are masons in important positions at the Royal Exchange, Corn Exchange, Baltic Exchange, Metal Exchange, the Bank of England, merchant banks, insurance companies, mercantile houses, the Old Bailey and the Inns of Court as well as Guildhall. Some institutions even have their own Lodges:

they include the Baltic Exchange, the Bank of England and the insurance market of Lloyds.[4]

The mumbo-jumbo of Freemasonry fits the character and culture of the City of London very neatly. Although one of the most important financial and business centres in the world, the City uses an enormous amount of medieval custom and tradition – or a tarted-up version of it, anyway – similar to the old customs and traditions of medieval stonemasons appropriated by latter-days 'masonic' gentry. Bank of England messengers wear fancy dress of pink waistcoats and top hats: the Worshipful Company of Butchers presents the Lord Mayor with a boar's head once a year; and the City Solicitor pays Quit Rents to the Queen's Remembrancer of a hatchet, a bill hook, six horses and sixty-one nails every October. The fact that these little events have completely lost their meaning and their original fourteenth-century context does not seem to bother the men who solemnly take part (scrapping the original medieval tradition that women participated too). The old Lord Mayor's procession carries on, but as a tourist attraction, with company and cigarette sponsorship prominent among the coaches and horses. And of course five self-appointed 'wise men' set the world price of gold at Rothschild & Sons every morning. The Rothschilds have, so Knight claims, been Freemasons for generations.[5] They made their original pile by cornering the market on key stocks and shares after hearing of the victory at Waterloo a day ahead of everybody else.

It would be a mistake, though, to see any one network as the single key to insider relationships in the financial world of the City. A masonic City Alderman told Stephen Knight:

There are so many competing bodies, especially in the City. What with Livery Companies, Rotary, Chamber of Commerce, Ward clubs, there are so *many* competing clubs. I would have thought that most people in the City attach much more importance to their Livery than they do to their Freemasonry – although of course the majority of Livery Club members are Freemasons as well.

Knight discovered also that a number of Livery Companies have their own freemasons' Lodges, while the City Livery Club has its own masonic temple. The Lord Mayor of London is selected each year from the City's twenty-six aldermen, who are nominated by the 15,000 Livery men. Almost all of these, Knight asserts, are also Freemasons. To join one of the Livery Companies, a man must be a Freeman of the City – an honour 'generally awarded by Freemasons to Freemasons, although there are many notable exceptions.'[6]

Livery Companies

So what are these Livery Companies, and why would the Freemasons see them as so important that they have effectively taken them over – evicting the women along the way? To explain their present position we have to look far back into history, while bearing in mind that their present-day character, and the context in which they operate, is very different from the centuries-old 'traditions' which they claim to be theirs.

Guilds and companies of self-employed craft workers are well known as having operated throughout Europe during the eleventh and twelfth centuries as the regulatory body for each craft – and a combination of welfare society, apprenticeship organiser and trade union, as well. They started as family groups but developed into larger, though fairly localised organisations including some very powerful ones in the City of London which also controlled their own trade in a wider area around London. Becoming part of the administrative structure of the old city by providing officers for the watch and also by raising forces to defend the city from attack, the trading guilds were granted royal Charters (the earliest in London being claimed by the Weavers Company dating back to 1155) and incorporated into the governing structure of the City of London. There was also a strong religious emphasis in many of the guilds, which had their patron saints, religious processions, mystery plays (from ministerium – a craft or guild) and of course their schools and other charitable activities – both for members and their own families, and for the poor of their city.

The religious mottoes and patrons were dropped when the religious tide changed: the Coopers, for instance, went from 'Laude Maria Virgo' to 'Love as Brothers'. The funds that had been bequeathed for singing masses for merchant souls were quietly transferred to general-purpose charitable trusts. The big funerals provided for prominent members evolved into elaborate 'feasts' which are now their principal activity as far as many latter-day members are concerned. The guilds also provided halls which acted as meeting places, and with their funds mounting from charitable bequests and especially donations of City land over the centuries, these halls came to be decked out with considerable splendour. Many were destroyed in the Great Fire of 1666, and others in the bombing of London in the Second World War, but a number still remain to give City men delusions of personal grandeur based on almost a thousand years of other people's craft organisation and legacies.

There are estimated to be eighty-three guilds or Livery Companies currently active in the City of London, with a dozen particularly prominent ones. In order of precedence, they are the Mercers', Grocers', Drapers', Fishmongers', Goldsmiths', Merchant Taylors', Skinners', Haberdashers', Salters', Ironmongers', Vintners' and Clothworkers'. (The sixth and seventh, Merchant Taylors' and Skinners', had a huge medieval row about precedence and so alternate in that sixth position – hence 'at sixes and sevens'.) While some guilds have completely disappeared, new ones are still being formed for particular groups, including the Scientific Instrument Makers', the Air Pilots' and Navigators', Master Mariners', Furniture Makers', Tobacco Pipe Makers' and Tobacco Blenders', Farmers' and Solicitors'. A few, like the Fletchers' (arrow-makers) are being revamped, this one with the pretext of a link with guided missiles. The Horners' are now claiming links with plastics rather than horn, and have strong links with the men in the British Plastics Federation. Another recent creation is the Company of Information Technologists which includes the top men in the IT business (and two women) to promote their new trade in the

City and finance research to benefit their own corporate interests.

The City of London Livery Companies, old and new, are grafted onto one of those relics of the past which have been long gone elsewhere – the other European guilds were abolished during or soon after the time of the French Revolution. A few of the new-old London ones do in fact retain some link with the original trade for which they were formed. The City and Guilds of London Institute, whose technical and craft certificates are recognised as the major qualification in many fields, derives from the guilds and retains its links with them although it is effectively an independent examining body for something like 150,000 candidates a year. Inspectors employed by the Fishmongers' Guild still impose fines for bad fish at Billingsgate. The Gun Makers' Company owns the London Proof House, where thousands of hand-guns are examined and stamped. The Apothecaries' and Spectacle Makers' Companies offer officially recognised qualifications. The Goldsmith's Company is one of three official assay offices for gold and silver, and this enormously rich company also commissions jewellery from young craftsmen for gifts, like the crown they donated to that well-known charity, Prince Charles. It also donates official 'plate' to new universities, and buys both antique and modern jewellery and plate for its own collection valued at around £8 million (which is sometimes loaned for exhibitions, mainly abroad).

Generally speaking, though, the City's Livery Companies have lost their craft links and functions altogether: the self-styled 'Fishmongers' have never gutted a fish and the 'Skinners' never skinned anything in their lives. These are now basically very grand dining clubs for men whose only trade is in money – with a charitable function attached, often simply a matter of observing the charity laws in disposing of the accumulated fortunes of the old (real) craft members.[7]

Astonishingly, the Livery Companies do not have to declare their assets or submit public accounts – yet they are among the biggest 'charities' in Britain. We know of one trust, run by the 'Great Twelve' listed above, which deals with an annual income of £600,000 and which does have to be accounted for to the Charity Commissioners. But the funds of individual guilds are a closely guarded secret. The Worshipful Company of Goldsmiths spend about £250,000 a year – although its declared trust income is only £88,000. The company owns a large part of the huge Barbican complex in the City, worth many millions of pounds. The Drapers' Company declares a trust income of £200,000 but its total real income is reputed to be £1 million (which makes this one, on its own, comparable in size to the Nuffield Foundation whose annual income is £1.5 million). The Drapers' Company owns part of Throgmorton Avenue, in the heart of the City, including the new NatWest Tower.[8] The Mercers' Company probably dwarfs even these: it owns large areas of prime land in the City and Westminster, including the Royal Exchange and the Covent Garden area – where it has proceeded with wholesale redevelopment against a strong campaign from the people living and working there, resulting in a very profitable tourist centre but one where few of the original inhabitants can afford to remain.[9] The Mercers' Company administers enormous charitable funds, the legacy of wealthy silk and luxury-cloth merchants intended for the relief of the poor people in London.

Are these enormous charitable funds in fact being squandered? It is now pointless, in a welfare state, to give out pensions and grants which are simply deducted from people's benefits if they are genuinely poor. There seems to be little or no consultation with others in the charity 'business' at home or abroad who are developing new strategies for intervention to meet new needs or to develop new approaches to old problems, which is one of the most important functions of genuine charities today. The Livery Companies are extremely unlikely to support refuges for battered women, campaigns to improve the take-up of benefits to which poor people are entitled, or research into the nature of poverty in our society as distinct from that of medieval times. There is an important school of thought, for instance, that poverty these days means exclusion from society and social life, where previously it meant not having basic needs like food and clothing.[10] The companies' charitable funds are run by money-men and company directors with little idea about real social need or current ideas in the field of poverty which they are – in theory – attempting to alleviate with the vast funds at their disposal.

Charitable giving in the City today is based very much on the who-you-know principle, experienced fund-raisers have told us, with the first point of reference being the names on the charity notepaper: are they 'one of us'? Far from giving to the poor, the Livery Companies are far more likely to giving scholarships to men or boys who are not in any real need, offering prestige gifts like flowers for a royal wedding or a crown to Prince Charles, or handing over large sums to élite male institutions dealt with elsewhere in this book, particularly the Oxbridge colleges and private schools for boys.

Links between the Livery Companies and certain private schools are indeed very close. The Grocers are sponsors of Oundle boys' school. The Mercers support St Paul's and Mercers', the Skinners back Tonbridge and the Merchant Taylors support – guess who – Merchant Taylors' School. The Haberdashers have Haberdashers' Aske's School, whose new buildings at Elstree cost an estimated £500,000. There are about thirty private schools which are endowed and actively supported by the Livery Companies with money that was given for poor students who would not otherwise receive any education at all.[11]

The élite men's historian Anthony Lejeune cites one John Colet as justifying the handing over of St Paul's School for poor boys to the Mercers' Company, an organisation of traders organised for mutual support and security: 'For my part, I find less corruption in such a body of citizens than in any order or degree of mankind.' The Mercers' Company today, though, has no trading connections whatever. Its members include the likes of Prince Philip, the Duke of

Kent, Robin McAlpine, the Governor of the Bank of England
and various wealthy and well-connected company Chairmen. It is quite simply a different organisation, for different purposes, and with a completely different group of
members. And as far as the charitable activities are concerned, it would be far more in the spirit of the bequests to
get all the people of London not just the few left living in the
old City – or even the country as a whole – to nominate
representatives (perhaps through existing channels of
national or local government) to administer funds set up by
wealthy people in the City of London (which then meant
the whole of London) for the people generally, especially the
poor and those who needed emergency aid. More innovative
and specialised charities should be advising on the best use
of the funds, and indeed the Goldsmiths and Mercers would
these days be giving money to support innovative organisations such as the Child Poverty Action Group or rape crisis
centres. Opening up the guild activities to public scrutiny
would also be much closer to the original form of guild
organisation, and a polar opposite to the élite men's Livery
Companies as they operate at the moment. Bringing women
in would also be truer to the original workings of the guilds,
which relied on the work and the participation of the whole
community – the Sisteren just as much as the Bretheren.

The old guilds did not distinguish between women and
men in terms of membership. In many cases the names of
women appear on the records as founder members, and practically all the guilds in the Middle Ages had women as
members on an equal footing with men. They were active,
working members who shared in the privileges as well as
the obligations, and of course contributed to the funds both
during their lifetimes and in the form of bequests at their
deaths. The historian Georgina Hill, writing at the end of
the nineteenth century, found that in the Drapers' Company the female members carried on business, with some of
them taking apprentices, in the same way as the men.

An ordinance of 1503 instructed: 'Every brother or sister
of the fellowship taking an apprentice shall present him to

the wardens and shall pay 13s 4d.' Girls could also of course be apprentices, as well as boys. And when a 'sister' died she was to be interred with full honours, have the best pall on her coffin, and be 'followed by the Fraternity to the grave with every respectful ceremony equally with the men'.

The Clothworkers, Fishmongers, Grocers, Brewers and many other companies spoke in their original articles of brothers *and* sisters, and there were specific references to equality: the 1419 Liber Albus, for instance, contained one ordinance against discrimination for married women: 'Such women shall be bound as a single woman to all that concerns her said craft . . . and if she is condemned she shall be committed to prison until she shall have made satisfaction . . .' Women also had separate craft organisations of their own trades. The 'Silkwomen' for example petitioned Edward IV 'praying protection against the competition through information of foreign manufactured silk goods'.

The last date at which a female apprentice was recorded with the Mercers' Company was 1779. A similar pattern applied to the other guilds also. Since that time they have become almost entirely a men's organisation, with a few exceptions which seem to prove that general rule. The Queen is a member of the Drapers' Company and the Queen Mother is a Freeman of the Shipwrights'. They are the only two women to have received the honorary Freedom of the City this century. There are a few women 'Freemen', but the Guild of Freemen of the City of London is strictly men-only. A few women belong to the companies, but hardly any as full Liverymen (voting members). Again, the exceptions seem to prove the rule: for example there are two women Liverymen of the Stationers' and Newspaper Makers' Company, but only because they had been members of the Newspaper Makers' before it was amalgamated with the Stationers' Company in 1933: no other women have joined since then. Where women do manage to enter, it may be under ancient rules that have not yet been formally repealed: one woman successfully gained access to the Goldsmiths' Company on the basis of her father's membership, under old rules, but this has not established any precedent for others to follow. Men employed by that company get the Freedom after ten years, women do not. In some companies the original equality has been corrupted into a system of associate membership for women along men's club 'lady associate' lines – as Freewomen or Freesisters *without* a vote.[12]

Only Liverymen can vote these days in elections for the Corporation of the City of London, although in the old days every member could do so. 'Taking up livery', which used to mean wearing the uniform of the guilds as of right on entry, now means being given the formal power to vote which not every member is allowed to have. Perhaps this does not matter so much with City elections something of a farce anyway – the medieval system was far *more* democratic, with real contests. Voting for the one nominee for Lord Mayor is now, according to one of the privileged electorate, 'like voting for Nkrumah': the real choice is made in some caucus meeting, possibly in the Lodges attached to the Livery Companies or to the Corporation itself.

The companies themselves seem to be run on a similar in-group basis: Anthony Lejeune describes them as being administered by Courts of Assistants composed of perhaps sixteen to twenty senior Liverymen (mostly Past Masters); on the fairly rare occasions when the whole Livery is convened it acts as a rubber-stamp to these decisions taken behind the scenes. A member of the Mercers', for instance, told him that only a handful of Liverymen attended, and only once could he remember a suggestion being opposed – 'but there's sherry, and you meet friends, and it's rather jolly'.[13]

Good clean fun and meeting useful friends seems to figure quite large in the companies' grand dinners, usually twice a year, supplemented by sherry parties, a ladies' night (for wives, not women who are members in their own right) and perhaps even a dance. The name of the game is prestige, wealth and status: a magnificent hall shimmering with gold and silver in the candlelight, and sometimes the television cameras too when a top politician is giving the after-dinner speech. And of course there's the romance and the fantasy, dressing up in voluptuous fabrics in gorgeous colours, trimmed with fur and medallions: the authorised élite man's equivalent to reading *Vogue* and buying your clothes at Harrods, perhaps, but with the added excitement of meeting other men who will be *extremely* good for business. You pass the Loving Cup round – the man who pledges with the cup standing up and bowing to the man next to him who, also standing, removes the cover with his right hand. Meanwhile the man on the other side stands to guard his back in case anyone is about to stick a knife in it. This charade is supposed to originate with the occasion when King Edward the Martyr was stabbed in the back while drinking from a cup of wine, so you can fantasise about your supposed medieval forefathers while you are about it.

Expensive, select and perhaps very useful – with about a quarter of the members working in the financial institutions of the City itself, the others useful business contacts from outside – the Livery Companies are not short of eager male recruits wanting to dress up as fletchers, cordwainers, mercers, upholders, tallow chandlers, poulters, paviors, makers of playing cards, loriners, girdlers, gold and silver wyre drawers or fanmakers. In some of the richest and grandest it is practically impossible for any 'outsider' to get in; heaven forbid that a real-life draper, for instance, would be admitted to the Drapers' Guild. If he was lucky, and quite well-off, he could pay an entrance fee – which could reach over £700 – to get in 'by Redemption' to a company a little lower down the social scale. The average candidate for redemption (as opposed to the younger men who already have family links with a company that allows them in 'by Patrimony') is, as one of the Clerks told Anthony Lejeune: 'an architect or a stockbroker, aged about 45, who's done well in his career and now wants an outside interest, something different with a bit of colour'. And if the man he's sharing the Loving Cup with has a hot tip about a pending takeover up his fur-lined sleeve, so much the better. As Lejeune tells us (and he should know): 'The Companies are a substantial buttress of what its enemies would call the "City Establishment" or the Old Boy Network: in other words, they perform an important, and very desirable, cohesive role.'[14]

Old boys

Compared to all this, perhaps, the use made by City gents of the Very Important Men's clubs might seem unexciting. But they too offer a solid social base, overlapping with the others, from which to develop networks of helpful contacts. Some of our own informants were particularly aware of the advantages to them as City men of certain clubs. One, a member of the Stock Exchange, told us about the East India club where he could meet other City and finance people 'who could potentially be useful'. Another, who belonged to the City of London club, explained: 'If you know a member in another firm and you have a problem, then you can have a private word with him.' However, he pointed out, City financial institutions like the Stock Exchange and Lloyds *also* functioned as clubs, with a 'social' side to their activities: members of these got to know each other very well through his combination of activities. You trade together, then you drink together (and vice versa).

Another, younger man saw his club as being part of the 'conveyor-belt' of the whole closed world of public school, Oxbridge and the City job.

'There is certainly a big conveyor-belt effect: at my club at least half of the members are public school/ Oxbridge/City. In my job all you have to do is be a wheeler-dealer, the fact that I went to Oxford makes no difference. It's no good employing people just because they went to your school if they can't wheel and deal, is it? You have to be fast and on the ball. *I'm* not particularly fast or on the ball, I was just lucky. The old boy network doesn't do any harm, I don't think.'

(But then, adapting Mandy Rice-Davis, he wouldn't would he?)

There is a great deal of double-think about the whole question of whether a public school or Oxbridge background, the whole old boy network in fact, gets you a job in a financial institution which you would not otherwise be considered for. One of the men we talked to admitted that, especially in the merchant banks and medium-sized brokers, 'there's a lot of the old school boy network, and people employed because they know people. A lot of the bigger brokers and especially the big companies just employ people mainly on talent – *especially* if they've been to Oxbridge . . .' It meant that people from 'the wrong background' were now acceptable – but only if they'd been through Oxbridge on the way!

There were, he told us, quite a lot of women who have come into positions in the City recently, on their merits, because of what he called 'the ethic thing that nowadays women and men are equal' although the importance of Oxbridge and personal connections was, if anything, even greater for the women than the men – which seems to suggest that merit is very far from being the only consideration. And many women, when they arrive in the City, take some time before it dawns on them that the most brilliant financial analysis and the finest judgements about the markets count for little when it comes to a hotly contested promotion or a crucial deal. Men familiar with the City have cited to us cases where women were working hard for something in blissful ignorance that it had already been decided ahead of time in a Lodge or club where they were simply *persona non grata*, and being laughed at behind their backs. For this group of men – who are very often dealing not in their own money but ours from insurance premiums, pensions funds and bank accounts as well as unit trusts – there is precious little accountability. It is in the interest of women in the City *and* the general public that it should all be opened up.

Studies of the financial and business institutions in Britain, and the City of London in particular, show what a closed world it actually is. Richard Whitley, in a study published in 1974, compared the backgrounds of directors of large companies in different sectors, including banking and insurance, over a number of decades. He found that on all counts – attendance at private school; the concentration in the 'Clarendon' schools and especially Eton and Harrow; attendance at Oxbridge; and family connections with other individuals in the same roles, including members of the aristocracy – the levels were very high for all the directors, varying according to which sector they were in. But they were exceptionally high in the world of finance – the Bank of England, High Street clearing banks, merchant banks and insurance companies – which is almost completely closed off at high level. So, for instance, 66 per cent of all industrial directors had been to fee-paying schools, but 80 per cent of those in financial companies. About two-thirds of the industrial directors who had been in higher education had been to Oxford or Cambridge, but 87 per cent of the financial directors. Élite VIM club membership was also looked at: almost twice as many financial directors as industrial ones belonged to a restricted list of these clubs. The most popular on this list were Brooks's, with forty-one financial directors, and White's with thirty-two, followed by the Carlton, Pratt's and the Turf club. However, many important clubs including the City of London were unfortunately not considered. Needless to say, perhaps, they were all men. The very occasional woman on a board of directors is not part of this series of interconnections.

Another important factor identified by Whitley was the degree of overlapping directorships of the big companies – in other words, one person being a director of several companies. No less than 93 per cent of the City firms were connected to each other by overlapping directorships, almost twice the integration score for all companies, and these in turn were connected to the other companies by a mass of overlapping directorships. Merchant bankers Hill Samuel (now taken over) and the Midland Bank were the most highly 'connected' institutions of all. Many of the connections are recent, and 'reflect a growth in influence on the part of the financial institutions' according to Whitley.

So the influence and importance of the financial sector, with its rigid male hierarchies and exclusive character at the top, is growing in the British economy. The only exception to this is the separate network of family or 'tycoon' firms like Marks & Spencer, Unilever, and Lucas.

Looking at personal relationships, based on common great-grandparents, he found that the links for industrial company directors were 'very low'; for family firms obviously very strong; and for financial institutions even more entrenched than that. Twenty-six of the twenty-seven financial firms were connected in this way, and the men concerned were frequently mentioned in *Burke's Peerage* and *Burke's Landed Gentry*. Putting all these sectors together, moreover, showed that

although Boards of the very large industrial companies are not nearly so integrated with the traditional upper status groups as are those of the large financial institutions, a considerable degree of connection between many large companies and financial firms does exist through the aristocracy. This may well have increased over the last 30 or so years as the management of large sums of money has become of increasing concern to the very large firm . . .

Whitley concludes that the very large industrial firms, and especially the financial ones, were recruiting their directors from a narrow segment of the population (he fails to note, incidentally, that they are all men).

These directors undergo a remarkably similar educational experience and, to some extent, have similar social circles as evidenced by club membership and kinship links. They tend, in other words, to be members of the same culture, or at any rate to have the background for sharing a common culture.[15]

It is an observation that applies generally to the élite 'men only' organisations discussed in this book.

A study of company chairmen carried out by Philip Stanworth and Anthony Giddens came to very similar conclusions to Whitley's. Two additional points made by these two are that among the Chairs (Chairmen) of major banks the exclusive character of their background has become even more extreme over time, not less. 80 per cent of each generation of leading bankers had been to private schools, but the share of élite Clarendon schools had increased from 38 per cent for those born between 1840 and 1859 to 71 per cent for those born 1900–1919. Eton in particular was predominant rising from 6 per cent to 47 per cent in that time. A similar pattern was observed for Oxbridge attendance, which rose from 44 per cent to 71 per cent of bankers in the period covered. In the merchant banks the pattern was more one of reaching a high peak and then falling off, but the authors found family connections to be extremely important here, with 47 per cent of the merchant bank Chairmen having begun their careers in firms directly controlled by their own family, or where they were important shareholders. In this sector, 'we were unable to locate one case of an individual emanating from a background outside the upper class'. There were a few high-street banking Chairmen from the middle class, but 98 per cent from the upper class.[16] It is indeed a small world, not to say an incestuous and of course a men-only world. Connections, not ability, have been the key.

What does this splendid isolation mean, in the way the clearing banks and merchant banks operate? It seems to be an important clue, in fact, to their decision-making. John Maynard Keynes observed: 'It is necessarily part of the business of a banker to profess a conventional respectability which is more than human. Life-long practices of this kind make them the most romantic and the least realistic of men.'[17] The *Financial Times*, effectively the bankers' club paper, commented that

something is seriously wrong with Britain's retail banking system. . . . It is class-based, diverse and sleepy. It is dominated by a handful of clearing banks whose profitability is the envy of commercial banks all over the world, yet its UK management is wholly in-bred and often less than sparkling.[18]

The whole of the City, Anthony Sampson suggests, has always been cut off from British life as a whole, and the British economy in particular (while using 'traditional' male channels of recruitment and operation). 'The Square Mile of the City', in his view, 'has become like an offshore island in the heart of the nation.' He sees this separation as extending deep into history, from the mercantile institutions such as the Bank of England, Lloyds insurance market and the older merchant banks which depended on international trade and the ships that docked in the Thames. In the industrial revolution, 'most City bankers remained aloof from industry and made new fortunes from buying and selling commodities, gold or minerals from the empire and beyond'. After the Second World War, when the Labour Government was nationalising important industries, 'City families were reclaiming their tribal territory with bowler hats and umbrellas' and the Government had to grant tax concessions to Lloyds and others to stop them leaving Britain altogether. All the British banks, including the regional ones, became increasingly centralised in the City of London.[19] In the late 1950s the London bankers found enormous new profits from the dealing in Eurodollars, with a minimum of regulation, and banks all over the world rushed to set up branches in the City of London to join in the deals – culminating in the so-called 'Big Bang' of computerisation and deregulation, when many of the smaller London brokers were bought out by American-based multinationals.

The bankers' romanticism perceived by Keynes showed itself in a rush to invest in unsound projects in the 1960s and 1970s – like 'fringe' banks, the property boom or ventures like Freddie Laker's airline (under-capitalised but taking on vast debts which the banks were clamouring to bestow on him). It was one of the fashionable new businesses and 'bankers move naturally in herds', Sampson suggests. What they do not do is analyse the industrial base or understand the needs of the companies in whose shares they are dealing at such break-neck pace. The 1980s mania for company mergers and takeovers, which did so much to keep a rising, even booming stock market (with plentiful opportunities for insider cashing-in) took place against a background of industrial decline and acute shortages of productive investment in the businesses concerned, leading to an industrial wasteland in many parts of Britain. Small firms in particular found themselves unable to get enough to realise their potential or carry out crucial research.

The boom, of course, ended with the crash of 1987 which involved financial markets world-wide but was a particular disaster in London. Following the 'Big Bang' hordes of yuppie whiz-kids, many with distinctly non-Establishment backgrounds and including even some women, had seemed to take over the City – although the much-publicised takeover was more apparent than real and the power remained very much in the same sets of hands or sold out to multinationals. As the newcomers moved into the dealing rooms with their 'golden hellos' the rest of the City remained fundamentally the same: the banks, Lloyds, the metal and other exchanges, pension funds and insurance companies. Following the crash, many of the newcomers were out as fast as they had come in. As one City woman observed wryly, 'It's much quieter round here these days.' The newcomers were back on the street, joining their counterparts throughout Britain who had already been made redundant from so much of British industry.

As Sampson puts it:

The traditional British élite, fortified by their ancient schools and Oxbridge colleges, have maintained their edge over others – at some cost to the country. Their values are less closely related to technology and industry than to pre-industrial activities such as banking and the army.[20]

In terms of investment 'the social divide between bankers and most industrialists makes them all the more hesitant'[21] – not to mention of course the divide between these bankers and any women who might be trying to start or expand a business, and thinking of approaching backers in the City.

Lord Poole, Chairman of Lazards, once said: 'I only lent money to people who had been at Eton.'[22] It is ironical in this context that one of the worst crooks operating in the City recently, Justin Frewen, is an Old Etonian. The old boy network was very helpful to him in swindling money from large numbers of small investors.

The City money that was not going into productive investment in Britain, apart from what had gone into essentially speculative dealing in stocks and shares (or invested in industry or banks abroad after exchange controls were lifted) had been diverted into the static form of mortgages to buy existing – not new – houses, which did nothing for the economy or the high levels of unemployment. There was also a boom in consumer credit, sucking in imports, and vast expenditure on the privatised industries such as British Gas and British Telecom which also failed to create a single new job.

It is a sad story, one of national economic decline – in some places, complete collapse – and the creation of two nations, North and South, poor and rich, the old industrial areas (in London itself as much as anywhere) and the wealthy stockbroker belts or newly affluent areas with all the new service jobs. Certainly it was a right-wing Conservative Government that was responsible for many of the policies, but to a large extent these were based on what the men in the City had always wanted, and were only too keen to implement once young whiz-kids from the old schools had worked out ways of making it all legal.

'The City' is after all an extremely powerful element in the British Government itself. Much discussion of domestic and international policy has come to an abrupt end with the assertion: 'The City wouldn't like it.' Certainly this was, in my personal experience, the counter to any suggestions within the Civil Service about reducing the trade and investment favours extended, without any rational basis, to South Africa. Domestically, too, the City has had a veto on economic policy which is used particularly against Labour Governments: it is the Governor of the Bank of England, formally, who conveys the bad news to the Prime Minister on the City's behalf. As Harold Wilson recalled, in conversation later with the Governor, there had been occasions when the latter had 'read the riot act to the government of the day'.[23]

There are two important qualifications which must be added to this overall picture of the financial world and the City as part of an old élite men's network. Firstly, and an important phenomenon especially since the Second World War, is the financial weight of 'new' sources of investment finance, the pension funds and the insurance companies – both of course using money contributed by millions of us. Ownership and control is a very vague concept with such large amounts of money and individual beneficiaries involved. In practice, though, it is a few key men at the top of the institutions who make the decisions. In many cases, especially with the pension funds, decisions are taken by the management of the companies whose employees contribute to the funds. Although pension fund trustees are in theory there to look after the employees' interests, there is so little regulation that a company's management can quite easily use it to shore up their own position – which may well be against the interests of the employees. An even stronger tendency recently has been for pension funds to invest large amounts of their money abroad, creating the paradoxical situation where women and men in Britain are contributing to a financial system which extracts the potential investment that could safeguard their existing jobs and create new ones, and instead financing competitors abroad. It means pensions for workers when they retire, at the expense of present and future jobs for themselves, their children and grandchildren.

These are the values of the City men, and not of the country as a whole. The funds are managed by a different group from the City men discussed so far: many of them have worked their way up through the pensions business and do not belong to the public school or Oxbridge set of the City proper. In many cases, however, there are strong links between the two: merchant bankers Hill Samuel, for instance, manage about £2 billion of pension funds' money, including co-management of the enormous British Rail fund with Warburgs, another bastion of the old guard. (Hill Samuel, incidentally, also advise many local authorities and devised many of their 'creative accounting' deals with City and foreign banks − but that's another story.) Smaller pension funds tend to go almost automatically for guidance to the 'old' system, usually a bank or stockbroking firm. Sampson comments that 'many City people still regard pension fund managers as wet behind the ears, and some have been able to take them for a ride'.[24]

The insurance companies are perhaps more self-sufficient in their investment activities. Their Chairmen include some of the old City establishment, although Sampson suggests that the boards have become slightly less influenced by bankers and old City families 'as the companies have become more confident of their own importance.' The most important group of men in the insurance companies, he suggests, are the investment managers who by training are almost all actuaries, a highly specialised branch of mathematical specialism for calculating probabilities. They, too, have little experience of the realities of the City. They are 'mostly quiet men from grammar schools' pre-occupied with their fiduciary role as trustees for the policy-holders.[25] This means going for the biggest profit with the smallest degree of risk, a recipe for investing where everybody else does and not investigating or backing anything new or untried. This, too, means heavy investment abroad rather than in jobs which would benefit the policy-holders putting up the money in the first place.

One of our own informants was very much one of these 'new men' from outside the City proper, a pension fund investment manager responsible for a portfolio worth about half a billion pounds. Although one of the most open of the financial men, he told us he was quite sure that women could not do his job properly. 'You have to be hard, you have to kick people's arse, you have to tell them off, you have to boss them about.' Women couldn't do that, he claimed, because of our 'general conditioning' or perhaps it 'could be that they're just weaker. They find it more difficult to be a complete shit, and you have to be a complete shit.'

There was in fact a 'girl' working with him, he said, who was doing very much the same kind of job. She tended to lose confidence when things went wrong, which they did all the time – and women for some reason couldn't accept the ribbing that was meted out routinely when people made mistakes, which was 'obviously' going to be sexist if a woman was involved.

'If it's done to a woman she makes out that people are being prejudiced against her when it's just part of the normal course, basically just taking the piss out of people who make a blunder. When you're ribbing someone you're ribbing them about their attributes anyway and being a woman is an attribute so . . . it's part of the process of bringing someone down.'

No wonder, then, that the women who managed to survive in his line of business were the 'super-confident' ones, especially those from very wealthy or upper-class families who were not vulnerable to this kind of pressure. For the others (like you, perhaps, and certainly like me) it would undermine our confidence and make it much harder to claim equal access to this world of big money.

The City: a man's world

It may seem an anachronism that one of the world's leading financial centres is so tightly controlled by a small, partly hereditary élite which is becoming even more tightly connected with the boys' private schools, Oxford and Cambridge, and the interlocking networks of men's organisations which refer back to medieval pomp and tradition. But in reality the system is not that different from that applying on Wall Street, in Hong Kong or any of the other major financial exchanges around the world. It works: the problem is, who for? Is it working against nobody? Are the exclusive clubs and cliques operating to protect and promote insider dealing, the antithesis of the market-place? 'Big Bang' has if anything increased concern about this with the lifting or controls on what any one company can do and the creation of 'Chinese walls' within them which are supposed to prevent conflicts of interest and a privileged exchange of information against the public interest.

One thing is clear, and this is only one of the major concerns: it operates to keep financial power in male hands, in the City of London above all. There is an intricate system of in-groups within in-groups: the Freemasons operate officially as a caucus within major institutions as well as within Livery Companies, which in turn bring together men who are in a position to help and promote each other's interests. What is particularly objectionable about the City of London is the pretence that there is an unbroken tradition of City guilds to which these powerful men (many of them not even working in the City itself) are the legitimate heirs, and their abuse of vast charitable funds bequeathed by women and men down the centuries, without any public accountability or disclosure. It is a system which is corrupt, not necessarily in the sense of individuals pocketing the cash – they hardly need to – but in the corruption of a real community, religious and charitable tradition to serve the ends of a very modern set of private financial interests.

They are also gaining, not losing their power. As owners of some of the prime sites in central London and the City itself, and also as controllers of the Corporation which can approve or reject applications for developing these sites, their trust funds are growing spectacularly. As local government, too, the Corporation is accumulating assets both inside and outside its territory: it controls many open spaces, notably Epping Forest and recently, the Conservative Government decided, Hampstead Heath as well; it also owns many housing projects in different parts of London. Far from it being an anachronism, the City with all its men-only and undemocratic new-old structures is becoming a power to be reckoned with in local government terms.

And the future? Increasingly, City firms since the Big Bang are becoming the property of US, Japanese and other conglomerates. Far from there being any sign of disdaining the exclusive clubbishness of the City, however, there is every sign that American, Swiss, Japanese and other men will be only too happy to dress up and get in on the ritual act. There could be a few more women in the jobs, but not in the Lodges, the Livery Companies or the clubs – which means working at a very big disadvantage, and worse, quite possibly not even knowing it.

Conclusion

Men's organisations, clubs and networks operate throughout our society in Britain – and no doubt investigations in other countries with a European culture would show a similar pattern. Freemasons operate in the United States, there are segregated sporting clubs in Australia, keen Rotarians in France and Germany – and many of these networks are spreading, along with western influence and business practices, into many countries of the so-called Third World.

Our society, which in theory is an open and democratic one with a high level of integration for women and men and a strong current of equal opportunities measures now flowing through it, turns out on closer examination to be closer to the opposite. The organisations and operations described in this book form part of the real 'covert' society which anthropologists describe as existing behind the 'overt' conventions – which people prefer to believe is how society works. Ostensibly social activities, interests and organisations, run on men-only or male-dominant lines, impinge with great force on the open world of employment, business deals and public appointments, as well as the whole political process. It works at every class level, and sometimes across class lines, and ranges from the informal setting to the highly structured organisation. And as women press with increasing effectiveness for equal rights and opportunities, the men-only world is becoming more important, not less.

Pub culture and the phenomenon of purposeful social drinking, which many women think we have fully integrated, turns out to be largely untouched by us except in a few of the trendier but definitely fringe establishments – and the brewery industry has counted up its profits and come down firmly on the side of men and their pints. Sport, especially of the men's mass-produced spectator variety, is booming – to the benefit of, and backed by, television companies. Sporting clubs openly discriminate against women, and especially where they provide useful 'contacts' as in the case of golf or yacht clubs they practise a whole range of petty and humiliating restrictions which constantly remind women of our subordinate status and keep us out of the main contact areas, such as the bar, at key times.

This is a pattern which we see very strongly in the working men's clubs, a misnomer since they were established for the whole working-class community. Virtually all now have women as members – but with second-class status, arbitrarily excluded from sporting and social activities, often when they are just becoming proficient especially in the lucrative pub and club games of snooker and darts. The petty humiliations imposed on women by many of the men on club committees, and in the Working Men's Club and Institute Union itself, should be seen as a national scandal. Even more so, if anything, should the men's stranglehold on the Conservative Clubs.

On a more secretive level there are the Rotarians and especially the Freemasons, which are strictly men-only (at least in Britain). The problem here lies in the deals members are able to do with each other in their exclusive gatherings, trading mutual advantage in what should be an open and public sphere. Both, but especially the Freemasons, provide an ideal context for organising control over other organisations.

Finally we have the élite men's networks, based on a lifetime of contacts and ways of recognising each other which are rooted in childhood, through the boys' private schools and in particular the 'leading' schools which have consolidated the advantages they can offer boys through investment in equipment, educational excellence and carefully cultivated contacts with the Oxford and Cambridge colleges as well as with any old boy likely to prove useful. It offers a job and a series of promotions, for life, for an old boy who continues to play the system via the men's clubs, perhaps the Church of England and the armed forces, or the financial centres in the City of London with their interlocking networks of men's organisations.

There is more than one pattern of operation for male control of important social and educational institutions. The first is of course the purely men-only organisations such as Rotary or the Freemasons, complete with ritual, shared beliefs (at least on a superficial level) and a feeling of social cohesiveness as men which keeps them alive and influential. Side by side with this are the clubs which are, or have been, part of the whole community, but have been taken over and controlled by a group of men acting together against women. This certainly includes the working men's clubs, some of the boys' schools and colleges now admitting girls and women but not on an equal basis, and the 'Very Important Men's' clubs which have second-class women members – often literally in the basement, or at slow times to help pay for an organisation still run very much for the benefit of men. Then there is the sad case of the City of London guilds or Livery Companies, dating back many centuries and rich with the legacies of their original trading members – women and men – which have been distorted into men-only contact networks, their charitable funds dispensed with considerable secrecy via friends and relations and not donated to those carrying out the wishes of the old guild members to help and support the poor.

It is the takeover of community organisations by cliques of men who take over and distort the original intention, while claiming the backing of 'tradition', which I find the most distressing aspect of the men-only scene. If it was the Militants caucusing to discuss 'entryism' and a planned takeover of a much bigger organisation, the Establishment would be beside itself with outrage. But these caucusing men *are* the Establishment! And that is precisely why they have been able to get into the positions of power, public as well as private, which they now hold. They have got there on the backs of the women who now find themselves excluded, subject to petty humiliation in our own organisations, and marginalised when we try to protest.

The possibilities of manipulation which these men-only structures provide are breathtaking, and as women we ignore them at our peril. Oddfellows or Freemasons or working men's club members can discuss appointments and policies in the local political parties, co-operative society or trade unions. Rotarians can discuss what the local Chamber of Commerce should be saying on local issues. There are caucuses within caucuses: masonic Lodges within Livery Companies, which in turn control the powerful Corporation of the City of London. As a system of control it is masterly (literally): the parasites control the host, which is often kept alive and functioning only by the dedication of women to community life and the idea of participation and mutual help. Where women are working to include people – especially those most in need, the isolated, children and the elderly – the men are organising separately to exclude them. As women put resources in, these men are taking them for themselves. It is a system of corruption so widespread and so obnoxious that until very recently, women have not really wanted to know about it.

For anyone committed to equality in our society, though, we *do* need to know. I feel that I have barely scratched the surface of the men-only phenomenon: many more women – and sympathetic men – will be needed to find out more, not just about the organisations covered in this book but also a vast range of others for which there was no time or space here. There are for instance the many professional and business organisations which admit only men to their decision-making committees, from the dog-breeders' Crufts to the magicians' Magic Circle. We need to know a lot more, and we shall need the support of men of goodwill and integrity who should refuse to participate at all, or who will renounce any promises – whether taken as a joke or in deadly earnest (or a mixture of the two) – to support the 'brotherhood' at the expense of the whole community, and particularly the women in it.

There are major issues about how women should respond to men-only control of important organisations, but we should not lose sight of the fact that this is first and foremost an issue for men. Those of them who work actively against women are probably a small minority, but the caucuses and cliques they organise are set up in the name of all men, who then benefit from the pro-male bias introduced. We only have to remind ourselves of the very privileged men listed in *Who's Who*, and members of VIM clubs – many of whom assured us they 'like' women, and are even in favour of equality with women, but are not disturbed or bothered by a set-up that keeps women out, or on the margins of the club, while they enjoy sole access to its central core. They need to be made aware of the shock, outrage, humiliation and anger which is the reaction of most women when we discover what has been going on behind their backs.

We in turn should start to judge much more harshly any man who belongs to, and takes advantage of, a men-only situation – and we should be more prepared to ask men about their affiliations. If we hesitate to ask, thinking perhaps it will embarrass the man or make him antagonistic to us, does this not also indicate something about the secret and powerful nature of the men's organisations – of which we are at some level aware, even while not knowing?

There are of course many women's organisations operating on a large scale, from the Women's Institutes to the Co-operative Women's Guild or the Church women's organisations. There are innumerable feminist groups and organisations, and women's sections within bigger structures such as the political parties and trade unions. With the exception of a few small groups which are modelled on men's organisations, like the women's Freemasonry, the women's organisations are fully open about their proceedings, their finances, and the way they select candidates and take policy decisions. They support community and mixed organisations, rather than seeking to destroy or exploit their resources for personal gain. In many cases men have joined – and not been exposed to the kind of humiliations so commonly imposed on women by men. It is high time that men's organisations met the basic standards of conduct set by the women's.

There is nothing intrinsically wrong about any group organising to discuss common interests and press their point of view in the public sphere, it seems to me – and that applies to men and women organising separately. What *is* wrong is secrecy, abuse of power, manipulation, exclusion or petty *apartheid* practised within the organisation – and in particular the use of private networks to manipulate what should be public affairs, whether business deals, recruitment into jobs, or 'public' appointments.

Women have to decide, individually and jointly, whether to participate in any organisation which is less than fully democratic, controlled by a male clique without reference to the membership as a whole. It is not a simple or easy choice: should we for instance abandon the one community organisation we have, like many working men's and sporting clubs, and with it our friends and the framework for community action with other people, who are less able to organise? If a club or organisation offers tangible business or job prospects, could we perhaps achieve more as women by taking advantage of any openings as they occur, and working towards gradual opening up to other women too? Are we not putting ourselves at a huge disadvantage by refusing a tempting invitation to join a men's club and rub shoulders with people who can give us a few of the unfair advantages so long confined to men only?

Each situation has to be considered on its merits, and particularly where community rather than individual benefits are involved it seems to me that women will and should be involved, however unjust the structure – but with the determination to open up these organisations to proper accountability and democratic control by all members. Time is on our side here, and so for once is the balance of economic advantage: community-based organisations now need women, our work and our financial contributions to keep going at all. We must not let the men-only men forget how much they rely on women, nor should *we* forget how to picket, sit in, disrupt and generally put a little honest pressure for the sake of democracy. It is crucial that we work together on this, both feminist and more traditional women, involving also those men who would like to see the clubs opened up but are nervous about stepping out of line with other men who are their main social contact. It is a series of battles that we *can* win, though not without cost.

It is the question of individual membership of élite organisations that is the problematical one, as is the similar drive to set up new élite mixed clubs like the Groucho, or women's 'old girl networks' which also operate on the basis of exclusion. For women faced with this dilemma it is not a simple question of joining a men's organisation, or one frankly imitating its old boy style, just for fun: a few may be very pleasant but many others will be uncomfortable, even nasty places to be. The argument for joining would be that if it is necessary for the job you are doing, or the legitimate ambition you are pursuing, then you should have access.

The problem is that this smacks of the old Queen Bee syndrome so much criticised by feminists: I'm all right, I don't have to help give other women a break – they can keep out, and a few will join me, some time or other, in this men's world. The acid test, I suggest, should be: is this organisation open to all women with my sort of job, or qualifications, or interests? If not, what am *I* doing here? And if I really want to press for greater openness from the inside, will I find any allies on the inside – or are they shut out altogether? I would argue for solidarity: take all of us, or none. No more divide and rule!

Finally, of course, there is the question of legislative change, or in some cases using the laws we already have. The working men's clubs can be dealt with by the Registrar of Friendly Societies, who should immediately set up an investigation of the clubs' misuse of rules and the WMCIU's refusal to use the proper procedures for any decisions the committee men do not want. Sporting clubs can be dealt with via the organisations controlling each sport. The Freemasons can be tackled, at least in part, by greater disclosure and employers can make it part of the conditions of employment that there is no participation in any organisation which is not open to all, where work or business colleagues or contacts are also present. The Livery societies should be required under the charity laws to disclose how they are using the vast funds bequeathed for the relief of poverty. Discrimination in private schools against girls can be challenged by their parents – possibly on the grounds that this is a commercial and educational service, where discrimination is already illegal on both grounds.

At the end of the day, though, it would be changes to the discrimination laws that would help the most. The Equal Opportunities Commission has already proposed, in March 1988, making 'private' clubs with both women and men as members subject to the law against sex discrimination – and knowing only too well that some men would respond to this by throwing the women out altogether, have proposed that this should relate to the situation at the beginning of 1988. Full marks here: no more lower category of membership for women only, no more lines painted on the floor, no more petty *apartheid*.

But there is also a need for another, parallel measure: to make it illegal to exclude women from any men-only organisation which serves as a place to discuss business, employment, public appointments or anything else which is itself already subject to anti-discrimination laws. We shall of course need informants and witnesses from the inside, but that has not proved too difficult in preparing this book.

Let's not deceive ourselves: the combined weight of the men-only organisations will be directed against any such legislative proposal. The working men's clubs would be lobbying alongside the Rotarians, the masons, the Conservative Clubs, and the VIM clubs. They are *very* well connected. They have enormous reserves of political influence. We shall just have to be better organised.

We do, after all, have majority support.

Correspondence about the organisations discussed in this book, and others operating on a discriminatory basis, would be welcomed by the author: c/o Everywoman, 34 Islington Green, London N1 8DU.

Appendix   Background of selected Establishment figures, 1986/7

	Total		Oxbridge		Public Schools: Leading[1]		First Rate[2]		West-End Clubs: 9 prestigious		Other	
	Number	Per cent	Number	Per cent	Number	Per cent	Number	Per cent	Number	Per cent	Number	Per cent
MPs[3]												
Con. M	377	96	181	48	91	24	36	10	137	36	35	9
F	14	4	3	21					0	—		
Lab. M	194	94	41	21	4	2	3	2	2		6	3
F	12	6	0	—								
Other M	51	96	6	12	1	2	1	2	2	4	1	2
F	2	4	0	—								
Diplomatic Service												
Ministers & Staff[4]	21	100	6	29	5	24	0	—	2	9		
Senior Officers & Staff[5]	22	100	17	77	8	36	2	9	5	23		
Chairmen Top 100 UK Companies[6]	85	100	29	34	12	14	10	12	20	24	12	14
Chairmen, Financial Institutions[7]	59	100	15	25	15	25	1	2	14	24	6	10

Sources: Dod's Parliamentary Companion, 1986; Times Top 1000 1986–87; Who's Who, 1986; Diplomatic Service List, 1986.

Notes

1 Pubs: 'Getting away from the wife'

1   Elizabeth Breeze, *Differences in Drinking Patterns Between Selected Regions* (DHSS Report/HMSO, 1984).
2   *UK Market for Beers, Wine and Spirits to 1990* (Staniland Hall).
3   'Trends in public usage and attitudes to pubs: Market Opinion Research International (MORI) 1984', *Brewing Review,* January 1986.
4   Brigid McConville, *Women Under the Influence* (Virago Press, 1983).
5   Camberwell Council on Alcoholism, *Women and Alcohol,* (Tavistock Publications, 1980).
6   Ann Whitehead, 'Sexual antagonism in Herefordshire', in *Dependence and Exploitation in Work and Marriage,* edited by Diana Leonard Baker and Sheila Allen (Longman, London, 1976).
7   Valerie Hey, *Patriarchy and Pub Culture* (Tavistock, London, 1986).
8   See Barbara Rogers, *The Domestication of Women* (Tavistock, London, 1981).
9   Roger Smith, 'Sex and occupational role on Fleet Street', in Baker and Allen's *Dependence and Exploitation.*

2 This sporting life

1   Ann Whitehead, 'Sexual antagonism in Herefordshire', in Diana Leonard Baker and Sheila Allen (eds), *Dependence and Exploitation in Work and Marriage* (Longman, 1976), p. 187.
2   Kathryn Stechert, *The Credibility Gap* (Thorsons, 1987) pp. 20–2.
3   Michael Korda, *Male Chauvinism! How it Works* (Ballantine, NY, 1973), pp. 54–5.
4   Malcolm Rigg, *Action Sport: An Evaluation* (The Sports Council, 1986).
5   Rosemary Deem, *All Work and No Play? The Sociology of Women and Leisure* (Open University Press, 1986).

6 'Male members only', *Cosmopolitan*, July 1986.
7 State of Victoria, Australia, *Report of Equal Opportunity Board into Discrimination in Sporting Clubs*, June 1983.
8 Tim Heald, *Networks: Who We Know and How We Use Them* (Coronet, 1983), Chapter 2.

3 Club hijack: working men only

1 Personal communications from club members.
2 *Yorkshire Evening Post*, 9 November 1982.
3 *Daily Mail*, 4 May 1982.
4 *Sheffield Morning Telegraph*, 30 April 1983.
5 *Scunthorpe Evening Telegraph*, 14 January 1982.
6 Personal communication. A relevant case is Jones v Royal Liver Friendly Society (1982) reported in *The Times*, 2 December 1982. The Registrar of Friendly Societies, the EOC or any individual affected by the action could take up the issue in court.
7 George Tremlett, *The First Century* (WMCIU, London, 1962).
8 *Wakefield Express*, 7 March 1980.
9 Tremlett, *First Century*.
10 *Blackpool Gazette*, 3 April 1982.
11 Accounts from the participants.
12 See the description of the strip circuit on Tyneside – regarded as the most entrenched 'male' area for clubs – in *The Guardian*, 4 June 1985.
13 Tremlett, *First Century*.
14 'People's Diary', *The Guardian*, 1 October 1986.
15 *The Guardian*, 8 and 9 August 1986.
16 Interview with BBC Cleveland, 4 April 1986.
17 The Registrar of Friendly Societies is at 15 Gt Marlborough St, London W1.

4 Freemasons and brothers

1 John James, *Chartres: The Masons who Built a Legend* (Routledge & Kegan Paul, 1985), pp. 104–8.
2 James, *Chartres*, p. 131.
3 Tim Heald, *Networks* (Coronet, 1983), p. 184.
4 Stephen Knight, *The Brotherhood: The Secret World of the Freemasons* (Grafton Books, 1985), pp. 15–21.
5 Quoted in Knight, p. 28.
6 Heald, p. 183.

7 Knight, pp. 121, 130–3.
8 Interviews quoted by Knight, pp. 132–3.
9 Russell Russell, 'Of mason men', *The Tatler*, July–August 1986.
10 John Sweeney, 'Top judges listed in Masonic Year Book', *New Statesman*, March 1986, N.D.
11 'Row over "rope and race" judge', *The Observer*, 15 March 1987.
12 Knight, pp. 155–86.
13 Sweeney, in *New Statesman*.
14 John Sweeney, 'Disarray among the masons', *New Society*, 28 March 1986.
15 Knight, pp. 184–5.
16 Knight, pp. 175–7.
17 Knight, pp. 187–8.
18 Russell, in *Tatler*.
19 Knight, p. 62.
20 For more detail see Knight, p. 49–114.
21 Private communication, reported in more detail in *Everywoman*, January 1987.
22 'Detectives ignore Met chief by joining masonic élite', *The Observer*, 30 November 1986.
23 *The Guardian*, 31 July 1986.
24 *Final Report to the London Borough of Hackney: Inquiry by Andrew Arden*, presented to the Council March 1987, p. 223.
25 *Labour Weekly*, 22 November 1985.
26 Knight, pp. 136–8, 223; Russell, in *Tatler*.
27 Knight, pp. 136–7.
28 Russell, in *Tatler*; 'Women's rights go on trial', *The Observer*, 16 June 1985.
29 Knight, pp. 206–10.
30 Knight, pp. 110–11.
31 'Freemasonry beliefs queried by churches', *The Guardian*, 27 May 1985.
32 Knight, pp. 120, 225.
33 Knight, pp. 3–4.
34 Russell, in *Tatler*.
35 Knight, p. 35.
36 Russell, in *Tatler*.
37 Knight, pp. 92–3.
38 Knight, pp. 144–5.
39 *The Guardian*, 22 August 1986.
40 Knight, pp. 145–9.
41 Russell, in *Tatler*.
42 *The Observer*, 30 November 1986.

43 George Armstrong, 'Maltese cross to bear', *The Guardian*, 8 April 1988.
44 'Unchivalrous world of the bogus Knights', *The Observer*, 15 March 1987.
45 'Orange parade triumph turns sour', *The Guardian*, 12 July 1986.
46 'People', *The Guardian*, 18 February 1986.
47 Knight, pp. 131, 138.
48 Knight, pp. 71, 79–80, 124.

5 Wheeling and dealing: Rotary Clubs

1 David Shelley Nichol, *The Golden Wheel* (Plymouth: Mac-Donald & Evans, 1984), pp. 235–69.
2 David Shelley Nichol, pp. 223–4.
3 *Newsweek*, 14 February 1982.
4 David Shelley Nichol, pp. 12–13.
5 *A Rotary Guidebook* (London: Rotary International in Great Britain and Ireland, 1985), p. 10.
6 *Electing a New Rotarian* (London: Rotary Information Service, 1986), p. 3.
7 Ibid., p. 8.
8 *A Rotary Guidebook*, p. 10.
9 Ibid., p. 10.
10 David Shelley Nichol, p. 46.
11 Ibid., pp. 108–9.
12 Ibid., p. 67.
13 Ibid., p. 100.
14 Ibid., p. 12.
15 Quoted in ibid., p. 264.
16 *A Rotary Guidebook*, p. 10.
17 *Information* (London: Rotary Information Service, 1985), pp. 5, 10.
18 *A Rotary Guidebook* (London: RIBI, 1985), pp. 58–9.
19 Mary Hockaday, 'Soroptimists United', *Everywoman*, June 1986, p. 27.

6 Speaking the right language: the education of Very Important Men

1 *The Observer*, 13 October 1985.
2 Tim Heald, *Networks* (Coronet, 1983), p. 101.
3 *The Times*, 25 September 1986.
4 'The Story of English', BBC-2, 23 September 1986.

5 Beryl Bainbridge, 'Southern Comfort', *The Observer magazine*, n.d.
6 As told to Tim Heald, p. 51.
7 Heald, p. 15.
8 Heald, pp. 42–3.
9 Clive Griggs, *Private Education in Britain* (Palmer Press, 1985), pp. 56–7.
10 Heald, p. 31.
11 'Harrow', *Boardroom* magazine, January–February 1986.
12 Heald, p. 28.
13 Heald, p. 21.
14 Heald, p. 58.
15 Heald, p. 49.
16 Geoffrey Walford, 'Introduction', in Geoffrey Walford (ed.), *British Public Schools: Policy and Practice* (Falmer Press, 1984), p. 1.
17 Irene Fox, *Private Schools and Public Issues: The Parents' View* (Macmillan, 1985), pp. 16–17.
18 Anthony Sampson, *The Changing Anatomy of Britain* (Hodder & Stoughton, 1982), pp. 428–9.
19 Heald, p. 53.
20 Sampson, p. 126.
21 Sampson, pp. 124–6.
22 Heald, p. 54.
23 D. Boyd, *Elites and their Education* (NFER, 1973).
24 J. Scott, *The Upper Class* (Macmillan, 1982).
25 A. H. Halsey, A. F. Heath and J. M. Ridge, *Origins and Destinations* (Clarendon Press, 1980), p. 171 and *passim*.
26 R. V. Clements, *Managers: A Study of their Careers in Industry* (George Allen & Unwin, 1958).
27 Boyd, p. 132.
28 ISCO, *Careers Bulletin* No. 158, summer 1977, pp. 3–4.
29 Walford, p. 2.
30 Griggs, pp. 147–8.
31 Heald, pp. 89–90.
32 Quoted in H. C. Barnard, *A History of English Education* (University of London Press, 1961), p. 242.
33 Griggs, pp. 136–7.
34 Jack Straw, 'Ministers boycott state schools', *New Statesman*, 12 September 1986.
35 Geoge Gale, 'Buy your way into the upper classes', *Daily Express*, 25 June 1981.
36 Letter to *The Guardian*, 16 July 1981.
37 Four-year study by researchers from Bristol Polytechnic and Newcastle University funded by the Economic and Social

Research Council, reported in *The Guardian*, 4 and 5 September 1986.

38 Ralph Miliband, *The State in Capitalist Society* (Weidenfeld, 1973).

39 Irene Fox, in *British Public Schools*.

40 Lord Hailsham, *The Conservative Case* (Penguin, 1959), pp. 113–14.

41 Edward Blishen, 'Charm schools', *The Guardian*, 2 January 1986.

42 Heald, pp. 50, 195–6.

43 Quoted in Sampson, p. 120.

44 *The Observer*, 5 October 1986.

45 Quoted in Sampson, p. 122.

46 Judith Okely, 'Privileged, schooled and finished: boarding education for girls', in June Purvis and Margaret Hales (eds), *Achievement and Inequality in Education* (Routledge & Kegan Paul, 1983).

47 Geoffrey Walford, *Life in Public Schools* (Methuen, 1986), p. 142.

48 *The Observer*, 23 March 1986.

49 *The Guardian*, 7 February 1984.

50 Geoffrey Walford, 'Girls in boys' public schools: a prelude to further research', *British Journal of Sociology of Education*, vol. 4, no. 1, 1983.

51 Walford, *Life in Public Schools*, p. 160.

52 Walford, 'Girls'.

53 Walford, 'Girls'.

54 Walford, *Life in Public Schools*, p. 161.

55 See especially Pat Mahony, *Schools for the Boys? Co-education Reassessed* (Hutchinson, 1985).

56 Edward Vulliamy, 'Touting for boys', *The Guardian*, 31 October 1986.

57 Heald, p. 71.

58 Greg Eglin in *British Public Schools*.

59 Heald, pp. 74–5.

60 Heald, p. 69.

61 *Times Higher Education Supplement*, 5 July 1985.

62 *Times Education Supplement*, 10 July 1985.

63 R. J. Norris, letter to *The Guardian*, 23 September 1986.

64 Heald, pp. 73–4.

65 Griggs, p. 54, citing a House of Commons Library report to Frank Field MP of 9 June 1980.

66 Anton Gill, *How to be Oxbridge: A Bluffer's Handbook* (Grafton Books, 1985) pp. 86–7.

67 Heald, pp. 194–5.

68 David Walter, *The Oxford Union* (Macdonald, 1984), pp. 13–16.
69 Sampson, pp. 146–7.
70 Frances and John Wakeford, 'Universities and the study of élites' in Philip Stanworth and Antony Giddens (eds), *Elites and Power in British Society* (Cambridge University Press, 1974), pp. 187–91.
71 Cited in Heald, pp. 97–9.
72 *The Guardian*, 7 November 1986.
73 Dan Corby in *The Guardian*, 18 December 1986.
74 Gill, p. 192.
75 Sampson, p. 144.
76 Gill, p. 207.
77 Cited in Sampson, p. 145.
78 'Women in Society', editorial in *The Cambridge Review*, 2 June 1983.
79 Kate Pretty, 'Women in isolation: a profile of women in the University of Cambridge', *The Cambridge Review*, 3 June 1985, p. 129.
80 Alan Franks, 'Why more women aren't fellows', *The Times*, 14 January 1985.
81 Kate Pretty, pp. 126–9.
82 Virginia Woolf, *Three Guineas* (Hogarth Press, 1986), p. 95.
83 Woolf, p. 70.

7 Very Important Men's clubs

1 Glyn Worsnip, 'A Gentleman's Place', programme on BBC Radio 4, 20 July 1986.
2 For Sara Keays's own account of what happened see her book, *A Question of Judgement* (Quintessential Press, 1985) and Barbara Rogers's interview with her in *Everywoman*, March and April 1986.
3 Anthony Sampson, 'The Private World of London's Clubs', *The Observer*, 31 December 1961 and 7 January 1962.
4 Tim Heald, *Networks* (Coronet, 1983), pp. 188–9.
5 Anthony Sampson, *The Changing Anatomy of Britain* (Hodder & Stoughton, 1982).
6 Sampson in *The Observer*.
7 Sampson in *The Observer*.
8 Heald, p. 189.
9 As told to Heald, pp. 168–9.
10 Michael O'Donnell, 'Whisper who dares', *The Guardian*, 20 August 1986.

11 Andrew Veitch, 'Obstetrics truce', *The Guardian*, 11 October 1986.
12 Sampson in *The Observer*, 7 January 1962.
13 Joyce Chesterton and Christopher Hall, 'Top clubs still flourish', *Daily Herald*, 31 October 1961.
14 Worsnip, 'Gentleman's Place'.
15 Everybody seems to tell this story, some of the clubmen suggesting that it was his own fault for 'provocation'.
16 Sampson in *The Observer*, 31 December 1961.
17 'Blue ribbons in the Carlton Club', *Sunday Telegraph*, 19 May 1985.
18 'Brooks's two centuries of continuity', *The Times*, 23 October 1964.
19 Worsnip, 'Gentleman's Place'.
20 Sampson in *The Observer*, 31 December 1961.
21 Anna Ford, *Men: a Documentary* (Weidenfeld & Nicholson, 1985).
22 Heald, pp. 190–1.
23 Heald, pp. 191–2.
24 Julia Langdon in the *Sunday Mirror*, 14 February 1988.
25 Interview, 26 February 1988. For more details see *Everywoman*, April 1988.
26 *The Times*, 1 July 1981; *Evening News*, 3 January 1980.
27 Sylvia Howes, 'Join the club', *Sunday Times*, 15 April 1984.
28 Anthony Lejeune, 'Can the clubs survive?' *Daily Telegraph*, 18 July 1969.
29 Interviewed by Worsnip, 'Gentleman's Place'.
30 *Daily Telegraph*, 16 May and 14 June 1975.
31 *Daily Mail*, 6 January 1972; *Daily Express*, 29 October 1985.
32 'Clubs for the dull set', *Sunday Times*, 28 February 1988.
33 Lejeune, 'Can the clubs survive?'
34 Ann Hills, 'The old girl network', *The Times*, 14 July 1983; Sylvia Howes, *Sunday Times*; Jane Kelly, 'Ladies club together', *Sunday Telegraph*, 19 May 1985.
35 Heald, p. 195.
36 Worsnip, 'Gentleman's Place'.
37 Heald, p. 192.

8 Crook and gun: men of the Church of England and armed forces

1 Quoted by Margaret Webster in *The Observer*, 1 March 1987.
2 Quoted in Margaret Duggan, *Runcie: The Making of an Archbishop* (Hodder & Stoughton, 1985), p. 43.
3 Webster in *The Observer*.

4 Kenneth Thompson, 'Church of England bishops as an élite', in Philip Stanworth and Anthony Giddens (eds), *Elites and Power in British Society* (Cambridge University Press, 1974).

5 Thompson, 'Bishops'.

6 Paul E. Welsby, *A History of the Church of England 1945–1980* (Oxford University Press, 1984), p. 218.

7 Tim Heald, *Networks* (Coronet, 1983), pp. 196–7.

8 Thompson, 'Bishops'.

9 Thompson, 'Bishops', pp. 204–5.

10 Stephen Knight, *The Brotherhood* (Grafton Books, 1985), pp. 232, 255–62.

11 Kennedy Thom, 'What gay Christians seek from the Church', *Crucible*, April–June 1980, pp. 63–4.

12 Cited in Dennis Barker, *Soldiering On: An Unofficial Portrait of the British Army* (Andre Deutsch, 1981), p. 108.

13 Clive Griggs, *Private Education in Britain* (Falmer Press, 1985), pp. 48–9.

14 See Barker, *Soldiering*, Chapter 13.

15 Barker, p. 110.

16 Peter Tatchell, *Democratic Defence: A Non-Nuclear Alternative* (Gay Men's Press, 1985), p. 80.

17 Barker, p. 220.

18 Barker, p. 220.

19 Knight, *Brotherhood*, pp. 38–43.

20 Tatchell, p. 73.

21 Tatchell, pp. 74–87.

22 Barker, p. 200.

23 *Military Contracts*, paper by At Ease (support group for people in the forces), c/o 1 Secker St, London SE1 8UF.

24 Anthony Sampson, *The Changing Anatomy of Britain* (Hodder & Stoughton, 1982), p. 253.

25 Heald, *Networks*, p. 130.

26 Heald, pp. 124–5. For more examples of this, see pp. 123–35.

27 For more detail see *Everywoman*, September 1986.

28 Interview with Flt Lt Diane Brown, Public Relations Officer for the WRAF.

29 Tatchell, p. 78.

30 *The Times*, 19 August 1983.

31 Barker, p. 20.

32 Colin Hughes in *The Times*, 20 February 1985.

33 See the discussion on this in Barker, Chapter 12.

34 Annette Goodeve quoted in *The Times*, 20 February 1985. There is also a fascinating account of how this system evolved, Myna Tristram's *Women of the Regiment: Marriage and the Victorian Army* (Cambridge University Press, 1984).

35 Barker, pp. 241–2.

36 Cynthia Enloe, *Does Khaki Become You? The Militarisation of Women's Lives* (Pluto Press, 1983), pp. 211–14 and *passim*.

9 Insider dealing: finance and the City

1 Robin Cook, 'The day of reckoning for the City', *The Guardian*, 28 November 1986; Hamish McRae, 'A new insecurity', *The Guardian*, 12 December 1986.
2 Stephen Knight, *The Brotherhood* (Grafton Books, 1985), pp. 216–21.
3 Knight, pp. 223–7.
4 Knight, p. 223.
5 Knight, p. 222.
6 Knight, p. 228.
7 'The Guilds of London', *Stock Exchange Gazette*, 28 April 1962; 'The romance of the City Guilds', *John O'London's Weekly*, 31 August 1929; Anthony Lejeune, 'The indestructible Livery Companies', *The Director*, November 1965.
8 Auriol Stevens, 'It costs so much . . .' *The Guardian*, 19 June 1969.
9 'The mercers roll up their sleeves', *City Limits*, 3–10 July 1986.
10 Peter Golding (ed.), *Excluding the Poor* (CPAG, 1986).
11 Ian Crichton, 'Livery Companies in the Jet Age', Press Association Feature No. 33576/D, 16 September 1961.
12 Auriol Stevens, *The Guardian*, 19 June 1969; 'Sisters of the City Guilds', *The Times*, 17 February 1964.
13 Lejeune in *The Director*, November 1965.
14 Lejeune.
15 Richard Whitley, 'The City and Industry: the directors of large companies, their characteristics and connections', in Philip Stanworth and Anthony Giddens (eds), *Elites and Power in British Society* (Cambridge University Press, 1974).
16 Philip Stanworth and Anthony Giddens, 'An economic élite: company chairmen', in *Elites and Power*.
17 Quoted in Anthony Sampson, *The Changing Anatomy of Britain* (Hodder & Stoughton, 1982), p. 272.
18 Sampson, pp. 263–5.
19 Sampson, pp. 430–1.
20 Sampson, pp. 283–4.
21 Quoted in Sampson, p. 280.
22 Quoted in Sampson, p. 267.
23 Sampson, p. 291.
24 Sampson, pp. 287–8.

Appendix Background of selected Establishment figures

1 'Leading schools': Ampleforth, Charterhouse, Eton, Harrow, Marlborough, Rugby, Shrewsbury, Westminister, Winchester.
2 'First-rate schools': Bedford, Bradfield, Bryanston, Cheltenham, Clifton, Downside, Fettes, Gordonstoun, Haileybury, Highgate, King's Canterbury, Lancing, Malvern, Millfield, Oundle, Radley, Repton, St Paul's, Sedbergh, Sherborne, Stoneyhurst, Tonbridge, Uppingham, Wellington.

		Per cent
3	Total No. of MPs = 650	100
	Total No. of Conservative MPs = 391	60
	Total No. of Labour MPs = 206	32
	Total No. of other MPs = 53	8
	Total no. of male MPs = 622	96
	Total no. of female MPs = 28	4

47 per cent of Cons. MPs (M & F) attended Oxbridge.
20 per cent of Labour MPs (M & F) attended Oxbridge.
2 women MPs (C.) listed West End club membership (7%)
N.B. excluding Thatcher.

4 First secretary and above.
5 Permanent under-secretaries and superintending under-secretary.
6 Eighty-five chairmen are listed in *Who's Who*.

7	Total No. of Finance Houses	=	30
	Total No. of Accepting Houses	=	16
	Total No. of Discount Houses	=	8
	Total No. of Clearing Banks (London)	=	5
			——
			59

Index